REFL

DAILY

ADVENT **2022** TO
EVE OF ADVENT **2023**

KATE BRUCE
VANESSA CONANT
STEVEN CROFT
JONATHAN FROST
LUIGI GIOIA
HELEN-ANN HARTLEY
MICHAEL IPGRAVE
MARK IRELAND
GRAHAM JAMES
LIBBY LANE
JAN McFARLANE
MARK OAKLEY
JOHN PERUMBALATH
JOHN PRITCHARD
SARAH ROWLAND JONES
ANGELA TILBY
JANE WILLIAMS

Including Holy Week Reflections by
PAULA GOODER

Church House Publishing
Church House
Great Smith Street
London SW1P 3AZ

ISBN 978 0 7151 2396 6

Published 2022 by Church House Publishing

Liturgical editor: Peter Moger
Series editor: Hugh Hillyard-Parker
Designed and typeset by Hugh Hillyard-Parker
Copy edited by Ros Connelly
Printed by CPI Bookmarque, Croydon, Surrey

Contents

About the authors 4

About *Reflections for Daily Prayer* 7

Building daily prayer into daily life 8

ADVENT
Monday 28 November to Saturday 24 December 10

CHRISTMAS
Monday 26 December to Thursday 5 January 34

EPIPHANY
Friday 6 January to Wednesday 1 February 44

PRESENTATION
Thursday 2 February 67

ORDINARY TIME BEFORE LENT
Friday 3 February to Tuesday 21 March 68

LENT
Wednesday 22 February to Saturday 8 April 84

EASTER
Monday 10 April to Saturday 27 May 124

PENTECOST (ORDINARY TIME)
Monday 29 May to Saturday 3 June 166

TRINITY (ORDINARY TIME)
Monday 5 June to Tuesday 31 October 172

ALL SAINTS TO ADVENT (ORDINARY TIME)
Wednesday 1 November to Saturday 2 December 300

Seasonal Prayers for Thanksgiving 328

The Lord's Prayer and The Grace 331

An Order for Night Prayer (Compline) 332

Table of Bible readings reflected on in this book 336

About the authors

Kate Bruce (pp. 82–93, 130–41) is a serving RAF Chaplain. She writes in the area of homiletics, and has published a number of books and articles in this field. She offers day conferences in preaching around the country, and preaches regularly in a variety of contexts. She enjoys running, and writes and performs stand-up comedy in her spare time. She is Visiting Fellow at St John's College, Durham.

Vanessa Conant (pp. 250–61) is the Rector of Walthamstow, a diverse urban parish in North East London. Trained at Trinity College, Bristol, Vanessa has served parishes in Hoddesdon and Edinburgh. She is interested in the connections between faith, climate and justice, and is very involved in community organizing in East London.

Steven Croft (pp. 34–45, 262–73) is the Bishop of Oxford. He was previously Bishop of Sheffield and team leader of Fresh Expressions. He is the author of a number of books including *The Gift of Leadership* and *Pilgrim Journeys*.

Jonathan Frost (pp. 154–65) is Bishop of Portsmouth. Previously, Jonathan served in cathedral, diocesan, chaplaincy and parochial contexts.

Luigi Gioia (pp. 10–21) is a theologian and researcher at Cambridge University and associate priest at St Paul's Knightsbridge in London. His book *Say It To God* (Bloomsbury 2017) was the Archbishop of Canterbury Lent Book 2018. His last book is *The Wisdom of St Benedict* (Canterbury Press 2021). His books have been translated into five languages.

Paula Gooder (pp. 118–129) is Chancellor of St Paul's Cathedral, London. She is a writer and lecturer in biblical studies, author of a number of books including *Women of Holy Week; Journalling the Psalms; The Parables* and *Phoebe: A Story*, and a co-author of the Pilgrim course. She is also a Licensed Lay Minister (Reader) in the Church of England.

Helen-Ann Hartley (pp. 58–69, 226–37) is the Bishop of Ripon in the Diocese of Leeds, a role she has held since early 2018. Prior to this appointment she was the Bishop of Waikato in New Zealand from 2014 until 2017, and before that she taught New Testament studies at Ripon College Cuddesdon and at the College of St John the Evangelist in Auckland, New Zealand.

Michael Ipgrave (pp. 166–77, 190–201) is Bishop of Lichfield, and has previously ministered in Rutland, Japan, Leicester and South London. He has a particular interest in ecumenical, Christian–Jewish and interfaith issues.

Mark Ireland (pp. 46–57, 178–89) loves helping people pray and engage with the Bible as disciples of Jesus. He also loves his wife Gill, skiing, fell-walking and eating cake. He is co-author of *Making New Disciples* and *How to Do Mission Action Planning* (both SPCK). He was a vicar and is Archdeacon of Blackburn.

Graham James (pp. 106–117, 214–25) was Bishop of Norwich for almost 20 years until his retirement in 2019. Since then he has chaired the Paterson Inquiry, an independent inquiry for the Government on patient safety in the NHS and private healthcare. Earlier in his ministry he was Bishop of St Germans in his native Cornwall and Chaplain to two Archbishops of Canterbury. He has now returned to Cornwall where he ministers as an honorary assistant bishop. More widely, he has recently been appointed to the Human Fertilization & Embryology Authority.

Libby Lane (pp. 70–81) is, since 2019, the Bishop of Derby. In 2015, she was consecrated as the Church of England's first woman bishop, serving as Bishop of Stockport in the Diocese of Chester. She is Chair of Cranmer Hall Theological College Committee and Vice Chair of The Children's Society.

Jan McFarlane (pp. 22–33, 274–85) is Assistant Bishop in the Diocese of Lichfield and Canon Custos of Lichfield Cathedral. She has served as Bishop of Repton, Archdeacon of Norwich, Director of Communications, Chaplain to the Bishop of Norwich, Chaplain of Ely Cathedral and Curate in the Stafford Team Ministry.

Mark Oakley (pp. 94–105) is Dean and Fellow of St John's College, Cambridge, and Honorary Canon Theologian of Wakefield Cathedral in the Diocese of Leeds. He is the author of *The Collage of God* (2001), *The Splash of Words: Believing in Poetry* (2016), and *My Sour Sweet Days: George Herbert and the Journey of the Soul* (2019) as well as articles and reviews, usually in the areas of faith, poetry, human rights and literature. He is a Fellow of King's College London, where he is also Visiting Lecturer in the department of Theology and Religious Studies.

John Perumbalath (pp. 238–49) is the Bishop of Bradwell in Chelmsford Diocese, having previously been Archdeacon of Barking. He has served as a theological educator and parish priest in the dioceses of Calcutta (Church of North India) and Rochester. He regularly guest lectures in the fields of faith and social engagement and in biblical studies.

John Pritchard (pp. 286–303) was Bishop of Oxford from 2007 to 2014. Prior to that he was Bishop of Jarrow, Archdeacon of Canterbury and Warden of Cranmer Hall, Durham. His only ambition was to be a vicar, which he was in Taunton for eight happy years. He enjoys armchair sport, walking, reading, music, theatre and recovering.

Sarah Rowland Jones (pp. 142–53, 316–27) was a mathematician, then a British diplomat with postings in Jordan and Hungary, before ordination in the Church in Wales. After 11 years as researcher to successive Archbishops of Cape Town, she returned to Wales, and is now the Dean of St Davids. She serves on international Anglican think-tanks, broadcasts regularly, and writes on spirituality, public theology and ecumenism.

Angela Tilby (pp. 304–15) is a Canon Emeritus of Christ Church Cathedral, Oxford, and Canon of Honour at Portsmouth Cathedral. She previously served in the Diocese of Oxford following a period in Cambridge, where she taught at Westcott House and was also vicar of St Bene't's Church. Before ordination she was a producer for the BBC, and she still broadcasts regularly.

Rachel Treweek (pp. 8–9) is the Bishop of Gloucester and the first female diocesan bishop in England. She served in two parishes in London and was Archdeacon of Northolt and later Hackney. Prior to ordination she was a speech and language therapist and is a trained practitioner in conflict transformation.

Jane Williams (pp. 202–13) is the McDonald Professor in Christian Theology at St Mellitus College. She is the author of a number of books, her most recent being *The Art of Advent* (2018) and *The Art of Christmas* (2021).

About *Reflections for Daily Prayer*

Based on the *Common Worship Lectionary* readings for Morning Prayer, these daily reflections are designed to refresh and inspire times of personal prayer. The aim is to provide rich, contemporary and engaging insights into Scripture.

Each page lists the Lectionary readings for the day, with the main psalms for that day highlighted in **bold**. The collect of the day – either the *Common Worship* collect or the shorter additional collect – is also included.

For those using this book in conjunction with a service of Morning Prayer, the following conventions apply: a psalm printed in parentheses is omitted if it has been used as the opening canticle at that office; a psalm marked with an asterisk may be shortened if desired.

A short reflection is provided on either the Old or New Testament reading. Popular writers, experienced ministers, biblical scholars and theologians all contribute to this series, bringing with them their own emphases, enthusiasms and approaches to biblical interpretation.

Regular users of Morning Prayer and *Time to Pray* (from *Common Worship: Daily Prayer*) and anyone who follows the Lectionary for their regular Bible reading will benefit from the rich variety of traditions represented in these stimulating and accessible pieces.

This volume also includes both a simple form of *Common Worship* Morning Prayer (see inside front and back covers) and a short form of Night Prayer, also known as Compline (see pp. 332–3), particularly for the benefit of those readers who are new to the habit of the Daily Office or for any reader while travelling.

Building daily prayer into daily life

In our morning routines, there are many tasks we do without giving much thought to them, and others that we do with careful attention. Daily prayer and Bible reading is a strange mixture of these. These are disciplines (and gifts) that we as Christians should have in our daily pattern, but they are not tasks to be ticked off. Rather they are a key component of our developing relationship with God. In them is *life* – for the fruits of this time are to be lived out by us – and to be most fruitful, the task requires both purpose and letting go.

In saying a daily office of prayer, we make the deliberate decision to say 'yes' to spending time with God – the God who is always with us. In prayer and attentive reading of the Scriptures, there is both a conscious entering into God's presence and a 'letting go' of all we strive to control: both are our acknowledgement that it is God who is God.

> *... come into his presence with singing.*
>
> *Know that the Lord is God.*
> *It is he that has made us, and we are his;*
> *we are his people, and the sheep of his pasture.*
>
> *Enter his gates with thanksgiving...*
>
> *(Psalm 100, a traditional Canticle at Morning Prayer)*

If we want a relationship with someone to deepen and grow, we need to spend time with that person. It can be no surprise that the same is true between us and God.

In our daily routines, I suspect that most of us intentionally look in the mirror; occasionally we might see beyond the surface of our external reflection and catch a glimpse of who we truly are. For me, a regular pattern of daily prayer and Bible reading is like a hard look in a clean mirror: it gives a clear reflection of myself, my life and the world in which I live. But it is more than that, for in it I can also see the reflection of God who is most clearly revealed in Jesus Christ and present with us now in the Holy Spirit.

This commitment to daily prayer is about our relationship with the God who is love. St Paul, in his great passage about love, speaks of now seeing 'in a mirror, dimly' but one day seeing face to face: 'Now I know only in part; then I will know fully, even as I have been fully known' (1 Corinthians 13.12). Our daily prayer is part of that seeing in a mirror dimly, and it is also part of our deep yearning for an ever-clearer vision of our God. As we read Scripture, the past and the future converge in the present moment. We hear words from long ago – some of which can appear strange and confusing – and yet, the Holy Spirit is living and active in the present. In this place of relationship and revelation, we open ourselves to the possibility of being changed, of being reshaped in a way that is good for us and all creation.

It is important that the words of prayer and Scripture should penetrate deep within rather than be a mere veneer. A quiet location is therefore a helpful starting point. For some, domestic circumstances or daily schedule make that difficult, but it is never impossible to become more fully present to God. The depths of our being can still be accessed no matter the world's clamour and activity. An awareness of this is all part of our journey from a false sense of control to a place of letting go, to a place where there is an opportunity for transformation.

Sometimes in our attention to Scripture, there will be connection with places of joy or pain; we might be encouraged or provoked or both. As we look and see and encounter God more deeply, there will be thanksgiving and repentance; the cries of our heart will surface as we acknowledge our needs and desires for ourselves and the world. The liturgy of Morning Prayer gives this voice and space.

I find it helpful to begin Morning Prayer by lighting a candle. This marks my sense of purpose and my acknowledgement of Christ's presence with me. It is also a silent prayer for illumination as I prepare to be attentive to what I see in the mirror, both of myself and of God. Amid the revelation of Scripture and the cries of my heart, the constancy of the tiny flame bears witness to the hope and light of Christ in all that is and will be.

When the candle is extinguished, I try to be still as I watch the smoke disappear. For me, it is symbolic of my prayers merging with the day. I know that my prayer and the reading of Scripture are not the smoke and mirrors of delusion. Rather, they are about encounter and discovery as I seek to venture into the day to love and serve the Lord as a disciple of Jesus Christ.

+ Rachel Treweek

Monday 28 November

Psalms **50**, 54 *or* **1**, 2, 3
Isaiah 42.18-end
Revelation 19

Isaiah 42.18-end

'Who is blind but my servant ...?' (v.19)

The physical inability to see always is the object of Jesus' special tenderness. Some of the most touching moments in the Gospels describe the healing of people who are blind from birth. Things get more complicated with metaphorical blindness, which is pervasive in Scripture. We know how severely Jesus decries the Pharisees' self-inflicted unwillingness to see: they think that they can see better than anyone else but fail to recognize God's action in history.

Scripture, however, knows yet another form of blindness, one that uniquely afflicts those who lovingly and painstakingly try to understand God's ways – to follow him, worship him, serve him. It is the blindness of the 'servants', that is the prophets, the contemplative souls and the saints. Authentic discipleship exposes us to this form of blindness, an often agonizing inability to see the salvation of God, to make sense of God's ways. Spiritual authors have described it as the 'night of the soul' and explained it with an image: when we have spent some time in a poorly lit room and step outside into a sunny garden, we are blinded not by the absence of light but by its abundance.

In Scripture, physical blindness can only be healed by a miracle. The moral blindness of the pharisees requires a conversion of the heart. The spiritual blindness of the disciple has no remedy other than patience, perseverance and prayer – this is the only way in which our eyes slowly adjusts to divine light.

COLLECT

Almighty God,
give us grace to cast away the works of darkness
and to put on the armour of light,
now in the time of this mortal life,
in which your Son Jesus Christ came to us in great humility;
that on the last day,
when he shall come again in his glorious majesty
to judge the living and the dead,
we may rise to the life immortal;
through him who is alive and reigns with you,
in the unity of the Holy Spirit,
one God, now and for ever.

Reflection by **Luigi Gioia**

Psalms **80**, 82 *or* **5**, 6 (8)
Isaiah 43.1-13
Revelation 20

Tuesday 29 November

Isaiah 43.1-13

'I am God, and also henceforth I am He' (v.13)

Interpreting the meaning of God's name, 'I am He', or Yahweh, has kept theologians and philosophers busy for centuries. Too holy for our forebears in faith to pronounce, it was invested with sacred power, as if it were a potent magic formula – something not to be repeated in vain, terrifying, even dangerous.

The prophet Isaiah seems unconcerned by these qualms. 'I am He' comes up insistently, almost obsessively in his prophecies. We have not only to believe, but also 'know, and understand' that 'I am He'. 'I am He' is an invitation: it means something like 'I am in charge of history, and you will see how only by staying with me'. The only way of knowing God is by waiting to see what he actually does, not just for a little while, but through the whole of history.

Who could have made sense of what Michelangelo was doing during the long years it took him to paint the Sistine Chapel? Pope Julius II, who had commissioned this work, often thought it would never come to anything. He knew the subject of the painting, but could not make sense of it until the scaffolding was removed and he could see the whole fresco.

Isaiah says that we are 'called by God's name': this means that who God is, what God does, becomes our identity over time. We will really know who God is only when we see what he has made of us once his work is completed. In the meantime, we stand, keep our eyes open, and wait.

COLLECT

Almighty God,
as your kingdom dawns,
turn us from the darkness of sin to the
light of holiness,
that we may be ready to meet you
in our Lord and Saviour, Jesus Christ.

Reflection by **Luigi Gioia**

Wednesday 30 November

Andrew the Apostle

Psalms 47, 147.1-12
Ezekiel 47.1-12
or Ecclesiasticus 14.20-end
John 12.20-32

Ezekiel 47.1-12

'Their fruit will be for food, and their leaves for healing' (v.12)

Where is the river Ezekiel saw in his vision – a river so deep that we cannot cross it, a river that brings freshness to stagnant waters, abundance of fruits and waters trees with healing leaves? John's Gospel seems to refer to this image when it describes water welling up from Jesus' side on the cross: Jesus spoke of his own body as the temple, and the waters of baptism flow from this temple, becoming a river that runs through the whole of history and brings life to people of all times and in all places.

John, however, gives an even more subtle twist to this image when he hints at the fact that Jesus himself is the river. Our thirst is not only for something God wants to give to us – it is a thirst for God himself: 'As a deer longs for flowing streams, so my soul longs for you, O God. My soul thirsts for God, for the living God' (Psalm 42.1-2). This is a thirst quenched only by going to Jesus and drinking of him: 'Let anyone who is thirsty come to me' (John 7.37). And as he quenches this thirst, he himself becomes a river that starts flowing through and from those who drink of him: 'Out of the believer's heart shall flow rivers of living water' (John 7.38).

Our thirst, our lack, our longings are what is needed to gush forth God and healing to the world.

COLLECT

Almighty God,
who gave such grace to your apostle Saint Andrew
that he readily obeyed the call of your Son Jesus Christ
and brought his brother with him:
call us by your holy word,
and give us grace to follow you without delay
and to tell the good news of your kingdom;
through Jesus Christ your Son our Lord,
who is alive and reigns with you,
in the unity of the Holy Spirit,
one God, now and for ever.

Reflection by **Luigi Gioia**

Psalms **42**, 43 *or* 14, **15**, 16
Isaiah 44.1-8
Revelation 21.9-21

Thursday 1 December

Isaiah 44.1-8

'Israel whom I have chosen!' (v.1)

Etymologies are often uncertain, but their very vagueness can be valuable and productive, because it leaves a place for the imagination. This is all the more true in the case of names, as with 'Israel'. The only aspect of the meaning of this name that is certain is its end, 'El', which is a diminutive of Elohim, the name of God. Insofar as this word is addressed to me today, I am Israel. God sees me so inseparably bound with him that he calls me by his name.

God has chosen us, loved us to the point that this has become who we are. We are called by God's name yes, but for what?

There is, however, a contradictory element to the name of Israel, which precludes any romantic idealization of this love. Israel can equally mean: 'She/He who struggles with God, or fights with God'. In the course of history, being chosen by God has been both a blessing and a curse – for the chosen people, for the Church and for each one of us.

God constantly loves us by challenging us, and we love him in return by trusting him, yes, but also at times by fighting back at him, crying out our frustration, our disappointment and our anger to him. Isn't this what always happens when two people love and choose each other for real?

COLLECT

Almighty God,
give us grace to cast away the works of darkness
and to put on the armour of light,
now in the time of this mortal life,
in which your Son Jesus Christ came to us in great humility;
that on the last day,
when he shall come again in his glorious majesty
to judge the living and the dead,
we may rise to the life immortal;
through him who is alive and reigns with you,
in the unity of the Holy Spirit,
one God, now and for ever.

Reflection by **Luigi Gioia**

Friday 2 December

Psalms **25**, 26 *or* 17, **19**
Isaiah 44.9-23
Revelation 21.22 – 22.5

Isaiah 44.9-23

'Save me: for you are my god!' (v.17)

Imagine a fishbowl immersed in a lake and two fish, one inside, the other outside. The fish inside the bowl represents those willing to be contained by one given religion; the fish free to swim in the whole lake stands for those who opt instead for spirituality. This fishbowl is how many people see religion today, not only those who say 'I am spiritual but not a believer', but many Christians too.

The time when our perceptions of God and our worldview were entirely controlled and 'contained' by powerful Church authorities is over, and few really regret it. We are unwilling to let any institution set boundaries to our faith or our lives. The personal quest for spirituality is perceived as more authentic. Wherever we stand on this, it is characteristic of our times. And now, as ever, the only way of dealing with it is by cultivating the old virtue of discernment.

It would be naïve to believe that the space inside the fishbowl is safer, that we are protected from wrong beliefs and wrong behaviours. Even the most rigid doctrines and regulations for living can end up replacing trust in God with something like we see in today's reading – a parody of the true object of our faith. The golden calf made by the people in the desert was not meant to be another god, but a manageable version of Yahweh. This is what made it so dangerous.

At the core of our prayer and our faith there should always be this question: who is the god to whom I say: 'Save me'?

COLLECT

Almighty God,
give us grace to cast away the works of darkness
and to put on the armour of light,
now in the time of this mortal life,
in which your Son Jesus Christ came to us in great humility;
that on the last day,
when he shall come again in his glorious majesty
to judge the living and the dead,
we may rise to the life immortal;
through him who is alive and reigns with you,
in the unity of the Holy Spirit,
one God, now and for ever.

Reflection by **Luigi Gioia**

Psalms **9** (10) *or* 20, 21, **23**
Isaiah 44.24 – 45.13
Revelation 22.6-end

Saturday 3 December

Isaiah 44.24 – 45.13

'I am the Lord, and there is no other' (45.5)

Understandably, we are wary of people who feel the need to flaunt their credentials all the time. Those who wield real power and influence, who possess real knowledge and expertise, are often the most understated and self-effacing. Admittedly, this too can be just a more refined form of self-importance, even if it is perhaps a more attractive character trait – and more effective.

What are we to make then of Isaiah's version of a God who feels the need to repeat obsessively 'I am the Lord (the one who really is in charge)', and 'there is no other, apart from me there is no God', and to remind us that he is our maker, that he can act in history as he pleases to 'bring prosperity and create disaster', and that nobody has the right to question him? Isn't this typical of people who are insecure?

We might wonder, with some reason, whether deep down God is not doubting himself. One of his major claims is that he is in charge of history, and the various Cyruses are just unwitting instruments of his will. Maybe. The least we can say is that the evidence is not compelling. Those who put together the Bible as we know it cannot have missed these contradictions, and yet they felt that such a dominant portrayal of God was necessary.

Did they foresee that this was precisely the background needed for the ultimate shattering of all human projections of God – the shocking self-effacing, self-emptying real identity of God revealed in Jesus Christ?

Almighty God,
as your kingdom dawns,
turn us from the darkness of sin to the
light of holiness,
that we may be ready to meet you
in our Lord and Saviour, Jesus Christ.

COLLECT

Reflection by **Luigi Gioia**

Monday 5 December

Psalm **44** *or* 27, **30**
Isaiah 45.14-end
1 Thessalonians 1

Isaiah 45.14-end

'Truly, you are a God who hides himself' (v.15)

St Augustine, together with all the Fathers of the Church, teaches that the Bible is a difficult book, and that this is not something to regret, but to rejoice in.

One of his arguments is that we only appreciate the things that require effort to obtain. Another is that we love difficulties because they stimulate our inventiveness and resourcefulness – hence our fascination for riddles, or for conquering the highest mountaintops. The longer we search and toil, the greater our desire grows. Desire widens our hearts and makes us capable of receiving greater delight and a fuller sense of fulfilment whenever we gain a deeper glimpse of meaning through our meditation.

There is a sense in which Scripture is best seen not as the place where God reveals himself, but where he *hides* himself. The good news is that he is in there, but crucially also that mastering the content of the Bible does not mean possessing God.

We have to be content with knowing that we never seek him in vain, and that whenever we wrestle with these pages, spend time with them, and persist in knocking, eventually some door opens, some meaning enlightens our mind, and some comfort is brought to our heart.

COLLECT

O Lord, raise up, we pray, your power
and come among us,
and with great might succour us;
that whereas, through our sins and wickedness
we are grievously hindered
in running the race that is set before us,
your bountiful grace and mercy
may speedily help and deliver us;
through Jesus Christ your Son our Lord,
to whom with you and the Holy Spirit,
be honour and glory, now and for ever.

Reflection by **Luigi Gioia**

Psalms **56**, 57 *or* 32, **36**
Isaiah 46
I Thessalonians 2.1-12

Tuesday 6 December

Isaiah 46

'I am ... declaring the end from the beginning' (vv.9,10)

Imagine waking up in a train without knowing how you ended up in it, nor where it is coming from or where it is going. After the initial surprise, you get acquainted with the other passengers, assess your situation, and start trying to make the best of it. Is this image not true of our lives, both individually and collectively?

We can speculate about our beginning, but have to rely on what other people tell us about it, or on what science helps us to discover. For a long time we believed we had been fully formed human beings from the beginning – which was thought to be no more than a few thousand years in the past. Then, to our great shock, we found out that we humans started as micro-organisms living on underwater rocks some 3.7 billion years ago.

However much we might believe that we possess real agency in our present life, our beginning does not belong to us. Nor does our end. We do not know when and how we will die, nor when and how history will end. However, we know that something, or someone, upholds and sustains us in being and, hopefully, in purpose.

We do not have hard evidence, of course, just a promise: 'My purpose will stand'. We do not know how this promise will play out, but it gives us confidence that for as long as we are on this train, our lives have purpose and direction.

COLLECT

Almighty God,
purify our hearts and minds,
that when your Son Jesus Christ comes again as judge and saviour
we may be ready to receive him,
who is our Lord and our God.

Reflection by **Luigi Gioia**

Wednesday 7 December

Psalms **62**, 63 *or* **34**
Isaiah 47
I Thessalonians 2.13-end

Isaiah 47

'I was angry with my people' (v.6)

'The people of Israel went into exile because God was angry with them.' The logic goes: 'Bad things happen to us when God is displeased or wants to teach us a lesson'. Much of what Isaiah says seems to corroborate this narrative, as do many other passages in Scripture, such as Psalm 119.71: 'It is good for me that I was humbled, so that I might learn your statutes.'

How can such a twisted version of God's action in history have made its way into Scripture? For a very simple reason: Scripture sometimes works as a window; at other times as a mirror. Sometimes, it opens our horizon on uncontaminated views of God's identity; at other times, it reflects back to us the image of the primordial, crude instincts that dictate how we would behave if we were God.

Most of Isaiah's preaching is devoted to the unmasking of what we falsely worship. Unwittingly, however, it also gives voice to our guilt. Unresolved or buried guilt is a potent agent of self-destruction. Guilt shouted at God, unfair as it might be, gives God a chance to heal it with the only effective antidote, that is his tenderness.

If you think that God may have been angry with you, shout the pain this causes you at him, and allow him to comfort you: 'When you walk through the fire you shall not be burned ... because I love you ... Do not fear, for I am with you' (Isaiah 43.2-5).

COLLECT

O Lord, raise up, we pray, your power
and come among us,
and with great might succour us;
that whereas, through our sins and wickedness
we are grievously hindered
in running the race that is set before us,
your bountiful grace and mercy
may speedily help and deliver us;
through Jesus Christ your Son our Lord,
to whom with you and the Holy Spirit,
be honour and glory, now and for ever.

Reflection by **Luigi Gioia**

Psalms 53, **54**, 60 *or* **37***
Isaiah 48.1-11
1 Thessalonians 3

Thursday 8 December

Isaiah 48.1-11

'I make you hear new things' (v.6)

Is there anything akin to impatience in God?

It is unwise to dismiss this question on the pretext that God is timeless, or to say that human attitudes that Scripture attributes to God, such as anger, jealousy, longing or frustration, are purely metaphorical.

When we think about God, we tend to stress his attributes of being all-powerful, all-knowing, and present through all time and in all places. When he talks about himself, God emphasizes his freedom: nobody can dictate what he can or can't do. God can – and in fact does – choose to be powerless when we refuse his love. He can – and does – let himself be affected, wounded, ignored and misrepresented by us. The aspects of his nature and identity he puts to the fore are his 'loving-kindness' and his 'faithfulness'. Even if a mother might forget her child, he will never forget us (Isaiah 49.15).

So yes, we can say God is impatient: he longs for the moment when we will give up our own projections of him and learn to overcome our expectations of a God who chooses to act not through might, but through powerlessness. And he is especially impatient for the time when we will finally trust him and come close enough to him to be able to hear the 'new things, the hidden things' (still) unknown to us.

COLLECT

Almighty God,
purify our hearts and minds,
that when your Son Jesus Christ comes again as judge and saviour
we may be ready to receive him,
who is our Lord and our God.

Reflection by **Luigi Gioia**

Friday 9 December

Psalms 85, **86** *or* **31**
Isaiah 48.12-end
1 Thessalonians 4.1-12

Isaiah 48.12-end

'There is no peace ... for the wicked' (v.22)

Often, we are tempted to think 'if only ...' – if only we were in a different place, or had a better job or more money; if only that annoying person was not in our lives; if only we had met the right partner, then we would be at peace. Peace eludes us, so we believe, because of our circumstances. Some external factors can indeed be the source of such trouble and anxiety that we are never really able to relax or rest. Deep down, however, we know that real, lasting peace depends on where we look for meaning and inspiration in our lives.

The 'wicked' in this context are those who do not pay attention to God's commandments. 'Commandments' – here as elsewhere in Scripture – do not stand primarily for orders, but for God's vision for humanity, his plan of salvation, his covenant.

Interestingly, Isaiah's invitation is not to *obey* them, but to *pay attention* to them, 'O that you had paid attention to my commandments! Then your prosperity would have been like a river'. The same idea recurs in Psalm 1, where the wicked 'are like chaff that the wind drives away' because they didn't learn to find that 'their delight is in the law of the Lord'.

Do we want peace? Let's pay attention, and look for delight.

COLLECT

O Lord, raise up, we pray, your power
and come among us,
and with great might succour us;
that whereas, through our sins and wickedness
we are grievously hindered
in running the race that is set before us,
your bountiful grace and mercy
may speedily help and deliver us;
through Jesus Christ your Son our Lord,
to whom with you and the Holy Spirit,
be honour and glory, now and for ever.

Reflection by **Luigi Gioia**

Psalm **145** *or* 41, **42**, 43
Isaiah 49.1-13
1 Thessalonians 4.13-end

Saturday 10 December

Isaiah 49.1-13

'For the Lord has comforted his people' (v.13)

Physical touch is the irreplaceable way through which our sense of worth and security develops in the first days, months and years of our existence. Hence it has a unique power to convey love and comfort at crucial times in our lives: holding the hand of a person who is ill, a gentle pat on the back to encourage someone, hugging a relative or a friend who is grieving.

And yet, an even greater comforting power than physical touch is contained in the words we say or the stories we tell. We often refer to words or stories as 'touching' because they move us, have an impact on us, change something in us – even though they do not involve any physical contact.

We are in relation with an invisible God, a God no one has ever seen. And yet, this is a God who reaches out to us, makes himself known and his presence felt by us, who touches us and so comforts us.

Most of what Isaiah is compelled to prophesy is made up of woes. He does announce freedom, restoration, salvation, but for the future. Here, however, there is one thing he pours on his listeners: God's own comfort. He knows that his human words have been given the extraordinary power to bring God's own 'touch', that this is the mission entrusted to him: 'Comfort, O comfort my people, says your God. Speak tenderly to Jerusalem' (Isaiah 40.1-2).

COLLECT

Almighty God,
purify our hearts and minds,
that when your Son Jesus Christ comes again as
judge and saviour
we may be ready to receive him,
who is our Lord and our God.

Reflection by **Luigi Gioia**

Monday 12 December

Psalm **40** *or* **44**
Isaiah 49.14-25
1 Thessalonians 5.1-11

Isaiah 49.14-25

'I have inscribed you on the palms of my hands' (v.16)

King Cyrus the Great has conquered Babylon. This is good news for the Israelites, exiled and longing for home. Surely God is looking out for his chosen people. But at the beginning of Chapter 49, there has been further talk of the 'servant'. Who is this servant? Does this talk of the servant mean that God has given up on Israel after all? Israel laments: 'The Lord has forsaken me, and my Lord has forgotten me.' Insecurity reigns.

No, says Isaiah to the people of Israel. God will never give up on you. Just as a mother cannot forget the child she has borne; just as the bride looks with longing at the one she is to marry, God will never let you go. 'I have inscribed you on the palm of my hands.'

I'm told that tattoo artists try hard to dissuade people from having the name of their beloved tattooed on their bodies in the madness of new love. They know they'll have work to do if and when the relationship breaks down. Better to be sure the relationship is permanent before permanently inking your body. God has no such doubts. Israel's name, my name, your name, tattooed on God's hand. Forever.

When someone asks me to pray for them and the need is urgent, I often write their name on the palm of my hand. It reminds me to pray for them throughout the day. It reminds me that God has got them and will never let them – or me, or you – go.

COLLECT

O Lord Jesus Christ,
who at your first coming sent your messenger
to prepare your way before you:
grant that the ministers and stewards of your mysteries
may likewise so prepare and make ready your way
by turning the hearts of the disobedient to the wisdom of the just,
that at your second coming to judge the world
we may be found an acceptable people in your sight;
for you are alive and reign with the Father
in the unity of the Holy Spirit,
one God, now and for ever.

Reflection by **Jan McFarlane**

Psalms **70**, 74 *or* **48**, 52
Isaiah 50
1 Thessalonians 5.12-end

Tuesday 13 December

Isaiah 50

'Morning by morning he wakens ... my ear to listen' (v.4)

The coming of the servant of whom Isaiah speaks doesn't mean that God is going to divorce his chosen people; instead, they are to learn more about the servant so that they may recognize him when he comes. So, in the third of Isaiah's four 'servant songs', we learn a little more of how the servant will deliver Israel, restore Jerusalem, and reunite the whole world with the creator God. And it's not going to be easy, Isaiah warns. The servant will teach God's people through careful listening to God, obedience and suffering.

First and foremost, God's servant will be thoroughly tuned in to God. And that means careful listening to God's voice, morning by morning. The very fact that you are reading this probably means that you have begun your morning listening to God's voice speaking through the Scriptures and possibly praying through one of the Church's liturgies.

Ministering in a Cathedral, we get through very many words in worship. It's easy to think that once we've got to the end of a service, we've prayed. But have we really listened? Sadly for many of us, our prayers rarely contain much silence, much attentive listening. The twentieth-century spiritual writer and teacher, Evelyn Underhill, said that the world is full of 'jangling noises' and that as Christians we know there are better melodies. But, she asks, how can we transmit the music of eternity unless we tune in to it each and every day?

COLLECT

God for whom we watch and wait,
you sent John the Baptist to prepare the way of your Son:
give us courage to speak the truth,
to hunger for justice,
and to suffer for the cause of right,
with Jesus Christ our Lord.

Reflection by **Jan McFarlane**

Wednesday 14 December

Psalms **75**, 96 *or* **119.57-80**
Isaiah 51.1-8
2 Thessalonians 1

Isaiah 51.1-8

'Look to the rock from which you were hewn' (v.1)

If God's chosen people are to fulfil their destiny, they must remain strong and refuse to be blown off course. Isaiah encourages them to remember their roots – how God has called them, cared for them in the wilderness and led them out of slavery in Egypt. To remember that God has been present for them in the past and will be there for them in the future. To remember 'the rock from which you were hewn' and 'the quarry from which you were dug'.

As a bishop in Derbyshire, I would often find myself driving back home late at night along roads with no street lights but brightly illuminated by the many working quarries dotted around that county. Late into the night, the quarrying continued, the ancient stone, there long before you and I existed, becoming gate posts, lintels, sills and flags, the bedrock of buildings that will stand long after you and I have gone. I often reflected as I drove what a tiny part we play in God's purposes and how it's as well to see our lives from the perspective of eternity.

No matter where we find ourselves today, we should look to the rock from which we were hewn and remember God's faithfulness to us in the past and his promise never to let us go. We can then step out boldly into the day, confident that the day is in God's hands, and our task is simply to follow.

COLLECT

O Lord Jesus Christ,
who at your first coming sent your messenger
to prepare your way before you:
grant that the ministers and stewards of your mysteries
may likewise so prepare and make ready your way
by turning the hearts of the disobedient to the wisdom of the just,
that at your second coming to judge the world
we may be found an acceptable people in your sight;
for you are alive and reign with the Father
in the unity of the Holy Spirit,
one God, now and for ever.

Reflection by **Jan McFarlane**

Psalms **76**, 97 *or* 56, **57** (63*)
Isaiah 51.9-16
2 Thessalonians 2

Thursday 15 December

Isaiah 51.9-16

'Awake, as in days of old' (v.9)

Isaiah gives the people of God a good shake. Wake up! Have you forgotten how God acts? Have you forgotten God's mighty power? Have you forgotten how God has created order out of chaos, symbolized by Rahab the sea monster? How God has defeated evil, symbolized by the dragon?

God will act and God's people need to be awake, alert, ready to follow. If like me, you sometimes need an alarm clock that bellows like a foghorn to wake you out of sleep, then these words will resonate. As we travel just past the midway point in our Advent journey, we hear again Isaiah's insistent alarm call.

Has our worship become something we sit through on automatic pilot? Has our prayer life become the dull recitation of familiar words? Have we become over-familiar with so many Bible texts that they've lost their impact? Have we already sung so many carols this Advent that the impact of Christmas itself risks losing its wonder?

If so, today we need to hear again Isaiah's call to wake up. In the words of the popular morning hymn, to 'shake off dull sloth and joyful rise to pay our morning sacrifice'. Are we expecting to see God in action today? To hear God's voice speaking to us? If not, why not? Are we guilty of domesticating our dragon-slaying, chaos-redeeming, sea-parting God?

COLLECT

God for whom we watch and wait,
you sent John the Baptist to prepare the way of your Son:
give us courage to speak the truth,
to hunger for justice,
and to suffer for the cause of right,
with Jesus Christ our Lord.

Reflection by **Jan McFarlane**

Friday 16 December

Psalms 77, **98** *or* **51**, 54
Isaiah 51.17-end
2 Thessalonians 3

Isaiah 51.17-end

'I have taken from your hand the cup of staggering' (v.22)

Isaiah now turns his attention from the exiles in Babylon to God's people struggling and suffering among the ruins of desolate Jerusalem. Their captors demonstrate their power by making the captives lie in the dust of the ruined city while they trample on their backs. Their humiliation is complete. Meanwhile God's people, staggering like those who are drunk, are so depleted that they have no sons and daughters to rescue them from their disgrace and to lead them safely home.

But they too are to wake up, to rouse themselves from the depression and despair that is akin to a drunken stupor. They are to get ready to welcome back the ones who will return from exile with singing. God will take the 'cup of staggering' from their lips – the cup that they have earned through their unfaithfulness to God – and their oppressors will drink it instead.

Drinking from a common cup has many resonances for Christians. 'Are you able to drink the cup that I drink?' Jesus asks his disciples (Mark 10.38). Jesus takes the cup destined for us – the cup filled with our waywardness and unfaithfulness and wrong-doing – and drinks it right down to the bitter dregs. And in its place, he gives us a cup of wine, as red as his blood so freely shed, filled to the brim with undeserved forgiveness, grace and love.

COLLECT

O Lord Jesus Christ,
who at your first coming sent your messenger
to prepare your way before you:
grant that the ministers and stewards of your mysteries
may likewise so prepare and make ready your way
by turning the hearts of the disobedient to the wisdom of the just,
that at your second coming to judge the world
we may be found an acceptable people in your sight;
for you are alive and reign with the Father
in the unity of the Holy Spirit,
one God, now and for ever.

Reflection by **Jan McFarlane**

Psalm **71** *or* **68**
Isaiah 52.1-12
Jude

Saturday 17 December

Isaiah 52.1-12

'Your God reigns' (v.7)

Isaiah's wake-up call now reaches a deafening crescendo as he rouses from deep slumber those in exile in Babylon and those left in the ruined city of Jerusalem. The exiles are to return with singing, and Jerusalem is to be restored. It's time to get ready.

Many of us will remember the first time of lockdown at the beginning of the Covid-19 pandemic when we were instructed not to leave our homes for fear of an invisible but deadly enemy. We got very used to slobbing around in casual clothes, with no one to see and nowhere to go. God's people have been lounging in their 'casuals', but it's now time to put on their 'beautiful clothes' in preparation for their release from captivity.

And so, on this eve of the fourth Sunday of Advent, we see, like the sentinels on the ruined walls of Jerusalem, a lone messenger appearing on the horizon. As he approaches, his garbled shouting is shaped into words that spread like wildfire through the city. 'Your God reigns!'

We remember another messenger, this time one with wings, who will carry good news to Mary, and whether the beautiful feet of the messenger brings to mind Handel's *Messiah* or Leonard Smith's *Our God reigns,* or any one of the many hymns or worship songs based on this triumphant passage, let us sing – literally sing – today of the God who has comforted his people and rescued us from all that holds us captive.

COLLECT

God for whom we watch and wait,
you sent John the Baptist to prepare the way of your Son:
give us courage to speak the truth,
to hunger for justice,
and to suffer for the cause of right,
with Jesus Christ our Lord.

Reflection by **Jan McFarlane**

Monday 19 December

Psalms 144, **146**
Isaiah 52.13 – end of 53
2 Peter 1.1-15

Isaiah 52.13 – end of 53

'Surely he has borne our infirmities' (53.4)

We come now to the fourth of Isaiah's 'Servant Songs'. In the first three songs, we learned that the servant would be a light to the gentiles (42.1-9) and that he would undergo much suffering. In this fourth song, we are told the meaning of his suffering – suffering so terrible it will result in him appearing less than human. But it is suffering with a purpose, as difficult as it is for us to understand.

In what theologians call 'the doctrine of substitution', the suffering servant, in whom Christians see the person of Jesus, takes upon himself the consequences of our sin, our failures, our disobedience, and he goes to his death in our place, silently, like a lamb led to the slaughter.

And then that startling verse – 'it was the will of the Lord to crush him with pain'. We instinctively recoil from those words. How could the God we understand as Love deliberately allow such suffering? We don't really know why such terrible suffering should be necessary, just as we don't know why good and innocent people suffer seemingly for no purpose today. It is an act of the will and an act of faith to accept that it had to be so, and that somehow such suffering is a necessary part of love. And so we trust and believe that Christmas and Easter are inextricably bound and 'through him the will of the Lord shall prosper'.

COLLECT

God our redeemer,
who prepared the Blessed Virgin Mary
to be the mother of your Son:
grant that, as she looked for his coming as our saviour,
so we may be ready to greet him
when he comes again as our judge;
who is alive and reigns with you,
in the unity of the Holy Spirit,
one God, now and for ever.

Reflection by **Jan McFarlane**

Psalms **46**, 95
Isaiah 54
2 Peter 1.16 – 2.3

Tuesday 20 December

Isaiah 54

'Enlarge the site of your tent' (v.2)

Today, fortunately, we have a much greater understanding of why some women are unable to conceive or carry a child to full term, and how some men too are unable to play their part in the reproductive process. Not to have children is, thankfully, no longer seen as shameful. But in Isaiah's day, not to bear a child was not only shameful but also seen as disastrous in failing to continue the family line and to be provided for in one's old age.

The people of Israel would have thought immediately of Sarah and Abraham and their long-standing fear that they would not bear children – until miraculously they conceived Isaac and were promised descendants as numerous as the stars in the sky. In the same way, Isaiah says, God's people will grow in number once more, and as a pregnant woman has to wear bigger clothes to accommodate the child growing within her, so God's people are to make room for new growth.

We know that in many parts of the world congregations are shrinking. Are we expectant? Do we trust that God is in charge and that if we remain faithful, others will be attracted to the Christian faith and will come to join us? Are we preparing by making room for them? What might we need to do to ensure they are both expected and welcomed? And what might we need to stop doing too?

COLLECT

Eternal God,
as Mary waited for the birth of your Son,
so we wait for his coming in glory;
bring us through the birth pangs of this present age
to see, with her, our great salvation
in Jesus Christ our Lord.

Reflection by **Jan McFarlane**

Wednesday 21 December

Psalms **121**, 122, 123
Isaiah 55
2 Peter 2.4-end

Isaiah 55

'Ho, everyone who thirsts, come to the waters' (v.1)

As we turn to chapter 55, and as Christmas Day draws near, we hear God's open invitation to everyone who is thirsty to come to the waters, and to drink and to eat, whether they can afford to or not. No one is to be excluded from the source of life. Rich and sustaining nourishment is available, freely, for all.

The blessings of the servant's completed ministry are to be extended to the ends of the earth. This would have been challenging news for those who understood themselves to be God's chosen people. They had developed a distinct identity – one that made clear who was in and who was out. And now, suddenly, they are expected to put down the barriers, open the gates and let everyone in.

What barriers do we, as practising Christians, put up to keep others out? We may not be consciously doing so, but are our churches failing to grow because we are determining who is in and who should be kept firmly out? Have we created our own rules and regulations to keep God's blessings to ourselves? Or do we truly believe that God's love and grace and arms flung open wide in welcome are for everyone?

Over these next few days, our churches will welcome those who don't usually come. Do we let them in grudgingly and on our own terms? Or are our arms held wide open in genuine welcome, knowing that the Christ-child was born for them too?

COLLECT

God our redeemer,
who prepared the Blessed Virgin Mary
to be the mother of your Son:
grant that, as she looked for his coming as our saviour,
so we may be ready to greet him
when he comes again as our judge;
who is alive and reigns with you,
in the unity of the Holy Spirit,
one God, now and for ever.

Reflection by **Jan McFarlane**

Psalms **124**, 125, 126, 127
Isaiah 56.1-8
2 Peter 3

Thursday 22 December

Isaiah 56.1-8

'To the eunuchs ... an everlasting name' (vv.4-5)

Nowadays, we don't often use the word 'eunuch', but in the time of Isaiah, the term was used for men who had been castrated or who lived celibate lives, or who, for whatever reason, were unable to procreate, and who were therefore treated as outcasts. But not so in the new world Isaiah's figure of the servant will usher in. Though unable to have children of their own, eunuchs who live faithful lives will have an honoured place and will bear spiritual children – those to whom they have passed on the faith. No longer regarded as 'a dry tree', they are given the opportunity of becoming faithful, fruitful vines.

This prophecy comes to fruition when in the New Testament, in the Acts of the Apostles, Philip encounters an Ethiopian eunuch on the road to Gaza. The eunuch asks Philip to explain the Scriptures to him, and he believes. He asks Philip to baptize him, which he does the minute that they spot some water. Philip understands that the good news of Jesus Christ is for everyone and that there are no barriers to baptism. Tradition has it that the eunuch went on to found the Ethiopian Church.

Who then are today's outcasts? Who do we consider to be those who might 'contaminate' our community of faith? What barriers do we put up to prevent them from coming in?

Or do we seek out the nearest water in which to baptize them?

COLLECT

Eternal God,
as Mary waited for the birth of your Son,
so we wait for his coming in glory;
bring us through the birth pangs of this present age
to see, with her, our great salvation
in Jesus Christ our Lord.

Reflection by **Jan McFarlane**

Friday 23 December

128, 129, **130**, 131
Isaiah 63.1-6
2 John

Isaiah 63.1-6

'I have trodden the wine press alone' (v.3)

The lectionary asks us to skip forward a few chapters, and we land on a seemingly random passage where all talk of joyful salvation is subsumed in a graphic description of a bloody battle. Once we've recovered from any sense of disorientation, we remind ourselves that salvation and judgement are two sides of the same coin.

The baby whose birth we will celebrate in two days' time comes to bring salvation to the world. But before we get caught up in the joy of the innocence and purity of a newborn baby, surrounded by gentle farmyard animals and shepherds, we're reminded that this baby is on a mission and that the salvation he comes to bring will be achieved at great cost. The ushering in of God's love and saving grace involves the destruction of all that is evil – and the fight will be fierce and bloody.

We see immediately the link between garments stained with red grapes and those whose blood has been spilled when, 'I crushed them in my wrath'. The warrior whose task is to defeat evil has to do so alone – there is no helper to be found – and we think immediately of Jesus dying on the cross, abandoned and alone. The link between bloodshed in the defeat of evil, and the grapes turned into wine that we drink 'in remembrance' of him, is plain to see.

COLLECT

God our redeemer,
who prepared the Blessed Virgin Mary
to be the mother of your Son:
grant that, as she looked for his coming as our saviour,
so we may be ready to greet him
when he comes again as our judge;
who is alive and reigns with you,
in the unity of the Holy Spirit,
one God, now and for ever.

Reflection by **Jan McFarlane**

Psalms **45**, 113
Isaiah 58
3 John

Saturday 24 December

Christmas Eve

Isaiah 58

'Look, you serve your own interest on your fast-day' (v.3)

Separated from the temple in Jerusalem, the exiles in Babylon continued to practise their religion by following prescribed traditions, such as keeping the Sabbath, and by adding rituals such as fasting. Isaiah challenges those who are keeping the rules and regulations of their religion in a futile attempt to draw God's attention to themselves. Even worse, such rituals were being used as a means of competing with one another, squabbling as to who was doing best. Isaiah is clear that this is not what God wants – such rituals serve only to anger him.

Isaiah insists that there is no such thing as a private religion. Our rituals must build us up in faith, and our faith must lead us out in action. Sharing our food with those who are hungry is the sort of fasting God requires.

Tonight, we will hear in the distance angels singing. We will remember shepherds heading towards the backyard of a pub to find a baby lying in a manger made to hold food for cows. We will kneel and adore him, King of Kings and Lord of Lords, who has turned up in the most unlikely of places. But we mustn't stay there for too long. We're called to be up and about, being his hands and his feet, doing his work and bringing his light and life into the most unlikely areas of our neighbourhood.

COLLECT

Almighty God,
you make us glad with the yearly remembrance
of the birth of your Son Jesus Christ:
grant that, as we joyfully receive him as our redeemer,
so we may with sure confidence behold him
when he shall come to be our judge;
who is alive and reigns with you,
in the unity of the Holy Spirit,
one God, now and for ever.

Reflection by **Jan McFarlane**

Monday 26 December

Stephen, deacon, first martyr

Psalms **13**, 31.1-8, 150
Jeremiah 26.12-15
Acts 6

Jeremiah 26.12-15

'It is the Lord who sent me to prophesy ...' (v.12)

We know little of Stephen: he was a Hellenist rather than a Hebrew, first named of the seven, content to wait at tables and singled out as 'a man full of faith and the Holy Spirit' (Acts 6.1,5). Luke sets in his mouth one of the longest speeches in Acts, retelling the whole story of Israel. In his final moments, as the rocks are made ready, Stephen is granted a vision of Jesus standing at the right hand of God. Stephen sets himself in the long line of the prophets, including Jeremiah who placed his life on the line to deliver God's word to Israel.

Each year at Christmas, in the midst of turkey and presents and carols, our challenge is to find a fresh vision of Jesus, the centre and fulcrum of history. The Church dares to believe that Almighty God, maker of heaven and earth, is born as a human child. One human life, in one time and place, transforms our vision of every human life at all times and in all places.

Stephen offers the whole of his life in response to his vision of Christ, both in his willingness to serve, in his witness to the faith, in his courage and in the manner of his death. These twelve days of Christmas offer an opportunity to be still at the turn of the year, to see more clearly the Lord we follow and to prepare ourselves for acts of witness to which Jesus calls us in the coming days.

COLLECT

Gracious Father,
who gave the first martyr Stephen
grace to pray for those who took up stones against him:
grant that in all our sufferings for the truth
we may learn to love even our enemies
and to seek forgiveness for those who desire our hurt,
looking up to heaven to him who was crucified for us,
Jesus Christ, our mediator and advocate,
who is alive and reigns with you,
in the unity of the Holy Spirit,
one God, now and for ever.

Reflection by **Steven Croft**

Psalms **21**, 147.13-end
Exodus 33.12-end
1 John 2.1-11

Tuesday 27 December

John, Apostle and Evangelist

1 John 2.1-11

'... whoever says, "I abide in him"' (v.6)

Where do you live? A home should be a place of sanctuary, security, and safety and should also be a place of love. St John offers the image of making our home in Jesus: abiding here.

We know that we are welcome in this home and that there is room for all. To abide here is to know that we are loved; to be at ease in the love and friendship of Christ. To abide is to stay awhile and to be able to rest and recover our identity, no matter how long or how difficult our journey home. To abide here is to be strangely warmed and to rediscover the fires of joy in the depth of winter.

But there is more to living here than resting by the fire, vital though that is. John finishes his sentence in this way: 'whoever says, "I abide in him" ought to walk just as he walked'. The place where we live sets the manner of our journeys.

The Epistle takes us back then to the gospel. If I am to walk as he walks – in love – then what will that mean for my diary, for my friendships, for my habits of conversation? As I abide in love, am I able to find the courage to let go of grudges and resentments and jealousies, to allow the light to overcome the darkness?

COLLECT

Merciful Lord,
cast your bright beams of light upon the Church:
that, being enlightened by the teaching
of your blessed apostle and evangelist Saint John,
we may so walk in the light of your truth
that we may at last attain to the light of everlasting life;
through Jesus Christ your incarnate Son our Lord,
who is alive and reigns with you,
in the unity of the Holy Spirit,
one God, now and for ever.

Reflection by **Steven Croft**

Wednesday 28 December

The Holy Innocents

Psalms **36**, 146
Baruch 4.21-27
or Genesis 37.13-20
Matthew 18.1-10

Matthew 18.1-10

'Whoever becomes humble like this child ...' (v.4)

Tragedies seem worse at Christmas. Natural disasters prompt sharper questions. Human wickedness seems darker still against the backdrop of the cards and carols. Remembering the Holy Innocents pulls us back from the world of fairy stories with happy endings and reminds us that the incarnation is a rescue mission. The Son of God is born to save God's people from their sins – and from the consequences of those sins. The incarnation is powerful medicine for a deadly sickness abroad in the world.

It is Matthew who tells the story of these murders and Matthew above all who reminds us of the immense value of each of these little ones. Children are to be the pattern of our discipleship. Children are the guests who must be welcomed as Christ is welcomed. Children are to be kept safe from harm and stumbling.

Today is a day to give thanks for little children; to renew our commitment to keeping them safe from all harm; to deepen our commitment to help and act where children are hungry or homeless; to play our part in the repair of the planet we will hand on to them in this critical generation.

The fourth day of Christmas is also a day to remember that, whatever our age or title or the size of our ego, the only way to share in the wonder of Christmas is the way of humility, the way of the little children.

COLLECT

Heavenly Father,
whose children suffered at the hands of Herod,
though they had done no wrong:
by the suffering of your Son
and by the innocence of our lives
frustrate all evil designs
and establish your reign of justice and peace;
through Jesus Christ your Son our Lord,
who is alive and reigns with you,
in the unity of the Holy Spirit,
one God, now and for ever.

Reflection by **Steven Croft**

Psalms **19**, 20
Isaiah 57.15-end
John 1.1-18

Thursday 29 December

Isaiah 57.15-end

'... and also with those who are contrite and humble in spirit' (v.15)

Where does God live? In many different places according to this part of Isaiah. God is the high and lofty one who inhabits eternity, whose name is holy. This verse echoes the great vision of God in the temple in Isaiah 6, a vision of God that causes the prophet to feel small and unclean and far away: 'I dwell in the high and holy place.'

But not only there. For if God were only remote, transcendent and distant, that would serve only to make us feel small and unclean and far away also.

God comes to dwell in a different place altogether: 'with those who are contrite and humble in spirit' – with Mary carrying her child; with the shepherds running from the fields to Bethlehem; with the wise men on their long, cold journey; with Anna and Simeon in the temple.

God comes to dwell with all those who know that they are wretched, pitiable, poor, blind and naked (Revelation 3.17). Indeed, God does more than dwell with us. God comes to make a home within us; to abide in us as we abide in God. God comes to lift us up; to make us clean by grace, to draw us near again to the fires of the maker's love.

'The sacrifice of God is a broken spirit; a broken and contrite heart, O God, you will not despise' (Psalm 51.18).

COLLECT

Almighty God,
who wonderfully created us in your own image
and yet more wonderfully restored us
through your Son Jesus Christ:
grant that, as he came to share in our humanity,
so we may share the life of his divinity;
who is alive and reigns with you,
in the unity of the Holy Spirit,
one God, now and for ever.

Reflection by **Steven Croft**

Friday 30 December

Psalms 111, 112, **113**
Isaiah 59.1-15*a*
John 1.19-28

Isaiah 59.1-15*a*

'... truth stumbles in the public square' (v.14)

Isaiah 59 offers us an extraordinary and clear reflection on the relationship between personal sin and its public consequences in the life of the community. The oracles begin with individual wrongdoing: acts of violence, immorality, lies and slander. These transgressions create a barrier, a separation, between individuals and God. But this is not the only consequence.

Private sin multiplies with public consequences through one person imitating another. Wrongdoing infects communities, generations and a wider culture. The darkness grows deeper on the whole community. Life then becomes a shadow existence, groping in the dark after truth and happiness. We long for something different; we reach for it, but we cannot name it: 'We all growl like bears; like doves we moan mournfully.' These are the consequences of social as well as individual sin.

There is no place then for the great virtues of public life and human community: like uninvited guests they stand outside the party, a forgotten memory: 'Justice is turned back, and righteousness stands at a distance; for truth stumbles in the public square, and uprightness cannot enter.'

'The people who sat in darkness have seen a great light' writes Matthew quoting an earlier part of Isaiah. But this darkness is a deep and complex shroud, a spider's web woven tightly over many generations, impossible to escape by our own goodness or ingenuity. Who is it that can save us?

COLLECT

Almighty God,
who wonderfully created us in your own image
and yet more wonderfully restored us
through your Son Jesus Christ:
grant that, as he came to share in our humanity,
so we may share the life of his divinity;
who is alive and reigns with you,
in the unity of the Holy Spirit,
one God, now and for ever.

Reflection by **Steven Croft**

Psalm **102**
Isaiah 59.15*b*-end
John 1.29-34

Saturday 31 December

Isaiah 59.15*b*-end

'... for he will come like a pent-up stream' (v.19)

There are many strands to the Book of Isaiah. The Book as a whole is like a complex, many-layered puzzle: the solution for us is unlocked with the Key of David, in the gift of Jesus, when the Church is able to grasp the meaning of the incarnation, cross and resurrection.

In today's passage, the prophet sees part of the answer to this web of darkness that is explored in the first part of Isaiah 59. The Lord will not leave the situation as it is. The Lord will be the source of salvation: healing for such ill can come from no one else. At the heart of the healing will be the restoration of justice.

In describing how salvation will come, the prophet reaches for the language of the warrior king, familiar from the psalms. God will come in great power and might, like a mighty wind or a pent-up stream, in storm and fury to judge the earth and set all things right.

For eyes that have seen the Christ-child, this language of the warrior king remains part of the language of salvation for the very end times; for the return of Christ as king. But the skein of darkness begins to unravel not through an Advent of power, but through an Advent of humility: quietly, silently, irresistibly, love enters the world to bring salvation in a single child, a light shining in the darkness, an antidote strong enough to bring healing to the troubled, broken world.

COLLECT

God in Trinity,
eternal unity of perfect love:
gather the nations to be one family,
and draw us into your holy life
through the birth of Emmanuel,
our Lord Jesus Christ.

Reflection by **Steven Croft**

Monday 2 January

Psalm **18.1-30**
Isaiah 60.1-12
John 1.35-42

Isaiah 60.1-12

'Arise, shine; for your light has come ...' (v.1)

One of the most powerful parts of the service of Holy Communion, for me, comes at the beginning of the Eucharistic prayer in the call: 'Lift up your hearts'. It's a call to those who are cast down. It is an invitation to offer bruised and broken hearts to the love of God to be mended. It's an invitation to lift our attention from the perspective of earth to the perspective of heaven. It's a call to find light in the midst of darkness and hope in the midst of fear.

Isaiah 60 has the same invitation: 'Arise, shine; for your light has come'; 'Lift up your eyes and look around'. The 66 chapters of the book of Isaiah are remarkable for setting passages of lament and judgement alongside passages of hope. In some sections of the book, the layers of hope are thin and scattered. This song in Isaiah 60 begins a series of passages that lift us up and point us forward and inward to realities of grace.

This makes the song one of great power as we celebrate the beginning of the New Year. Scripture invites us to turn over a new page, whatever our journey has been, and look upwards and outwards with hope to God's promise and to all that lies ahead. Lift up your hearts!

COLLECT

Almighty God,
in the birth of your Son
you have poured on us the new light of your incarnate Word,
and shown us the fullness of your love:
help us to walk in his light and dwell in his love
that we may know the fullness of his joy;
who is alive and reigns with you,
in the unity of the Holy Spirit,
one God, now and for ever.

Reflection by **Steven Croft**

Psalms **127**, 128, 131
Isaiah 60.13-end
John 1.43-end

Tuesday 3 January

Isaiah 60.13-end

'... you shall call your walls Salvation, and your gates Praise' (v.18)

'Where there is no vision, the people perish' says Proverbs (29.18 AV). The oracles in this part of Isaiah probably come from a time when the exiles have returned from Babylon. Jerusalem is a ruin. The hard work of reconstructing the temple, the city and the identity of the nation is about to begin.

So the prophet casts a vision for this rebuilding, recalling the time of Solomon and the first building of the temple. Costly materials – both timber and precious metals – will flow into Jerusalem again for this work of reconstruction. The disgrace and shame of the past will be forgotten. More than that, the great virtues of common life forced out of the city in 59.14-15 will return again. Violence will be banished now.

God's glory will abide in this city, symbolized by the temple. The light of both sun and moon will be eclipsed: 'for the Lord will be your everlasting light, and your days of mourning shall be ended'.

As with all visions on this side of eternity, these promises were only partly realized (though even this was a remarkable achievement for the exiles). But the prophet's song lives on, preserving the possibility of a better life, inspiring common endeavour and nourishing in every generation the building of a new Jerusalem in this world and the next.

How might we draw on them on this day to inspire fresh hope?

COLLECT

God our Father,
in love you sent your Son
that the world may have life:
lead us to seek him among the outcast
and to find him in those in need,
for Jesus Christ's sake.

Reflection by **Steven Croft**

Wednesday 4 January

Psalm **89.1-37**
Isaiah 61
John 2.1-12

Isaiah 61

'The spirit of the Lord God is upon me' (v.1)

God remakes and reshapes us from within, through God's indwelling and abiding Spirit. But what are the hallmarks of that anointing and reshaping?

Isaiah 61 offers one of the most important lists of qualities and actions. This oracle will come to be seen as a prophecy of the Messiah, God's anointed one, the Christ. According to Luke 4, when Jesus stands up to speak in the synagogue in Nazareth he will read these very words and then say, remarkably, 'Today this scripture has been fulfilled in your hearing' (Luke 4.21).

But what are the hallmarks of God's anointing, the character and actions that flow from God's indwelling Spirit? Good news for the oppressed. Binding up the broken hearted. Comfort for those who mourn. Repairing the devastation of many generations.

There must be no single or narrow interpretation of these rich verses, no false dichotomy between a spiritual and physical poverty or captivity. The fruit of the Holy Spirit's work is the outworking of the grace and mission of God in the whole world: the prophet is sent, the Christ is sent, the Church is sent to bring good news to the poor.

As another year begins, we will need to drink deep draughts of the Spirit's refreshing waters and rediscover our calling: we too, in this present moment, find we are sent to bring good news to the poor.

COLLECT

Almighty God,
in the birth of your Son
you have poured on us the new light of your incarnate Word,
and shown us the fullness of your love:
help us to walk in his light and dwell in his love
that we may know the fullness of his joy;
who is alive and reigns with you,
in the unity of the Holy Spirit,
one God, now and for ever.

Reflection by **Steven Croft**

Psalms 8, **48**
Isaiah 62
John 2.13-end

Thursday 5 January

Isaiah 62

'You who remind the Lord, take no rest, and give him no rest' *(vv.6-7)*

In the midst of this powerful series of prophecies of restoration, we rediscover what it means to be intercessors. The Lord has promised to restore Jerusalem, to bring in the kingdom. But that prophecy was not yet fulfilled even after the exiles' return, and we still wait for its fulfilment.

Is this waiting a passive, patient thing, just hanging around until the time is right? By no means. We are called to engage in God's mission, inspired by God's Spirit. But we are called also, year by year, to pray, to intercede, to be sentinels, to cry out to the Lord of heaven and earth.

Sentinels have two jobs. The first is to scan the horizon. Intercession for the Church and the world must be nourished by listening and learning and seeing well. Intercession cannot be entirely spontaneous; there must be planning and preparation. But all of that must then feed into continuous, consistent, disciplined prayer, bringing before God the needs of the whole world, with others. This intercessory prayer is part of the call of every disciple and the principal vocation of many. Sentinels must not fall asleep on duty.

Take time on this twelfth day of Christmas to reflect on the pattern of your prayer, both public and private and how you might set your resources in order for the coming year.

COLLECT

God our Father,
in love you sent your Son
that the world may have life:
lead us to seek him among the outcast
and to find him in those in need,
for Jesus Christ's sake.

Reflection by **Steven Croft**

Friday 6 January
Epiphany

Psalms **132**, 113
Jeremiah 31.7-14
John 1.29-34

John 1.29-34

'... the Lamb of God who takes away the sin of the world!' (v.29)

If Christmas is about appreciating again the wonder of the incarnation, the season of Epiphany is about sharing that wonder with the world. The pattern of the Church year emerged gradually as a support to the Church's ministry of evangelism and accompanying new believers to baptism and confirmation.

Lent is the season of preparation for baptism at Easter or in the Easter season. Epiphany is therefore a time for every church to issue a big, warm, open invitation to the whole world to 'come and see' (echoing John 1.39), to explore Christian faith for the first time, to return to faith after years of wandering.

John the Baptist sets the example to the whole Church with his testimony about Christ. As soon as John sees Jesus coming towards him he declares: 'Here is the Lamb of God who takes away the sin of the world!' The words are perhaps too familiar to us, and we lose their wonder and significance. At their first meeting, John draws down all of the significance of thousands of years of sacrifice in the temple to his understanding of the wonder of who Jesus is. The one who has given his life to a symbolic washing in the River Jordan – a baptism – goes onto declare that it is Jesus who truly takes away the sin of the entire world.

This is a testimony in which every Christian can share and a model for our evangelism and witness to Christ.

COLLECT

O God,
who by the leading of a star
manifested your only Son to the peoples of the earth:
mercifully grant that we,
who know you now by faith,
may at last behold your glory face to face;
through Jesus Christ your Son our Lord,
who is alive and reigns with you,
in the unity of the Holy Spirit,
one God, now and for ever.

Reflection by **Steven Croft**

Psalms **99**, 147.1-12 *or* **76**, 79
Isaiah 63.7-end
1 John 3

Saturday 7 January

Isaiah 63.7-end

'I will recount the gracious deeds of the Lord' (v.7)

The whole book of Isaiah is set in a wonderful counterpoint to the book of Psalms, which echoes and counter-echoes across the tradition: deep calling to deep. Isaiah 63.7-14 is a beautiful psalm of thanksgiving, worthy of a place in the Psalter.

Psalms of thanksgiving are not only for good times, when life is going well. The skies are growing darker again in Isaiah 63 after the uniform hope of the previous three chapters. It is in times of trial and difficulty, most of all, that we need to look within and to look back and rehearse the praiseworthy acts of the Lord, the abundance of God's steadfast love.

For the Israelites, this looking back is a continual recalling of the exodus, the great act of salvation and the creation of a new people. Recalling the exodus is a reminder of the presence of God in the wilderness. Like many of the psalms, this part of Isaiah does not look back with rose-tinted spectacles: the trial and testing and mis-steps in the journey are remembered as timely reminders for the present day.

For the Church, the centre of our thanksgiving is not the exodus but the passion and resurrection of our Lord Jesus Christ. Our central act of thanksgiving is the Eucharist: this is where we remember and where we are re-membered, put back together, after the difficulties and distractions of another week. Thanksgiving is so much more than politeness: it is the key to living a reflective, fruitful, hopeful life.

COLLECT

Creator of the heavens,
who led the Magi by a star
to worship the Christ-child:
guide and sustain us,
that we may find our journey's end
in Jesus Christ our Lord.

Reflection by **Steven Croft**

Monday 9 January

Psalms **2**, 110 *or* **80**, 82
Amos 1
1 Corinthians 1.1-17

1 Corinthians 1.1-17

'To the church of God that is in Corinth ...' (v.2)

Corinth in the time of Paul was a thrusting, wealthy and successful seaport and centre of trade, home to the highly competitive Isthmian Games. As this letter reveals, the fledgling church in that city reflected some of the characteristics, good and ill, of its surrounding culture.

Paul commends them as being enriched in Christ 'in every way', and for 'not lacking in any spiritual gift'. Yet in a letter written barely 25 years after the Baptism of Christ (celebrated yesterday), we already see the sacrament of baptism dividing believers from one another, as members of the church seem to have been split into factions, owing allegiance to the person who baptised them instead of to Christ.

All this is vaguely comforting – to know that even the earliest Church was not pure and perfect. But it is also vaguely disturbing. Sometimes I have been drawn into arguments in the church I serve, thinking that I was contending for the truth of the gospel. But with hindsight was I simply following a particular personality, and reflecting the competitive, consumerist culture of the society in which I live?

Lord, help me to be aware today when my behaviour simply reflects rather than challenges the cultural assumptions of the society around me. And help me to live in such a countercultural way 'that the cross of Christ might not be emptied of its power'.

COLLECT

Eternal Father,
who at the baptism of Jesus
revealed him to be your Son,
anointing him with the Holy Spirit:
grant to us, who are born again by water and the Spirit,
that we may be faithful to our calling as your adopted children;
through Jesus Christ your Son our Lord,
who is alive and reigns with you,
in the unity of the Holy Spirit,
one God, now and for ever.

Reflection by **Mark Ireland**

Psalms 8, **9** *or* 87, **89.1-18**
Amos 2
1 Corinthians 1.18-end

Tuesday 10 January

1 Corinthians 1.18-end

'God chose what is foolish in the world to shame the wise ...' (v.27)

As a marketing strategy, it is pants. Paul knows exactly what each part of his audience wants, and he gives them the opposite. To Jews who wanted signs and to Greeks who sought wisdom, he offers only a crucified saviour. Yet God was at work through Paul's foolishness, and a congregation grew in Corinth not made up of the intelligentsia, but rather of those whom the world looked down on – those without power, position or noble birth.

I heard a vicar the other day talk very honestly about the fruits of his evangelism. He said the breakthrough came when he let go of the pride of wanting to lead and preach to a large congregation. Instead, he set himself to look out for the groups in his community who would never feel at home in a formal Sunday morning service. He began to gather them in small groups, feed them, and open the Scriptures with them. Several small worshipping communities emerged. They didn't come on Sunday, but he made sure they were equally part of the church family.

And what about me? Do I have a subconscious idea in my mind of the kind of person I would like to bring to faith in Jesus? Someone like me perhaps, who might boost the numbers at the kind of service I like?

Lord, help me to recognize that the people you are calling may be very different.

COLLECT

Heavenly Father,
at the Jordan you revealed Jesus as your Son:
may we recognize him as our Lord
and know ourselves to be your beloved children;
through Jesus Christ our Saviour.

Reflection by **Mark Ireland**

Wednesday 11 January

Psalms 19, **20** *or* **119.105-128**
Amos 3
1 Corinthians 2

1 Corinthians 2

'I decided to know nothing among you except Jesus Christ, and him crucified.' (v.2)

Corinth was known for its schools of rhetoric, teaching skills of oratory that could 'spin' a message and manipulate a crowd. Paul knew the rules of the game, as he shows later in the letter; he could easily have used these dark arts, so beloved of today's spin doctors, to gain and convince an audience. Instead, Paul presents a gospel of a humiliated, crucified Christ to a city of entrepreneurs who cherished success and loved winners.

Like Paul in Corinth, we live in a consumer culture, with crowds itching to be told the kind of message they want to hear. That's why we love the echo chambers of social media, repeating back to us our prejudices. How tempting it is to present Christ as a social influencer might, as offering self-fulfilment, a pick-and-mix spirituality, or a way to inner peace or mindfulness.

Paul will have none of it. He eschews the path of media celebrity and gets his hands (very) dirty as a skilled leather worker and tent maker. His pulpit is the tanner's workshop, not the lecture hall, and his message (in a very Roman city) is all about a condemned man crucified by the Roman authorities.

I praise God for the many new local congregations emerging today, led not by religious professionals like me, but by lay people who simply have a passion for Jesus and try to live as his disciples in their daily work.

COLLECT

Eternal Father,
who at the baptism of Jesus
revealed him to be your Son,
anointing him with the Holy Spirit:
grant to us, who are born again by water and the Spirit,
that we may be faithful to our calling as your adopted children;
through Jesus Christ your Son our Lord,
who is alive and reigns with you,
in the unity of the Holy Spirit,
one God, now and for ever.

Reflection by **Mark Ireland**

Psalms **21**, 24 *or* 90, **92**
Amos 4
1 Corinthians 3

Thursday 12 January

1 Corinthians 3

'... fire will test what sort of work each has done' (v.13)

How much of what we have laboured for will endure after we have gone? It is a question I begin to think about more now that I have passed 60.

Paul as a master builder, who built on the foundation of Christ, had to watch as someone else built on what he started. Over the years, I have laid the foundations of a number of pieces of Christian work, and watched as others have taken my place. Some have built far better than I could, and the work has flourished and endured. Others have undone aspects of the work which I laid down, sure that what they were doing was God's will. That was hard.

And yet, years later, I come across small fruits of things I did years ago, even when that piece of work has been tested as through fire. Sometimes I am told of something I had quite forgotten doing, or a message I once gave, that has changed someone's life for good. Those may be the times when I have built with gold, silver or precious stones.

But what about the times when I have built with wood or hay or straw? I can think of occasions when something I inherited in a healthy state has not flourished under my leadership. Probably there are those who have struggled to watch my clumsy attempts to build on what they had so carefully laid down. Lord, have mercy.

COLLECT

Heavenly Father,
at the Jordan you revealed Jesus as your Son:
may we recognize him as our Lord
and know ourselves to be your beloved children;
through Jesus Christ our Saviour.

Reflection by **Mark Ireland**

Friday 13 January

Psalms **67**, 72 *or* **88** (95)
Amos 5.1-17
1 Corinthians 4

1 Corinthians 4

'... stewards ... should be found trustworthy' (v.2)

It is a strange irony that we appear to be losing the language of stewardship in the church, at the very time when the idea of stewardship is striking such a chord in discussions about climate change and the future of the planet.

Fewer churches and denominations couch their teaching on financial giving in terms of us being stewards – not owners – of all that God provides, and 'stewardship campaigns' tend to be replaced by calls to Christian generosity. Generosity presupposes ownership, which is not for us to claim.

The climate crisis has reminded people the world over that human beings are not the owners of creation but its stewards. We have been given responsibility and the ability to care for all species and the whole natural world on this planet, which Pope Francis has called 'our common home'.

What difference will it make today to our personal spending, and to our willingness to make difficult decisions about a greener lifestyle, if we choose to think of ourselves in this way, not as the owners of possessions but as 'servants of Christ and stewards of God's mysteries'?

Paul reminds us that one day we will be judged for our stewardship, 'when the Lord comes, who will bring to light things now hidden ...'

Lord, help me today to be a trustworthy steward of all that you have entrusted to me, as one who must one day give an account of my stewardship.

COLLECT

Eternal Father,
who at the baptism of Jesus
revealed him to be your Son,
anointing him with the Holy Spirit:
grant to us, who are born again by water and the Spirit,
that we may be faithful to our calling as your adopted children;
through Jesus Christ your Son our Lord,
who is alive and reigns with you,
in the unity of the Holy Spirit,
one God, now and for ever.

Reflection by **Mark Ireland**

Psalms 29, **33** *or* 96, **97**, 100
Amos 5.18-end
1 Corinthians 5

Saturday 14 January

1 Corinthians 5

'Drive out the wicked person from among you' (v.13)

This passage is made more difficult because we do not have the Corinthian church's side of the correspondence, so it is not clear why they were tolerating this particular case of sexual immorality, which was of a kind that would bring them into disrepute with Roman society. Some scholars have argued that the offender was perhaps a rich and influential member of the church, the kind of celebrity convert that the church was inclined to boast about.

Paul urges that the offender be publicly put out of the church, in order to save his spirit and to avoid such immoral behaviour spreading within the fellowship. Excommunication was seen as remedial, not permanent.

Interestingly though, Paul does not urge believers to disassociate from unbelievers who might be leading an immoral or unethical life, lest they might have withdrawn from society altogether. Here is the tension we still live with today – how do Christians keep themselves pure whilst at the same time engaging fully with friends and colleagues who may live by a very different moral code? Paul reminds us not to make judgements about those outside the church – that is God's job (v13).

Lord, help me neither to cut myself off from the world, in which case I cannot be salt and light, nor try so hard to fit in that I lose all distinctiveness.

COLLECT

Heavenly Father,
at the Jordan you revealed Jesus as your Son:
may we recognize him as our Lord
and know ourselves to be your beloved children;
through Jesus Christ our Saviour.

Reflection by **Mark Ireland**

Monday 16 January

Psalms 145, **146** *or* **98**, 99, 101
Amos 6
1 Corinthians 6.1-11

1 Corinthians 6.1-11

'Do you dare to take it to court before the unrighteous ...?' (v.1)

Scripture can be mishandled. 'The benefit of clergy' was a principle in the medieval church, which gave the right to clergy accused of crimes not to be tried by secular courts, but rather to have their case heard by an ecclesiastical court. It was a cause of scandal when clergy received more lenient treatment from their peers than they would have done from a secular court.

Those arguing in favour of the benefit of clergy claimed scriptural warrant from this passage, where Paul criticizes the Corinthians for taking their internal disputes before secular courts, resulting in a poor witness to unbelievers. However, Paul was not talking about criminal law, but about civil law. In criminal matters, it is for the courts to decide, and no one is above the law.

Elsewhere, the New Testament asserts that teaching elders in the church should be judged with greater strictness because of their position (James 3.1).

The long shadow of the benefit of clergy still hangs over the Church in our own day, where those in Church leadership have sometimes failed to refer allegations of abuse to the police to investigate, as they are required to do; instead, they have tried to deal with matters themselves, listening more to the fluent words of a bad priest than the faltering testimony of a wounded survivor.

Correct exegesis matters. Lord, help me to rightly handle your Word today.

COLLECT

Almighty God,
in Christ you make all things new:
transform the poverty of our nature by the riches of your grace,
and in the renewal of our lives
make known your heavenly glory;
through Jesus Christ your Son our Lord,
who is alive and reigns with you,
in the unity of the Holy Spirit,
one God, now and for ever.

Reflection by **Mark Ireland**

Psalms **132**, 147.1-12 *or* **106*** (*or* 103)
Amos 7
1 Corinthians 6.12-end

Tuesday 17 January

1 Corinthians 6.12-end

'Do you not know that your body is a temple of the Holy Spirit?' (v.19)

Paul is responding to some of the slogans popular among Christians in Corinthians. Some of them at least seem to have embraced the Greek idea that the body was separate from the soul, and therefore it didn't matter much what you did with your body, because it was only the soul that lived for ever.

Paul's response is to remind them that Christ has not only redeemed their souls but their bodies as well. If our bodies are temples in which the Holy Spirit dwells, how can we consider either neglecting our body by being careless about what we eat or by being careless in our sexual relationships? The word Paul uses to describe 'becoming one body', either in marriage or with a prostitute, denotes either glueing two pieces of wood together or welding two pieces of metal together.

Christ's body was bruised and broken that we might be redeemed, so that we are indeed 'bought with a price'. Therefore our bodies belong to him, and we are to glorify him with our bodies. And if all Christians are temples of the Holy Spirit, then to sin with our body is not just a social failure but a sacrilege – a profaning of what is holy.

How might I treat my body differently, and fellow Christians differently, in the light of this truth?

COLLECT

Eternal Lord,
our beginning and our end:
bring us with the whole creation
to your glory, hidden through past ages
and made known
in Jesus Christ our Lord.

Reflection by **Mark Ireland**

Wednesday 18 January

Psalms **81**, 147.13-end
or 110, **111**, 112
Amos 8
1 Corinthians 7.1-24

1 Corinthians 7.1-24

'... let each of you lead the life that the Lord has assigned' (v.17)

I have recently been reading the 17th-century classic, *The Rare Jewel of Christian Contentment* by Jeremiah Burroughs, which has made me appreciate afresh the value of contentment and how many problems we bring on ourselves by being discontented with our lot.

In this passage, Paul commends two states of life for believers: marriage and singleness. This teaching would have been incredibly hard for Paul's readers, since the port city of Corinth was a by-word for licentiousness in the ancient world. In today's world, relationships are complicated and varied, but Paul's point is still relevant, that in our relationships believers are to live by different values from those around us, since we know our bodies to be temples of the Holy Spirit.

Paul's view of marriage, set out in verses 2-6, is way ahead of its time in terms of a mutual relationship in which both men and women are encouraged to use the gift of sex to bring joy and life to the other, rather than simply for the husband's gratification.

Paul was also countercultural in affirming that a single life could (like his own) be deeply fulfilling. Paul may well have been a widower at the time of writing, since it would have been unusual for a leader of the Pharisees to have been single.

For Paul, the secret of contentment is not to envy others, but to embrace one's own state – whatever it is – as a gift from God and use it to God's glory.

COLLECT

Almighty God,
in Christ you make all things new:
transform the poverty of our nature by the riches of your grace,
and in the renewal of our lives
make known your heavenly glory;
through Jesus Christ your Son our Lord,
who is alive and reigns with you,
in the unity of the Holy Spirit,
one God, now and for ever.

Reflection by **Mark Ireland**

Psalms **76**, 148 *or* 113, **115**
Amos 9
1 Corinthians 7.25-end

Thursday 19 January

1 Corinthians 7.25-end

'... those who marry will experience distress in this life' (v.28)

Paul is often accused of having a bit of a downer on marriage, however context is all important. As verses 26 and 31 indicate, Paul's guidance on whether or not to get married is given in the light of 'the impending crisis'. If Christ is about to appear in glory and the world to be dissolved, then changing one's relationship status is not the first priority.

As a young man, I thought God might be calling me to be single, but then at the age of 40 I was 'surprised by joy', or rather in my case, 'surprised by Gill'. Paul's concern that marriage could distract a person from their focus on the Lord's work needs to be balanced with the testimony of countless Christian couples down the centuries, that marriage to someone who shares your faith hugely enriches ministry as well as the whole of life.

Paul is well ahead of his time in this passage in the freedom he accords to women. He sets widows with independent means free from the social expectation that they 'ought' to marry, and says that if they choose to do so, they can choose anyone they wish who is 'in the Lord', that is, who is a fellow believer.

Sometimes I ponder the disparity between Paul's high view of singleness in this passage and the way single people sometimes feel in churches, almost as a problem to be solved, rather than a gift to be valued.

COLLECT

Eternal Lord,
our beginning and our end:
bring us with the whole creation
to your glory, hidden through past ages
and made known
in Jesus Christ our Lord.

Reflection by **Mark Ireland**

Friday 20 January

Psalms **27**, 149 *or* **139**
Hosea 1.1 – 2.1
1 Corinthians 8

1 Corinthians 8

'Knowledge puffs up, but love builds up' (v.1)

There are a variety of factors at play as Paul arbitrates on a dispute in the Corinthian church. The best-quality meat came to the market after it had been sacrificed in pagan temples. The temples were also popular venues for social and business entertaining, so upwardly-mobile Christians who eschewed meat from the temple would put themselves at a social disadvantage. And since the pagan gods were not gods at all, what harm was there?

However, meat was a luxury in Corinth, and so poorer members of the congregation who could not afford meat for themselves would have been scandalized by the seemingly irreligious behaviour of the richer believers. And many of these 'weaker' members had themselves been redeemed from the power of these pagan deities and knew it was important for them to keep well clear.

Paul's pastoral strategy here is to accept that the 'strong' do have knowledge, but to remind them that with that knowledge they also need love for their weaker brothers and sisters for whom they bear a responsibility within the body of Christ.

Knowledge brings responsibility no less when we shop in the supermarket today. Richer Christians should be asking: is this food ethically sourced, with low food miles, with recyclable packing? Meanwhile, those who are poor usually do not have the luxury of such choices. Perhaps this should make me think more carefully about the quality of the things I buy for the local food bank?

COLLECT

Almighty God,
in Christ you make all things new:
transform the poverty of our nature by the riches of your grace,
and in the renewal of our lives
make known your heavenly glory;
through Jesus Christ your Son our Lord,
who is alive and reigns with you,
in the unity of the Holy Spirit,
one God, now and for ever.

Reflection by **Mark Ireland**

Psalms **122**, 128, 150
or 120, **121**, 122
Hosea 2.2-17
I Corinthians 9.1-14

Saturday 21 January

1 Corinthians 9.1-14

'... we put up with anything rather than hinder the gospel of Christ' (v.12, NIV)

When I was a diocesan missioner, I often met PCCs anxious about the lack of children and families in church but unwilling to change. After listening for a while, I would often sum up the discussion by saying, 'So what you really want is more children and young people coming to the kind of services that you like?'

How different from Paul's attitude in today's reading! Paul was willing to put up with anything rather than hinder the gospel of Christ. What would our churches be like if we thought first about the needs of the newcomer, or the person we want to invite to church for the first time?

Paul insists that, as spiritual father to many of the Corinthians, he would have every right to ask for them to support his ministry financially. But then he makes clear that he has voluntarily given up this right so as not to hinder the work of the gospel.

He was perhaps aware that if he had been supported financially, it would have been mostly through members of the richer or 'strong' faction in the church, which might have made him beholden to them and weakened his ministry to the 'weak' faction.

Lord, I am sorry for the times when I want things in church to be done my way. Rather, help me, like Paul, to put others first so as not to hinder the gospel of Christ.

COLLECT

Eternal Lord,
our beginning and our end:
bring us with the whole creation
to your glory, hidden through past ages
and made known
in Jesus Christ our Lord.

Reflection by **Mark Ireland**

Monday 23 January

Psalms 40, **108** *or* 123, 124, 125, **126**
Hosea 2.18 – end of 3
1 Corinthians 9.15-end

1 Corinthians 9.15-end

'What then is my reward?' (v.18)

If there's one character trait that we don't usually associate with the apostle Paul, it's shyness. Paul was undoubtedly confident. I suspect you'd know him when you met him, or maybe could hear him before he walked into a room?

I wonder, though, if that's a fair representation of who he was? In this chapter of his first letter to the Corinthians, Paul is working hard to defend his apostolic identity. There were some that said he wasn't really an apostle because he didn't actually accompany Jesus during his public ministry. Yet Paul's whole purpose in life was shaped because Paul encountered the risen Jesus on the Damascus Road. Paul had seen Jesus, and because of that he could call himself an apostle.

At the same time, Paul's style of ensuring he was supported in his ministry was significant. Whereas the Twelve may well have largely put down their nets to devote themselves to full-time evangelism, Paul earned a living as a tent-maker and used that income to ensure he wasn't a burden on the communities he spent time with. This is the point he is making here: Paul was not a drain on local resources, and so the gospel was free for all at point of delivery. This was as counter-cultural then as it is now: good news for all at no cost – and no small print either.

COLLECT

Almighty God,
whose Son revealed in signs and miracles
the wonder of your saving presence:
renew your people with your heavenly grace,
and in all our weakness
sustain us by your mighty power;
through Jesus Christ your Son our Lord,
who is alive and reigns with you,
in the unity of the Holy Spirit,
one God, now and for ever.

Reflection by **Helen-Ann Hartley**

Psalms 34, **36** *or* **132**, 133
Hosea 4.1-16
1 Corinthians 10.1-13

Tuesday 24 January

1 Corinthians 10.1-13

'God is faithful, and he will not let you be tested beyond your strength' (v.13)

When I lived and worked in New Zealand I drew considerable wisdom from my Māori colleagues. They used to say to me that you face the future with your back to it. I often stopped to think about that phrase and its implications.

I think this is what Paul is getting at in this passage, which he begins by reminding his readers of what their ancestors had to endure. At first glance, this doesn't seem to be entirely positive, and you'd be forgiven for wondering if Paul is being overly harsh in his summary.

The glimmer of hope comes towards the end, where Paul reminds us of God's faithfulness. I have always found this idea to be a compelling part of what faith is about: God goes before us in good times and in bad, and because of that, we have the strength to look beyond whatever our present challenge might be. God doesn't take the difficult stuff away – that's for us to navigate and endure. God in Jesus gives us hope, and hope breaks into our concern and distress and offers us a way through it. We might well want to take issue with the statement that God won't let us be tested beyond our strength, but it is perhaps an invitation about learning to trust along the way. Perhaps that is the point of this passage: trust God, and God will not let you down.

COLLECT

God of all mercy,
your Son proclaimed good news to the poor,
release to the captives,
and freedom to the oppressed:
anoint us with your Holy Spirit
and set all your people free
to praise you in Christ our Lord.

Reflection by **Helen-Ann Hartley**

Wednesday 25 January

Conversion of Paul

Psalms 66, 147.13-end
Ezekiel 3.22-end
Philippians 3.1-14

Philippians 3.1-14

'I press on towards the goal for the prize of the heavenly call of God in Christ Jesus' (v.14)

Most Saturday mornings, I take part in my local park run. I love the feeling of community it provides, and the encouragement and support of fellow runners and the much-valued volunteers around the course. I often tell people that as I make my way round the 5-km course that it's the vision of the warmed cheese scone and flat white that I enjoy in the café afterwards with friends that keeps me going!

On the hilly elements of the course, I find myself digging deep and pressing on to reach my goal. Paul too knew the challenges of athletic endeavour; he often evokes the imagery of competitive sport in his letters, and here in Philippians we have one such example. Paul's dramatic personal change completely turned his life in a different yet renewed direction, giving him absolute focus and determination in following Jesus. Paul was not converted from one religion to another; he remained proud of his heritage.

Yet there can be no denying the transformation that Jesus brought about in Paul's life, and his continued desire to grow in his knowledge of Jesus and thus in his own faith. Paul also knew the importance of continuing education for formation. His drive to know more serves as an example to us in our daily walk as disciples. For that is the meaning of that word: one who learns, and who does so in the company of others.

COLLECT

Almighty God,
who caused the light of the gospel
to shine throughout the world
through the preaching of your servant Saint Paul:
grant that we who celebrate his wonderful conversion
may follow him in bearing witness to your truth;
through Jesus Christ your Son our Lord,
who is alive and reigns with you,
in the unity of the Holy Spirit,
one God, now and for ever.

Reflection by **Helen-Ann Hartley**

Psalms **47**, 48 *or* **143**, 146
Hosea 5.8 – 6.6
1 Corinthians 11.2-16

Thursday 26 January

1 Corinthians 11.2-16

'For just as woman came from man, so man comes through woman; but all things come from God' (v.12)

I have a vivid memory many years ago, of visiting Mount Tabor. I was wearing a t-shirt and shorts, and it became clear that the latter prevented me from venturing further than the front gate area. There was a box beside the entrance filled with random clothes, which saved the day, but it did mean making my way round this sacred place in an ill-fitting long skirt.

This passage calls to mind that incident, since what seems to be the issue is the wrong clothing or possibly the wrong hair-do. Either way, it is vital to read this passage with two things in mind: first, that we are dealing with a very specific context to which we do not have full access in terms of our understanding; and second, that Paul is doing his best to argue his way through this, but ultimately resorts to dismissing the matter on the grounds that it is contentious. That's one way of dealing with tricky issues.

Despite the complexity of Paul's line of thought, it is clear that in Corinth, women and men shared the same liturgical function of praying and prophesying. It is perhaps easy to overlook this, and it is important that we don't. At the end of the day, God is the source of all being and authority, and we would do well to direct our energies to recalling our roles in giving honour to all people regardless of status and personhood.

COLLECT

Almighty God,
whose Son revealed in signs and miracles
the wonder of your saving presence:
renew your people with your heavenly grace,
and in all our weakness
sustain us by your mighty power;
through Jesus Christ your Son our Lord,
who is alive and reigns with you,
in the unity of the Holy Spirit,
one God, now and for ever.

Reflection by **Helen-Ann Hartley**

Friday 27 January

Psalms 61, **65** *or* 142, **144**
Hosea 6.7 – 7.2
1 Corinthians 11.17-end

1 Corinthians 11.17-end

'So then, my brothers and sisters, when you come together to eat, wait for one another' (v.33)

Upon receiving an invitation to dinner, I am often perplexed at the request to arrive at 6.30 for 7 in the evening. Just what is the right time to arrive within that window? I recall turning up in good time for an engagement, only to find that other attendees were running behind schedule and as a result we didn't sit down to eat until after 10pm. Clearly, there was an issue in Corinth with people eating at different times, resulting in dishonour to Christ's body. The Church in Corinth was socially diverse, and it is perhaps not surprising that the radical collapsing of status was causing all sorts of issues.

Paul has to remind the community of why Christ's body matters, and he does this by recalling the words at the institution of the Lord's Supper. This is a rare example of Paul directly quoting Jesus, and in so doing providing us with the earliest account of the Eucharist, words we still use to this day. That is a remarkable continuity of tradition, accompanied by another unchanging reality: that with a diverse and broad Church comes debate and disagreement. That is probably why whenever I read 1 Corinthians, I always find it resonates in a very contemporary way. It remains the case, however, that despite the fracture at times, Christ's body in its suffering bears witness to the resurrection, and therein lies the hope and promise of future restoration and wholeness.

COLLECT

Almighty God,
whose Son revealed in signs and miracles
the wonder of your saving presence:
renew your people with your heavenly grace,
and in all our weakness
sustain us by your mighty power;
through Jesus Christ your Son our Lord,
who is alive and reigns with you,
in the unity of the Holy Spirit,
one God, now and for ever.

Reflection by **Helen-Ann Hartley**

Psalm **68** *or* **147**
Hosea 8
1 Corinthians 12.1-11

Saturday 28 January

1 Corinthians 12.1-11

'... the manifestation of the Spirit for the common good' (v.7)

An abiding memory of the first national lockdown in the UK back in March 2020 was the Thursday evening 'clap for carers' on our doorsteps. There was something profoundly moving in that intentional time of coming together, acknowledging the sectors of society that were going above and beyond the call of duty to care for the sick and dying, and to keep essential services running.

I think of all that when I read this passage in which Paul is celebrating the spiritual gifts. It is the same Spirit given to each person, manifesting vision and purpose for the wellbeing of all creation. This, in so many ways, is the manifesto of God's kingdom. Though Paul doesn't explicitly mention the kingdom, there is a strong sense of its presence in this passage, through the Spirit holding things for the fulfilment of God's purposes in each one of us.

This passage also speaks of the path of unity, and the role of diversity in this. Somehow, so we might ask ourselves, everything is held together. We know, as did Paul and the Corinthians, that the path towards unity is demanding and costly. Paul points the hearers of this letter back to God: God is the answer to how everything fits together, and a key part of making the body function is recognizing the role that each person plays as being of equal importance.

Given the challenges that this fledgling community faced with its different groups of people all drawn together in Christ, perhaps the greatest challenge was the giving way to other gifts, all for the greater good of the gospel. That is a challenge we share today.

COLLECT

God of all mercy,
your Son proclaimed good news to the poor,
release to the captives,
and freedom to the oppressed:
anoint us with your Holy Spirit
and set all your people free
to praise you in Christ our Lord.

Reflection by **Helen-Ann Hartley**

Monday 30 January

Psalms **57**, 96 *or* **1**, 2, 3
Hosea 9
1 Corinthians 12.12-end

1 Corinthians 12.12-end

'... the body does not consist of one member but of many' (v.14)

In this passage, Paul builds on the image of the body and its many parts with humour, as he imagines the eye speaking to the hand, and so on. Whilst there is a list – the apostles come first and the interpretation of tongues comes last – what matters is that all work together. Only when that happens will God's purposes be brought to fruition. This serves as an important lesson to the Corinthian community as much as it does to us today. How can I seek to ensure that all are included and valued in the working out of God's mission?

The use of the image of the body to illustrate common life together was one that was fairly common in Paul's day. What is especially significant and even subversive, however, is that Paul uses it both to celebrate diversity and crucially to ensure that one part is not seen as superior over another.

Paul's breaking-down of the barriers of status goes to the heart of the gospel that is good news for all. It's hard to overestimate the challenge this would have presented to the diverse Corinthian community, which consisted of different groups who had come together in a common identity in Christ.

Reading this passage, with its playful humour and provocation, it's hard not to sense the resonances with many Christian communities today, and the dangers of simply being with people whom we perceive to be most like us.

COLLECT

God our creator,
who in the beginning
commanded the light to shine out of darkness:
we pray that the light of the glorious gospel of Christ
may dispel the darkness of ignorance and unbelief,
shine into the hearts of all your people,
and reveal the knowledge of your glory
in the face of Jesus Christ your Son our Lord,
who is alive and reigns with you,
in the unity of the Holy Spirit,
one God, now and for ever.

Reflection by **Helen-Ann Hartley**

Psalms **93**, 97 *or* **5**, 6 (8)
Hosea 10
1 Corinthians 13

Tuesday 31 January

1 Corinthians 13

'And now faith, hope, and love abide, these three; and the greatest of these is love' (v.13)

It may come as a disappointment to selectors of suitable readings for marriage services that the kind of love Paul is talking about here isn't romantic love. The Greek word used here, *agape* is a reason for acting that we can choose or ignore. It requires effort and commitment. Whilst this is obviously appropriate for intimate relationships, it has an important and lasting wider meaning that Paul wants to convey as vital for the Corinthian community. Indeed, when it comes down to it, love may be the answer to all of the problems that community was facing, if only they could see it that way.

Yet again, Paul's work sounds remarkably contemporary. A few years ago, following the terrorist attack against the Muslim community in Christchurch, New Zealand, I took part in an interfaith vigil outside Bradford City Hall. Drawing upon a Māori tradition of singing a brief song to support a theme under discussion, I sang these words of Paul and invited others to join in or hum along. As our voices resonated in that public space, there was a strong sense of connection and of God's love binding us together in our diversity. It was a powerful reminder to me of the call to seek unity in all that we do, for the sake of building up our common life.

COLLECT

God of heaven,
you send the gospel to the ends of the earth
and your messengers to every nation:
send your Holy Spirit to transform us
by the good news of everlasting life
in Jesus Christ our Lord.

Reflection by **Helen-Ann Hartley**

Wednesday 1 February

Psalms **95**, 98 *or* **119.1-32**
Hosea 11.1-11
1 Corinthians 14.1-19

1 Corinthians 14.1-19

'... nothing is without sound' (v.10)

In this passage, Paul is articulating the importance of prophecy for the whole community over and against the unintelligibility of speaking in tongues. While we don't know exactly what 'prophecy' means, it seems to imply words that build up, encourage and console. These end-results develop what precedes this passage in the extensive reflections on love. Prophecy strengthens the life of the community and thus develops the bonds of love.

Paul doesn't discourage or indeed ban speaking in tongues, but he very clearly gives higher importance to that which will benefit the whole. The phrase 'there's a time and place', comes to mind as a way of explaining what Paul is seeking to achieve in his argument here. We live in a world that is literally full of noise: in real life, and in online life. Some of it is positive; much of it is not. The result is often competing and confusing narratives that put pressure on people to believe one way or another or to conform to a particular ideology.

At the end of the day, Paul wants the Corinthian community to be built up together, and that requires giving priority to certain gifts for the greater good. This also means enabling a collective discernment, that is shared. The individualistic nature of speaking in tongues only benefits the speaker. Paul acknowledges the enthusiasm of the Corinthians, but urges this to be directed to more corporate benefit. Only then will the vision of a community of diversity truly prevail, and God's will be fulfilled.

COLLECT

God our creator,
who in the beginning
commanded the light to shine out of darkness:
we pray that the light of the glorious gospel of Christ
may dispel the darkness of ignorance and unbelief,
shine into the hearts of all your people,
and reveal the knowledge of your glory
in the face of Jesus Christ your Son our Lord,
who is alive and reigns with you,
in the unity of the Holy Spirit,
one God, now and for ever.

Reflection by **Helen-Ann Hartley**

Psalms **48**, 146
Exodus 13.1-16
Romans 12.1-5

Thursday 2 February

Presentation of Christ in the Temple

Romans 12.1-5

'... to present your bodies as a living sacrifice, holy and acceptable to God, which is your spiritual worship' (v.1)

In the latter part of his letter to the Romans, Paul moves to themes of practical application, building on the deeper theological reflections earlier in the letter. In the midst of personal and collective trials, Paul urges the Christians in Rome, and us, to inhabit the reality of God's mercy and present ourselves as a living sacrifice to God.

You cannot miss the references to the temple here, and thereby to the festival we celebrate today. Candlemas and the return of the light reminds us that in spite of all our messiness at times, there is nonetheless treasure within. When you take away the layers of stuff that happens, then beauty can be revealed. When you respond to confrontation with re-formation, that's when God is at work. What is discarded might seem wasteful, and it is not without pain. But it comes from a deep desire to understand that the revelation of hope is contained in the reality of God's love that is open to each person. No life is beyond the reach of God. No life is such that it cannot hold beauty.

The late Australian poet Clive James was once asked about the process of writing poetry. He said this: 'All I can do is turn a phrase until it catches the light.' As we lift our lives to God afresh, let today be an opportunity to reflect the light of Christ in ways that can illumine hope in all that we seek to do.

COLLECT

Almighty and ever-living God,
clothed in majesty,
whose beloved Son was this day presented in the Temple,
in substance of our flesh:
grant that we may be presented to you
with pure and clean hearts,
by your Son Jesus Christ our Lord,
who is alive and reigns with you,
in the unity of the Holy Spirit,
one God, now and for ever.

Reflection by **Helen-Ann Hartley**

Friday 3 February

Psalms 17, **19**
Hosea 13.1-14
1 Corinthians 16.1-9

1 Corinthians 16.1-9

'Now concerning the collection for the saints ...' (v.1)

The sharing of resources from the wealthier sections of the community to the poor in Jerusalem was vital to Paul's message. Here, towards the end of his first letter to the Corinthians, Paul draws down to a level of practical detail that in many ways is timeless. So often, however, we find it hard to imagine what this looks like on the ground: who should we give to, and how much? Is my neighbour over there giving more than I am, and what does that make me look like: generous or mean?

Whatever the questions we might ask when such a scenario presents itself to us, a former colleague of mine, theologian Nicholas King wonders if what lies at the heart of these verses is an identified issue of trust in the Corinthian community. Paul instructs his audience to put money aside rather than bring it to a gathering of the faithful, and expresses uncertainty that he will be able to travel with the money to Jerusalem.

This wider issue of trust is a dynamic that many Christian communities struggle with today: why should I give to 'them' rather than to 'us here'? I am sure you can think of examples in your own context. What then is it that moves us from suspicion to trust, and from fear to hope?

COLLECT

Almighty God,
by whose grace alone we are accepted and called to your service:
strengthen us by your Holy Spirit
and make us worthy of our calling;
through Jesus Christ your Son our Lord,
who is alive and reigns with you,
in the unity of the Holy Spirit,
one God, now and for ever.

 Reflection by **Helen-Ann Hartley**

Psalms 20, 21, **23**
Hosea 14
1 Corinthians 16.10-end

Saturday 4 February

1 Corinthians 16.10-end

'The churches of Asia send greetings. Aquila and Prisca, together with the church in their house, greet you warmly in the Lord' (v.19)

I love the endings to Paul's letters because here we often read the names of individuals whom Paul knew and worked with. In the case of Aquila and Prisca, they were the couple who had hosted Paul when he founded the Church at Corinth. They, like Paul, were tent-makers, and it is likely they worked in business together, using their trade as an opportunity to proclaim the gospel as well as to earn a living.

As you read the other names in this passage, stop and wonder for moment: who were they, what did they do, and how can I give thanks for the contributions of all those whom I know in my local Christian community? When we read Paul's letters, and because Paul's voice can be so strident at times, we forget that Paul was networked with many people. It makes me imagine the conversations that happened 'off the page', the arguments, the laughter, the joys and the tears.

Having journeyed through this whole letter, perhaps this is an opportunity to try to imagine what sort of letter Paul might write to the community you are part of: what are the issues Paul might speak into, and how can Paul's insights about the gifts of the Spirit and the importance of God's love enable fresh perspectives on seemingly intractable conflicts?

COLLECT

God of our salvation,
help us to turn away from those habits
which harm our bodies and poison our minds
and to choose again your gift of life,
revealed to us in Jesus Christ our Lord.

Reflection by **Helen-Ann Hartley**

Monday 6 February

Psalms 27, **30**
2 Chronicles 2.1-16
John 17.1-5

John 17.1-5

'... the hour has come' (v.1)

Before the narrative moves to the drama of the passion, we are privileged to overhear Jesus at prayer. He has been preparing himself and his disciples for what lies ahead. And now he cannot but throw himself on the mercy of his heavenly Father. Jesus knows the hour has come.

This prayer is charged with the scandal of Jesus' truth: the particularity of this vulnerable fragile man in an actual place in time and geography, claiming that in him, through the pain and mess of what is to come, the fullness of God's glory will be revealed.

It is ridiculous, fraught with risk, that all the hope of eternity comes down to this hour. The particularity reminds of us again of God's choice in taking flesh. At every point of this story, Jesus chooses. He has all authority, but he chooses to give it up for this hour. Knowing what is coming, he chooses to walk towards it that the work given may be finished.

The hour has come. Jesus knows what that will mean and chooses to trust that he can see it through. In fact, he will be stretched beyond his limit and broken. And yet, in the scandalous particularity of the dead flesh of a first-century Palestinian man nailed to a cross on a hill outside Jerusalem, the work is finished, and the glory of God is, indeed, glorified.

COLLECT

Almighty God,
who alone can bring order
to the unruly wills and passions of sinful humanity:
give your people grace
so to love what you command
and to desire what you promise,
that, among the many changes of this world,
our hearts may surely there be fixed
where true joys are to be found;
through Jesus Christ your Son our Lord,
who is alive and reigns with you,
in the unity of the Holy Spirit,
one God, now and for ever.

Reflection by **Libby Lane**

Psalms 32, **36**
2 Chronicles 3
John 17.6-19

Tuesday 7 February

John 17.6-19

'I am asking on their behalf ...' (v.9)

If embodying the whole glory of God in the particularity of Jesus is risky, his prayer that those who follow him be entrusted with manifesting that glory was surely reckless. And it was. The disciples betrayed, denied, abandoned him.

What is expected is extraordinary: that these fallible, flawed, failed women and men are to be bearers of the glory of God. They were to be Jesus' legacy, the continuation of his work. No wonder Jesus pleaded with his heavenly Father to protect them.

Jesus bequeathed a new community to the world, who would continue to struggle and wrestle with what it means to be bearers of the good news of the kingdom. It might have been less messy and ambiguous to have left a clear instruction manual or to have imposed a programme to follow. He chose instead to trust those who had been entrusted to him to work it out as they went.

'I'm asking on their behalf' Jesus prayed, and they needed it. And despite all that followed, the disciples were not lost. They remember who Jesus is and all that is promised in him, and, as reckless as the trust seemed, Jesus was glorified in and through them. The grace and mercy of God made known in the limitless love of Jesus expanded to embrace those for whom he prayed, and that love sent them out to live and work for his praise and glory.

COLLECT

Eternal God,
whose Son went among the crowds
and brought healing with his touch:
help us to show his love,
in your Church as we gather together,
and by our lives as they are transformed
into the image of Christ our Lord.

Reflection by **Libby Lane**

Wednesday 8 February

Psalm **34**
2 Chronicles 5
John 17.20-end

John 17.20-end

'... so that the world may know' (v.23)

Jesus' remarkable prayer goes on to pray into the future, for those who will believe because of them. That prayer in itself demonstrates the depth of Jesus' faith in his heavenly Father, and in his disciples: it assumes there will be those who believe in the future – it assumes there will be a future.

If we too are to be recipients of the grace of Jesus' prayer, it is because Jesus trusts us as well. We too are Jesus' legacy. Fallible, flawed, failed as we are (just like the first disciples were), we are known, loved, called and entrusted with the glory of the good news of the kingdom. Recklessly, Jesus entrusts his future glory to you and me.

It is as a community, belonging to one another as we belong to Jesus, learning from mistakes and misunderstanding, discovering joy in the midst of broken reality that we can be the answer to Jesus' prayer. Jesus' prayer makes it clear that it is the evidence of the love among, between and overflowing from us that will make him known.

We cannot contain or restrict God's work to the institution of the Church, and no one denomination has a monopoly on the grace of God. Nonetheless, Jesus prayed that in the ways that we are with one another, who we are as much as what we do, his love would be made clear so that the world may believe.

COLLECT

Almighty God,
who alone can bring order
to the unruly wills and passions of sinful humanity:
give your people grace
so to love what you command
and to desire what you promise,
that, among the many changes of this world,
our hearts may surely there be fixed
where true joys are to be found;
through Jesus Christ your Son our Lord,
who is alive and reigns with you,
in the unity of the Holy Spirit,
one God, now and for ever.

Reflection by **Libby Lane**

Psalm **37***
2 Chronicles 6.1-21
John 18.1-11

Thursday 9 February

John 18.1-11

'... he went out with his disciples ... to a place where there was a garden' (v.1)

Every aspect of Jesus' story is grounded in the earthed reality of specific places: our salvation is literally down to earth. The passion narrative is no different. Jesus and the disciples go to pray in a known place, a garden across the Kidron Valley. It had become a precious place to gather, a place of learning, of belonging and of sanctuary.

The betrayal of Jesus in that place was also a betrayal of all those associated memories and experiences.

But Jesus was determined to draw all the possible poison into himself. Even in the midst of his betrayal, he works to limit damage and violence. Again and again, he draws all the attention to himself, striving to limit the harm both to the people about him and the place they treasure.

The places of our lives can be redolent with meaning, and there is particular pain when contexts that are precious are despoiled. Pain-filled memories can seep into every corner of our lives with insidious venom that we seem powerless to contain. Just as Jesus drank to the dregs the cup handed to him then, drawing out the poison into himself for the protection, healing, salvation of all those caught up in the passion around him, so he desires to protect, heal and save today. He will not let even one of us be lost.

COLLECT

Eternal God,
whose Son went among the crowds
and brought healing with his touch:
help us to show his love,
in your Church as we gather together,
and by our lives as they are transformed
into the image of Christ our Lord.

Reflection by **Libby Lane**

Friday 10 February

Psalm **31**
2 Chronicles 6.22-end
John 18.12-27

John 18.12-27

'Simon Peter ... followed Jesus' (v.15)

I find the Passion in John's Gospel all the more horrific because our vision of Jesus' narrative, his false trial and torture, is slightly out of focus in the background, while the story of Simon Peter's denial and betrayal is played out centre stage.

We see Simon Peter arriving in the dark and cold, edging towards the fire in an attempt to get warm. His physical circling closer to the heat of the brazier is reversed in the voiced distancing of himself from Jesus. And by the time the cock crows, although he may feel to be benefiting from proximity to the fire, Simon Peter believes he has cut himself off from the true source of light and comfort by his denial of Jesus.

Simon Peter is a great example of sainthood: not because of what he gets wrong so often – though he does go wrong a lot – but because he gets stuff wrong for the right reasons. Here, for example, despite his fear and in the face of all that was at risk, Simon Peter was still following.

And that is all Jesus ever asked of him – follow me. Simon Peter heard that invitation at the outset of Jesus' ministry and he will hear it again after the resurrection. It is all that is asked of us, however many times we fail – follow me.

COLLECT

Almighty God,
who alone can bring order
to the unruly wills and passions of sinful humanity:
give your people grace
so to love what you command
and to desire what you promise,
that, among the many changes of this world,
our hearts may surely there be fixed
where true joys are to be found;
through Jesus Christ your Son our Lord,
who is alive and reigns with you,
in the unity of the Holy Spirit,
one God, now and for ever.

Reflection by **Libby Lane**

Psalms 41, **42**, 43
2 Chronicles 7
John 18.28-end

Saturday 11 February

John 18.28-end

'... so as to avoid ritual defilement' (v.28)

It is obscene what we sometimes choose to care about. Appalling, in the face of gross injustice, abuse and violence, our endless capacity for self-justification and self-delusion.

How often, to preserve our dignity and respectability, to promote our own self-interest, have we too clothed our sin in the terrible hypocrisy of piety?

There is a great deal of to-ing and fro-ing in this account of the trial of Jesus. There is a flurry of movement around his contained, controlled figure at the still heart of this story. Those who are wanting to manage and control events to their own advantage move into a maelstrom of vociferous individual posturing, corporate positioning and organizational shifting of blame, and the irrationality of a roused mob.

What is being arranged is the unjust, illegal institutional murder of an innocent man. The concern of those who are doing the arranging is that they are not seen to be reputationally damaged. But none of those who claim authority in this story 'avoid ... defilement'.

It is all too easy to cast stones at those in this account who abuse their influence. But we all cloak our own grasping at power in our mini-kingdoms, wherever they are, in such hypocrisy and are ruthless, in our own ways, in wanting to hold on to control. In truth, we are no different, and fail to live up to our prayer that God's kingdom would come.

COLLECT

Eternal God,
whose Son went among the crowds
and brought healing with his touch:
help us to show his love,
in your Church as we gather together,
and by our lives as they are transformed
into the image of Christ our Lord.

Reflection by **Libby Lane**

Monday 13 February

Psalm **44**
2 Chronicles 9.1-12
John 19.1-16

John 19.1-16

'Pilate took Jesus and had him flogged' (v.1)

Where does power lie here?

It seems, on the surface, wholly to lie with Pilate. He was representative of the emperor whose sway was understood as absolute across all the known world. At Pilate's say-so, Jesus was subjected the terrible casual violence of torture – not just physical, but psychological, emotional and spiritual too. Pilate boasts of his power of life or death over Jesus.

John helps us see beneath the surface. Pilate, even by his own lights, does not have the power to act as he desires. He does not want to kill Jesus, but cannot withstand the pressures brought to bear upon him. In the end, Pilate capitulates to others' influence and hands Jesus over. He has no power at all.

And Jesus? He seems to be entirely without agency. Throughout this passage, action goes on around him and is taken against him. But the king without a kingdom, the one flogged, mocked, struck, condemned and handed over, is the one who holds real power. Jesus is not a victim but one who sets the path to resolution by choosing reconciliation rather than confrontation. Jesus does not hold any temporal power but the greater and eternal of authority of God's kingdom, where neither bullying cruelty nor violent aggression hold sway but only the choice of love and grace and mercy.

COLLECT

Almighty God,
you have created the heavens and the earth
and made us in your own image:
teach us to discern your hand in all your works
and your likeness in all your children;
through Jesus Christ your Son our Lord,
who with you and the Holy Spirit reigns supreme over all things,
now and for ever.

Reflection by **Libby Lane**

Psalms **48**, 52
2 Chronicles 10.1 – 11.4
John 19.17-30

Tuesday 14 February

John 19.17-30

'... it was written in Hebrew, in Latin, and in Greek' (v.20)

In a warped precursor to Pentecost, it is ensured that all those gathered in Jerusalem can understand the mocking charge under which Jesus is sentenced and condemned.

But even this indignity is good news. It is a reminder that Jesus' crucifixion is for all. Everyone is included in the reach and consequence of this death. It was intended to be an end, to indicate failure and deny hope. What we know it signifies – indeed, as good news for the whole world – is that here is not an end but a completion, not failure but hard-won reconciliation, not hopelessness but salvation.

Whatever it looks like, this is not the work of the earthly temporal powers of religion or state, but the transforming work of God's kingdom. This crucified God is abandoned by the passing world who recognize no king here. Yet, at his weakest and most vulnerable, Jesus assumes the title he never claimed for himself. Here, at the foot of the cross, even in the throes of his dying agony, Jesus' kingdom community is being formed.

Jesus said that whoever does the will of his heavenly Father is his mother and sister and brother. These beleaguered, frightened few, standing vigil with Jesus as he dies are doing the will of God. In them, Jesus inaugurates a new community that will draw in the whole world. Here is the kingdom of God.

COLLECT

Almighty God,
give us reverence for all creation
and respect for every person,
that we may mirror your likeness
in Jesus Christ our Lord.

Reflection by **Libby Lane**

Wednesday 15 February

Psalm **119.57-80**
2 Chronicles 12
John 19.31-end

John 19.31-end

'They took the body of Jesus and wrapped it ... in linen cloths' (v.40)

Generally, men don't come out well in the crucifixion narrative. The men in the story engage in treachery and betrayal, in abandonment and denial, in false accusation, collusion, expediency, aggression, torture and violence.

Joseph and Nicodemus, though, offer a counterpoint to that. They are brave, generous, tender, humble. These men, up to this crucial point, have kept themselves in the shadowy background, but choose here to step into focus. To use John's own metaphor, they move from darkness into light.

Nicodemus had previously kept himself from known association with Jesus. He came to visit Jesus 'by night' to discuss and consider, but, like many since, although perhaps longing to believe, could only observe from a distance, too uncertain to commit. Joseph of Arimathea was a 'secret' disciple, frightened for his reputation and hiding his conviction because of what others might think of him. There are many who would identify with Joseph in that.

So, what changed? What brought these men of influence out into the public gaze to risk all for Jesus now he was dead? Perhaps it was the very brutality of his death that shone a light on their prevarication and dissembling. Perhaps the manner of his death finally revealed the unavoidable truth of his life to them.

Millions since, women and men alike, have similarly stood at the foot of the cross and been won by the overwhelming, compelling power of love.

COLLECT

Almighty God,
you have created the heavens and the earth
and made us in your own image:
teach us to discern your hand in all your works
and your likeness in all your children;
through Jesus Christ your Son our Lord,
who with you and the Holy Spirit reigns supreme over all things,
now and for ever.

Reflection by **Libby Lane**

Psalms 56, **57** (63*)
2 Chronicles 13.1 – 14.1
John 20.1-10

Thursday 16 February

John 20.1-10

'... for as yet they did not understand the scripture' (v.9)

We often think it was easier for those who knew Jesus in the flesh. We think being there must mean they could see more clearly and understand more fully. But in this narrative, we realize that for the disciples, for Peter, John, Mary, after Jesus died, the possibility of redemption is too difficult to grasp. In the pre-dawn darkness, they are blinded by their fear and grief and shame.

We can sense the urgency, confusion and horror in their behaviour that Sunday morning – running back and forth, in and out of tomb, exchanging garbled messages, almost tripping over one another in their need to make sense of what is happening and contain their terror.

What they feel is emptiness, what they seem to see is nothingness. They are confronted by an absence: Jesus is not there. It is all too much, and so they retreat to the comforting shadows of their individual places of security. No doubt, that will sound familiar to anyone who has faced grief, or trauma, or depression.

In the darkest places of our lives, sometimes all we encounter is an absence where God is not. It can be very hard to trust that the dawn is coming. But come it does, and, as for those first disciples, wherever we have retreated to, even there, the gentle light of the risen Christ will search us out.

COLLECT

Almighty God,
give us reverence for all creation
and respect for every person,
that we may mirror your likeness
in Jesus Christ our Lord.

Reflection by **Libby Lane**

Friday 17 February

Psalms **51**, 54
2 Chronicles 14.2-end
John 20.11-18

John 20.11-18

'... she told them that he had said these things to her' (v.18)

Despite her grief and fear, Mary will not give up.

She had doggedly followed Jesus to the bitter end. She sustained her courage through the observance of the sabbath. She would not abandon even the brokenness of his dead body. And when even that last refuge, of offering the only thing left in the tender rituals of expected anointing, was denied her, she would not give up.

Peter and John had abandoned her again when they couldn't make sense of the empty tomb. Persistent and determined, she would not retreat but stayed nearby. Although her report of the disappearance of Jesus' body was disbelieved and unresolved, she refused to be silenced.

Mary keeps talking, testing what she understands, exploring the possibilities. She tries everyone who might be able to help – the disciples, angels, what she thinks is the gardener. She will not give up in her desire to find her way through the darkness that engulfs her. That faithful tenacity is rewarded, and Jesus finds her and calls her afresh. Her eyes are opened and she recognizes the risen Christ.

And Mary persists. The disciples had not believed or understood her earlier report of the empty tomb, but she will not give up. With her renewed vocation, she goes to find again those who did not have her courage or determination to share the good news entrusted to her.

COLLECT

Almighty God,
you have created the heavens and the earth
and made us in your own image:
teach us to discern your hand in all your works
and your likeness in all your children;
through Jesus Christ your Son our Lord,
who with you and the Holy Spirit reigns supreme over all things,
now and for ever.

Reflection by **Libby Lane**

Psalm **68**
2 Chronicles 15.1-15
John 20.19-end

Saturday 18 February

John 20.19-end

'Jesus said to them again, "Peace be with you ..."' (v.21)

I love the 'agains' in this passage. They make it plain that Jesus does not just give us one chance.

Jesus recognized and accepted the disciples' fear, and knew it would take time and repetition for them to understand and believe. He spoke peace to their brokenness, and offered practical physical reassurance to their fear. Jesus reiterated his peace, and gave them renewed identity and purpose even though they were ill equipped to receive or act upon it yet.

And he repeated that grace for Thomas. Jesus would not leave him behind. Thomas was not more doubting than the rest. None of the disciples could understand, believe or act until Jesus was there in person among them – showing, telling, reassuring, encouraging them as many times as it took.

Jesus came again for Thomas, not grudgingly but lovingly. And Thomas' response was more immediate, more public, more active than that of his brothers who, despite Jesus' repeated reassurance of peace, were still hidden silently away behind locked doors.

As we read this passage, we are in Thomas' shoes before Jesus came again to the house where they were hiding – not present for Jesus' resurrection appearance in the flesh but offered the testimony of those who were. Jesus will not leave us behind either. That we too might know his blessing, Jesus will come to find every one of us and speak his peace, again and again, as often as it takes.

COLLECT

Almighty God,
give us reverence for all creation
and respect for every person,
that we may mirror your likeness
in Jesus Christ our Lord.

Reflection by **Libby Lane**

Monday 20 February

Psalm **71**
Jeremiah 1
John 3.1-21

Jeremiah 1

'I see a branch of an almond tree' (v. 11)

Jeremiah offers some useful Lenten focal points.

Jeremiah sees an almond tree. There is word play in Hebrew between '*shaqued*' (almond branch) and '*shoqed*' (watching). This almond branch speaks profoundly to Jeremiah of God's concern for human affairs and his interaction in the midst of our muddle. Sometimes we might be tempted to look around us and wonder where God is. The almond branch image reassures. God is present.

God is active. He calls specific people at specific times to specific tasks. Jeremiah is called to a purpose God has had for him, long before his conception. God does not abandon Judah to her foolish apostacy; God cries long and often through Jeremiah for the people to return to the covenant. Even in our failure, God's mercy is present in judgement – which is ultimately designed to chasten and restore.

God equips. Jeremiah quakes at his calling, pleading youthful inexperience. As God did with Moses and Isaiah years earlier, reassurance is given that will brook no resistance. Though Jeremiah's calling will be hard, God will make him like 'a fortified city', 'an iron pillar' and a 'bronze wall' in the face of his people's hostile resistance.

Whatever we face today – personally and collectively – as we set our course for Lent, remember this: God is present, God is active and God equips.

COLLECT

Almighty Father,
whose Son was revealed in majesty
before he suffered death upon the cross:
give us grace to perceive his glory,
that we may be strengthened to suffer with him
and be changed into his likeness, from glory to glory;
who is alive and reigns with you,
in the unity of the Holy Spirit,
one God, now and for ever.

Reflection by **Kate Bruce**

Psalm **73**
Jeremiah 2.1-13
John 3.22-end

Tuesday 21 February

Jeremiah 2.1-13

'... my people have exchanged their glory for something that does not profit' (v.11)

Imagine a farmer in an arid climate. There is a spring on their land, bubbling up with irrigating life force. One day you find the farmer digging out a hole and lining it with lime plaster.

'What are you doing?'

'I'm making a place where rainwater will collect so I can water my crops.'

This is a foolish farmer! With a spring of water bubbling up, why exchange it for a cistern that will crack and leak?

Similarly, the people exchange the God who brought them out of Egypt, carried them and cared for them, for a useless thing – a false god, Ba'al. How has this happened? They stopped seeking God. Priests, legal authorities, rulers and prophets stopped remembering their heritage. The people forgot their story. The passion of their youthful love for God evaporated like the morning dew. They chased worthless idols and became like the thing they pursued: worthless.

Did we once revel in the bubbling fountain of divine life that welled up in our spirits? Has that love grown cold? Have we hewn out our own wells? Have we forgotten the bread that satisfies, replaced Jesus with a few stale rusks? Have we swapped the warmth of the sun for a two-bar electric fire? Time for a spiritual stocktake.

COLLECT

Holy God,
you know the disorder of our sinful lives:
set straight our crooked hearts,
and bend our wills to love your goodness and your glory
in Jesus Christ our Lord.

Reflection by **Kate Bruce**

Wednesday 22 February

Ash Wednesday

Psalm **38**
Daniel 9.3-6, 17-19
I Timothy 6.6-19

1 Timothy 6.6-19

'... command them not ... to set their hopes on the uncertainty of riches, but rather on God who richly provides' (v.17)

Jeremiah takes aim at the people's attempts at self-reliance through the metaphor of digging cisterns. A futile example of cistern digging is accumulating riches believing this will bring peace and happiness. Money is neutral, but 'the love of money is a root of all kinds of evil'. It breeds self-reliance, airbrushing out the truth of our dependence on God for each breath and every heartbeat. When we fall for self-reliance, we become trapped in the need to grasp, hoard and stockpile. We become defensive, suspicious and manacled to the myth of scarcity. Generosity withers. Community founders. Individualism runs rampant.

Ash Wednesday urges us to put down the spade and examine our own cistern-digging habits. Is it cash in the attic and money in the bank that helps us sleep at night? Foolishness. We 'brought nothing into the world, so that we can take nothing out', except our relationship with God. Invest here.

God 'richly provides us with everything for our enjoyment'. There is no need to grasp and accrue and hoard. But how easily we forget. How easily we mistrust and think we'd better have an insurance policy. How readily we forfeit the freedom and peace that comes from seeking God first. Ash Wednesday sets before us our false cisterns and the eternal fountain and says: 'Choose life.'

COLLECT

Almighty and everlasting God,
you hate nothing that you have made
and forgive the sins of all those who are penitent:
create and make in us new and contrite hearts
that we, worthily lamenting our sins
and acknowledging our wretchedness,
may receive from you, the God of all mercy,
perfect remission and forgiveness;
through Jesus Christ your Son our Lord,
who is alive and reigns with you,
in the unity of the Holy Spirit,
one God, now and for ever.

Reflection by **Kate Bruce**

Psalm **77** *or* **78.1-39***
Jeremiah 2.14-32
John 4.1-26

Thursday 23 February

Jeremiah 2.14-32

'... long ago you broke your yoke and burst your bonds' (v.20)

Variously, Judah was a vassal of Assyria, Egypt and finally Babylon, in an era of political ferment. Jeremiah berates the people for pursuing Assyria and quaffing the waters of the Nile. They seek protection from that which is not God. Here is a spiritual tendency with which we can readily identify.

Jesus stated, that 'My yoke is easy and my burden is light' (Matthew 11.30). How readily we throw this yoke off and saddle ourselves with unhelpful baggage. We see this when we flee from God and rely on the weak crutches of our dependencies and competencies.

Apostacy is the flagrant refusal to follow the steer of Christ's yoke. We see it in the Church when political leaders are courted for power and patronage, even when their values and behaviour are obviously incompatible with the gospel. We see this in many examples of people victimized in order to protect the brand of big-name leaders and the cult of success.

Forsaking God's path is 'evil and bitter'. Don't trust Egypt or Assyria. No good thing can come of it. Rather, trust the one who said: 'Come to me, all you that are weary and are carrying heavy burdens, and I will give you rest. Take my yoke upon you, and learn from me; for I am gentle and humble in heart, and you will find rest for your souls.' (Matthew 11.28-29)

COLLECT

Holy God,
our lives are laid open before you:
rescue us from the chaos of sin
and through the death of your Son
bring us healing and make us whole
in Jesus Christ our Lord.

Reflection by **Kate Bruce**

Friday 24 February

Psalms **3**, 7 *or* **55**
Jeremiah 3.6-22
John 4.27-42

Jeremiah 3.6-22

'I will heal your faithlessness.' (v.22)

There were two sisters: Israel, who lived in the north, and Judah who dwelt in the south. Israel did as she pleased and thus destroyed the one relationship that really mattered. Judah looked on, but learned nothing from her sister's situation. Judah pleased herself. When things looked bad, she put on a penitent act. Israel had no example to follow, but Judah did – and hence had less excuse for her disobedience and dissembling.

Judah presents an acceptable face. This ties in with the historic reforms of King Josiah, designed to bring Judah back to God. He was a man after God's heart, but his reforms did not bring about deep transformation in the spiritual life of the nation. Sunday best to look the part, but 'the Lord looks on the heart' (1 Samuel 16.7).

When you look at my heart, God, what do you see?

We are messy and muddled, and God knows this. There is no need to hide or dissemble before God. God sees us as we are and, like Israel and her sister, calls us to return, to be honest about our weakness and failure. God can work with this. It's the stubborn refusal to repent that blocks God, the insistence of false innocence that ties God's hands.

This Lent we cry out 'Create in me a clean heart, O God' (Psalm 51.10) and trust that God will heal our faithlessness.

COLLECT

Almighty and everlasting God,
you hate nothing that you have made
and forgive the sins of all those who are penitent:
create and make in us new and contrite hearts
that we, worthily lamenting our sins
and acknowledging our wretchedness,
may receive from you, the God of all mercy,
perfect remission and forgiveness;
through Jesus Christ your Son our Lord,
who is alive and reigns with you,
in the unity of the Holy Spirit,
one God, now and for ever.

Reflection by **Kate Bruce**

Psalm **71** *or* **76**, 79
Jeremiah 4.1-18
John 4.43-end

Saturday 25 February

Jeremiah 4.1-18

'... or else my wrath will go forth like fire' (v.4)

Divine wrath? I'd rather dwell on the love of God, the warmth and welcome of God. But, airbrush out God's anger and we create a toothless deity. God is not a bit piqued because people aren't paying him attention. God is not a prima donna in a huff. God's fury comes because failure to worship causes evil to sprout up. Wickedness prospers and innocents pay.

We don't have to go far to see how neglect of God allows evil to flourish, but let's begin at home, with the Church. We have not protected children or the vulnerable. Throughout the worldwide Church, voices have been silenced in order not to sully reputations. Gender injustice is rife. Racism abounds. Difference is demonized. Do we care more about where the flower stand goes than about the plight of the hungry on the doorstep? As unpalatable as it is – this failure has its roots in not attending to the worship of God. I don't mean with bells and smells, or choruses and clapping; I mean in the deep places of the human heart.

Jeremiah offers this startling image: 'remove the foreskins of your heart.' Don't simply go through the motions of attending to right religious practice – circumcise your heart. In humility, bring the internal world of the self before God – that God might transform our vision, imagination, wounds, habits, attitude, language and action.

COLLECT

Holy God,
our lives are laid open before you:
rescue us from the chaos of sin
and through the death of your Son
bring us healing and make us whole
in Jesus Christ our Lord.

Reflection by **Kate Bruce**

Monday 27 February

Psalms 10, **11** *or* **80**, 82
Jeremiah 4.19-end
John 5.1-18

Jeremiah 4.19-end

'They are skilled in doing evil, but do not know how to do good' (v.22)

In the musical *Oliver*, Fagin sings about reviewing his situation. He's always been a robber – can he change? He examines what this might mean but is anxious about it. He concludes: 'I'm a bad 'un and a bad 'un I shall stay!' He elects to stick with the security of the life he knows. He is a pickpocket and villain; skilled in doing evil, he does not know how to do good.

To be skilled takes focus and practice. The people of God have intentionally decided not to know God. This causes Jeremiah deep anguish. He sees the coming judgement, the boiling pot from the north tipping over (1.13). Enemies will lay waste to cities, as desolation comes upon the land. Ultimately, the northern power, Babylon, a tool of divine judgement, carried the people into exile.

God wants his people to return to him, and his judgement – hard though it is – aims to bring them back from the stupidity of evil into restored relationship. Like Fagin they resist. The consequences will be terrible. But even in the depths of this horror, we find a diamond of hope. God is clear, judgement will come, but a doorway of light glimmers. 'I will not make a full end.' Given the deliberate evil of the people, who deserve only condemnation, God's grace is striking.

Is it time to review our situation?

COLLECT

Almighty God,
whose Son Jesus Christ fasted forty days in the wilderness,
and was tempted as we are, yet without sin:
give us grace to discipline ourselves in obedience to your Spirit;
and, as you know our weakness,
so may we know your power to save;
through Jesus Christ your Son our Lord,
who is alive and reigns with you,
in the unity of the Holy Spirit,
one God, now and for ever.

Reflection by **Kate Bruce**

Psalm **44** *or* 87, **89.1-18**
Jeremiah 5.1-19
John 5.19-29

Tuesday 28 February

Jeremiah 5.1-19

'They have spoken falsely of the Lord ...' (v.12)

Our reading today plunges us further into God's fury and anguish on the lips of Jeremiah. Rich and poor alike have abandoned God, setting their faces against repentance. Jeremiah is clear that this attitude will have a consequence, but the people delude themselves into believing that God winks at their apostacy.

Buckle up. Jeremiah's words demand our attention and pose hard questions. In honesty, we may find we have more in common with the people Jeremiah is addressing than we like to admit. Wherever we find ourselves today, God comes calling. 'Do not forsake me. Whatever you face, do not shut me out. Do not fool yourself that you can rely on your own resources. Do not speak falsely of me.'

Now is a good moment to remind ourselves that we draw breath because God gives us life. Our heart beats because God wills it so. Without God we are dust. Where our hearts are stony and rebellious, cry out to God to train and discipline them. When we see the clay of our life as a misshapen pot, cry that the potter would throw us on the wheel and remake us.

God can do nothing with a rebellious heart, but a penitent spirit is malleable. God of grace – remake us.

COLLECT

Heavenly Father,
your Son battled with the powers of darkness,
and grew closer to you in the desert:
help us to use these days to grow in wisdom and prayer
that we may witness to your saving love
in Jesus Christ our Lord.

Reflection by **Kate Bruce**

Wednesday 1 March

Psalms **6**, 17 *or* **119.105-128**
Jeremiah 5.20-end
John 5.30-end

Jeremiah 5.20-end

'... your sins have deprived you of good' (v.25)

When the Tempter crooks a beckoning finger, it always whispers attraction. 'This will be good. This will be pleasing. This will satisfy.' Imagine you are desperately thirsty; the Tempter offers to quench your need with a mug of liquid. Anticipating relief, you gulp it down. It is always brine. Our sins always deprive us of good, even if they come with the promise of great reward. Ponder the temptation of Jesus in the wilderness, which can be summed up as: 'feed yourself and please yourself'. Clear-sighted, Jesus tipped the brine away.

The devil dances to a discordant beat. When we attend to this cacophony, we become deaf to heaven's music: the songs of faith, hope and love, the tunes of kindness, compassion and generosity fade away. Jeremiah's audience are gyrating to a destructive rhythm: thieving and treachery are the norm; the rich have grown fat and sleek in their corruption; the religious leaders are weak and false; the land is in peril. Revelling in their sense of superior selfhood, none realize the proximity of the axe of judgement.

Open a news app and skim the headlines. It is not difficult to see how sin, individual and societal, creates cultures in which the vulnerable are preyed upon, where the powerful line their own pockets, and where truth is spun to say what suits.

Jeremiah speaks truth: sin will always deprive us of ultimate good.

COLLECT

Almighty God,
whose Son Jesus Christ fasted forty days in the wilderness,
and was tempted as we are, yet without sin:
give us grace to discipline ourselves in obedience to your Spirit;
and, as you know our weakness,
so may we know your power to save;
through Jesus Christ your Son our Lord,
who is alive and reigns with you,
in the unity of the Holy Spirit,
one God, now and for ever.

Reflection by **Kate Bruce**

Psalms **42**, 43 *or* 90, **92**
Jeremiah 6.9-21
John 6.1-15

Thursday 2 March

Jeremiah 6.9-21

'They have treated the wound of my people carelessly' (v.14)

Remember the asphalt surfaces of school playgrounds? If you fell, tiny bits of stone embedded themselves in scraped knees. Being patched up involved the painful removal of this grit from the graze, with the ubiquitous, stingy application of witch hazel. Wounds cleaned up by kind hands.

We are far enough into Jeremiah's book to know that the wound he mentions is more grievous than a scraped knee; there is raging infection in the land, a pandemic transmitted by dishonesty, disorder and denial. Economic dishonesty elevates the idol of greed. Apostasy ushers in spiritual disorder. The careless attitude of those tasked with tending the spiritual health of the people has fostered denial of the truth.

This wound needs a powerful salve: 'Look for the ancient paths, where the good way lies; and walk in it.' Jeremiah's primary audience ignored his words. Are *we* listening? This Lent, come back to the pathways of prayer, dive into the river of Scripture, submit to confession and spiritual direction.

We need the presence of God in the attentiveness of each other. It takes great courage to allow someone to tend our hidden wounds, but this is vital. Where we are honoured with such trust – there is no room for carelessness as we pick out the stubborn grit of sin and failure, bringing the sting of truth and the salve of kindness.

COLLECT

Heavenly Father,
your Son battled with the powers of darkness,
and grew closer to you in the desert:
help us to use these days to grow in wisdom and prayer
that we may witness to your saving love
in Jesus Christ our Lord.

Reflection by **Kate Bruce**

Friday 3 March

Psalm **22** *or* **88** (95)
Jeremiah 6.22-end
John 6.16-27

Jeremiah 6.22-end

'... mourning as for an only child, most bitter lamentation' (v.26)

In the Jewish Museum in Berlin is an art installation, *'Shalekhet'* ('Fallen Leaves'), by Menashe Kadishman. It consists of faces made from chunks of metal, piled on each other. You are invited to walk across them – a profoundly unsettling experience. They knock together making a sound like iron wheels on railway tracks. It's the sound of violence, oppression, theft, abuse, and terrible, terrible fear. It is the sound of exile.

In 586 BC, Judah experienced the culmination of a series of deportations. Nebuchadnezzar II of Babylon sacked Jerusalem and destroyed the temple. Judah is smashed politically, socially, economically and spiritually. Jeremiah sees this on the horizon, and states the uncomfortable truth: God has rejected them. It is the cry of exile.

The only response to this devastation is honest, bitter lament. This is not how things should be. What have we done? Where is God? Lament prevents us from running too quickly to Pollyanna-ish declarations of hope: the 'peace, peace, when there is no peace' (Jeremiah 6.14) of the false prophets. This simply hides the wounds and silences those who know first hand the absence of peace.

However, lament does not keep us trapped forever in the despair of exile, or trouble of any kind. Lament is a doorway into hope, because it is spoken to someone. It is addressed to God: 'How long, *O Lord*.' That's the point of exile.

COLLECT

Almighty God,
whose Son Jesus Christ fasted forty days in the wilderness,
and was tempted as we are, yet without sin:
give us grace to discipline ourselves in obedience to your Spirit;
and, as you know our weakness,
so may we know your power to save;
through Jesus Christ your Son our Lord,
who is alive and reigns with you,
in the unity of the Holy Spirit,
one God, now and for ever.

Reflection by **Kate Bruce**

Psalms 59, **63** *or* 96, **97**, 100
Jeremiah 7.1-20
John 6.27-40

Saturday 4 March

Jeremiah 7.1-20

'Do not trust in these deceptive words: "This is the temple of the Lord, the temple of the Lord, the temple of the Lord."' (v.4)

Imagine someone standing outside a place of worship, declaring that Sunday best and rote liturgical chuntering are deceptive, as is the requisite repetition of choruses or the intonation of psalms, *if the heart is absent from worship*. Their voice cuts through the inevitably frosty response with a reminder that God desires reformation of the heart, no more attending worship one day and offering cakes to idols the next. You're imagining Jeremiah.

'Let me dwell with you in this place' says God. Has God been pushed out of his own temple? The idea of God dwelling with his people is present in Revelation 21, in an intimate picture: 'See the home of God is among mortals. He will dwell with them; they will be his peoples' (Revelation 21.3). Like Jeremiah's audience, we are being called into this intimate, uncompromising relationship with God. You can't hobble between God and your preferred idol. The idols have to go.

Perhaps we find it difficult to let go of our props and supports? Then tell God about this.

We cannot transform ourselves, but we can be open to the transformative power of God dwelling in us. God speaks persistently – we must respond, even if that response is simply: 'God help me. Remake me. Potter, throw me on your wheel again.'

COLLECT

Heavenly Father,
your Son battled with the powers of darkness,
and grew closer to you in the desert:
help us to use these days to grow in wisdom and prayer
that we may witness to your saving love
in Jesus Christ our Lord.

Reflection by **Kate Bruce**

Monday 6 March

Psalms 26, **32** *or* **98**, 99, 101
Jeremiah 7.21-end
John 6.41-51

Jeremiah 7.21-end

'Obey my voice, and I will be your God' (v.23)

Many years ago, there was a production of the musical *Godspell* that began with a number of actors coming to the front of the stage and singing loudly about their philosophy of life. One sang about capitalism, one about socialism, another about humanism, and so on. Their songs started to conflict with eath other and made such a racket that the audience didn't know who to listen to any more. All of a sudden, a very loud ram's horn sounded, and in walked a man carrying a bucket of water. He began splashing it around, first on the actors and then on everyone else. It was John the Baptist, and he was telling us to wash our mouths and ears out, and to prepare ourselves to hear the one true song that really matters.

John was in the tradition of prophets like Jeremiah. In today's reading, we find Jeremiah voicing God's desire for his people to hear him, to listen to his melodies of fidelity and peace, so that they can wake up to who they have become, and to the destructive and inhumane things they are doing. Alarmingly, we discover this includes the ritual sacrifice of children.

In all the noise of now, it can be hard to hear yourself, or the world that is making you. Jeremiah reminds us that at such a time, truth can perish and there will be a lot of collateral damage in our relationships and society.

COLLECT

Almighty God,
you show to those who are in error the light of your truth,
that they may return to the way of righteousness:
grant to all those who are admitted
into the fellowship of Christ's religion,
that they may reject those things
that are contrary to their profession,
and follow all such things as are agreeable to the same;
through our Lord Jesus Christ,
who is alive and reigns with you,
in the unity of the Holy Spirit,
one God, now and for ever.

Reflection by **Mark Oakley**

Psalm **50** *or* **106*** (*or* 103)
Jeremiah 8.1-15
John 6.52-59

Tuesday 7 March

Jeremiah 8.1-15

'... they did not know how to blush' (v.12)

In the poetry of this chapter, Jeremiah relates God's bewilderment at his people as he identifies what is at the heart of their problems. They have 'held fast to deceit', 'do not speak honestly', and, like horses charging into battle, are blind to the dangers facing them. At the same time as all this, people like to think of themselves as wise and peaceful and so have no ability to self-scrutinize. They don't even blush at their behaviour.

Towards the end of today's passage, it seems to dawn on folk that the crisis in which they find themselves may be caught up in the way they have been living their lives. It feels as if God may be punishing them and therefore they are, at last, prompted to ask 'what for?'

It is easy in life to conclude from time to time that God 'has given us poisoned water to drink' as some divine retribution on us. What is harder to see is that so often we bring pain on ourselves, that our behaviour can catch up with us, that hidden truths come to light, that relationships break down as people begin to see who we really are or what we've been up to.

Sometimes, life throws things at us out of the blue, but at other times, we are simply victims of our own worst selves.

COLLECT

Almighty God,
by the prayer and discipline of Lent
may we enter into the mystery of Christ's sufferings,
and by following in his Way
come to share in his glory;
through Jesus Christ our Lord.

Reflection by **Mark Oakley**

Wednesday 8 March

Psalm **35** *or* 110, **111**, 112
Jeremiah 8.18 – 9.11
John 6.60-end

Jeremiah 8.18 – 9.11

'O that my head were a spring of water, and my eyes a fountain of tears' (9.1)

There is scholarly debate as to who is speaking and crying in this passage. Is it Jeremiah asking us to hear 'the cry of my own poor people'? Or is it a personified Jerusalem whose 'joy is gone'? Or maybe it is the people themselves acknowledging that 'for the hurt of my poor people I am hurt'? However, for some, it is as clear as day that it is God who is weeping, pained by the fact that those he loves 'refuse to know me'. As evidence of this, Jeremiah cites the deceit, selfishness and hypocrisy of atomized individuals who have no commitment to God's vision for human society and the principles that are required to bring it into reality.

Tears are mentioned a few times here. Today, they can be something we try to hide. We worry that they expose our vulnerability, need, or deep unhappiness, in a world in which we are supposed to have none of these things. In the Christian tradition, however, tears are often greeted as a gift. They are eloquent and honest. They bypass the words we can use to hide and reveal our soul, to others and to ourselves, unfiltered.

The poet and priest John Donne prayed in one of his Holy Sonnets, in the spirit of Jeremiah, that, as 'a little world made cunningly', tears might drown his destructive worldview and wash his eyes out to see, and to live, better.

COLLECT

Almighty God,
you show to those who are in error the light of your truth,
that they may return to the way of righteousness:
grant to all those who are admitted
into the fellowship of Christ's religion,
that they may reject those things
that are contrary to their profession,
and follow all such things as are agreeable to the same;
through our Lord Jesus Christ,
who is alive and reigns with you,
in the unity of the Holy Spirit,
one God, now and for ever.

Reflection by **Mark Oakley**

Psalm **34** *or* 113, **115**
Jeremiah 9.12-24
John 7.1-13

Thursday 9 March

Jeremiah 9.12-24

'I act with steadfast love, justice, and righteousness in the earth, for in these things I delight' (v.24)

When the writer and theologian Ronald Knox was told by a friend to 'pull himself together', Knox replied: 'I'm not sure I have a together.' This experience in which we feel we lack an integrated or centred self, as individuals or as a community, is at the heart of what is known as 'lament'. When something happens to us that shatters our view of things, and which doesn't fit in with our outlook on life, we need to move slowly towards appropriating what has happened so that our view of things changes, widens, to include our new experience. This move is often painful and costly. To help it along, we lament.

To lament means to be honest about the hurt of our world crashing around us, about the anger we may feel, or the doubt in a God who would do such a thing. The purpose of lament, in the spiritual life, is to help get us back to a place of praise.

In today's reading, God calls on 'the mourning-women to come'. He invites their 'dirge' so that 'eyes may run down with tears'. It is only through such lament that his people will recognize what exile and loss has done to them and, then, how it might be shaped into a new life where they will understand and know him.

COLLECT

Almighty God,
by the prayer and discipline of Lent
may we enter into the mystery of Christ's sufferings,
and by following in his Way
come to share in his glory;
through Jesus Christ our Lord.

Reflection by **Mark Oakley**

Friday 10 March

Psalms 40, **41** *or* **139**
Jeremiah 10.1-16
John 7.14-24

Jeremiah 10.1-16

'There is none like you, O Lord' (v.6)

Today's reading makes a similar point to that found in Psalm 115. The gods worshipped in Jeremiah's day are 'like scarecrows'; they are human creations in a human likeness, and we set them up to be adored. In doing so, it is ourselves that we end up bowing down to. In contrast, we are told here that there is none like the Lord and that 'he is the living God'. The gods of others might be made of silver and gold, but there are many things more valuable than money. Of supreme value is to know the true God, who made the earth with wisdom, and to understand that other substitutes we pursue will always let us down because 'they are worthless, a work of delusion'.

One might read the book of Jeremiah and conclude that God is to be feared because he is fierce and out to punish us. What Jeremiah is teaching, though, is that we are not to worship God because he is vindictive, but because he is real. We find this reality hard to bear because so much of our own composition is made up of cover-ups, superficialities and avoidances. So we replace the reality of God with a range of convenient replacements – and for some of us this might be the self-congratulation of being part of the 'right' religion – but all of them must fall away if we are to stand before the 'the true God' to see, and be seen, with the transparent and faithful eyes of love.

COLLECT

Almighty God,
you show to those who are in error the light of your truth,
that they may return to the way of righteousness:
grant to all those who are admitted
    into the fellowship of Christ's religion,
that they may reject those things
    that are contrary to their profession,
and follow all such things as are agreeable to the same;
through our Lord Jesus Christ,
who is alive and reigns with you,
in the unity of the Holy Spirit,
one God, now and for ever.

Reflection by **Mark Oakley**

Psalms 3, **25** *or* 120, **121**, 122
Jeremiah 10.17-24
John 7.25-36

Saturday 11 March

Jeremiah 10.17-24

'Correct me, O Lord, but in just measure' (v.24)

The hurt voice of an exiled people is loud in this passage. They see they have forgotten life-giving truths, that their leaders have wounded them, and that now they are all scattered. They can sense what lies ahead. The severity of their wound, and exile, must now be borne, it seems, as a punishment for their confident stupidity in ignoring the covenant with their God. Perhaps if they repent, they reflect, God will eventually also punish those who have laid waste their land and homes?

The prayer at the end of this passage is that they might be corrected, but in just measure and not in anger. It is a courageous thing to pray to be amended because, as the great truths of our faith remind us, there has to be a fall before there is a redemption, and death before life. In other words, if we are to be rescued there needs to be some rupture; salvation is a 'falling awake', as it were.

If our prayer is that we be changed, are we prepared? What needs to be lost if we ourselves are not to be lost in a maze of our own making?

COLLECT

Almighty God,
by the prayer and discipline of Lent
may we enter into the mystery of Christ's sufferings,
and by following in his Way
come to share in his glory;
through Jesus Christ our Lord.

Reflection by **Mark Oakley**

Monday 13 March

Psalms **5**, 7 *or* 123, 124, 125, **126**
Jeremiah 11.1-17
John 7.37-52

Jeremiah 11.1-17

'What right has my beloved in my house, when she has done vile deeds? (v.15)

Today's passage is sometimes known as Jeremiah's 'covenant sermon'. His message is that people should listen again to God because they have an extraordinary ability to ignore the lessons of the past and so repeat the mistakes of their ancestors in following other gods. It is a radical sermon because Jeremiah announces the collapse of the Mosaic covenant on account of this disloyalty. This covenant is rooted in the promise that, if the people are faithful to him, God will always be their God and will give them a land to build their community life in. However, just as they decide not to listen to God anymore, so God now refuses to listen to them. Their relationship is shattered.

Anyone who has gone through a painful separation with a lover knows what chaotic emotions take over. They range from regret or shame, to hate, hurt and fantasies of revenge. Nothing is more dislocating that the departure of someone you had built hopes and dreams with. What happens to your unemployed love, now? We speak, at such times, of our hearts 'breaking'.

So, it seems, does God, who makes a comparison with such a break-up and to the perplexed heartache it creates.

COLLECT

Almighty God,
whose most dear Son went not up to joy
but first he suffered pain,
and entered not into glory before he was crucified:
mercifully grant that we, walking in the way of the cross,
may find it none other than the way of life and peace;
through Jesus Christ your Son our Lord,
who is alive and reigns with you,
in the unity of the Holy Spirit,
one God, now and for ever.

Reflection by **Mark Oakley**

Psalms 6, **9** *or* **132**, 133
Jeremiah 11.18 – 12.6
John 7.53 – 8.11

Tuesday 14 March

Jeremiah 11.18 – 12.6

'... you are near in their mouths yet far from their hearts' (12.2)

The clear theme that emerges here is that of divine justice. Jeremiah lays out something of his inner life, and how it feels, as a prophet, like being a lamb led to slaughter. By sharing his feelings, we see that Jeremiah both embodies the pain of his exiled people, and the pain of his God, who is being ignored by those he loves and made a covenant with. Jeremiah symbolizes both his community and his God, representing each to the other, and so bears the cost of the one asked to help repair their relationship.

Jeremiah is asking why he finds himself the victim of devised schemes, but he is also asking questions as to why the unpleasant and guilty people seem to flourish in life. Jeremiah is frustrated at how so many are treacherous, but he concedes that God still made them, even though God is now 'far from their hearts'.

Today we can find ourselves asking similar questions about why it is that the good can suffer and the wicked do quite nicely. What matters ultimately is the quality of the human heart, and our ability to love rather than judge our neighbour. By loving, we counter all that works against what is just and begin to become the answer to our own questions about God's way of shaping this world.

COLLECT

Eternal God,
give us insight
to discern your will for us,
to give up what harms us,
and to seek the perfection we are promised
in Jesus Christ our Lord.

Reflection by **Mark Oakley**

Wednesday 15 March

Psalm **38** *or* **119.153-end**
Jeremiah 13.1-11
John 8.12-30

Jeremiah 13.1-11

'... now the loincloth was ruined; it was good for nothing' (v.7)

This is a bit strange. It sounds as if God is asking Jeremiah to go and hide a pair of his pants in the earth, by the water, and wait for them to be unwearable. That appears to be exactly what Jeremiah does. Perhaps we need some weird behaviour by people of faith to break through the 'common sense' articulacy of a culture that is misguided and headed for ruin? I look forward to the preachers of today using a pair of Y-fronts to challenge the misguided decisions of government!

The prophetic act here is serious, though. God is asking his people to see that he 'clings' to them, like thin material on sweat, but in 'stubbornly following their own will', they are losing their identity as a community and becoming purposeless. This pride of theirs needs dealing with if they are to see sense and become 'a people, a name, a praise, and a glory' that he has always longed for them to be. If it takes burying a loincloth to understand the depths of God's frustration, and the ways he will prise them away from their ridiculous gods, then so be it.

How we do the same in our own day is a challenge to how imaginative our discipleship is, or should be.

COLLECT

Almighty God,
whose most dear Son went not up to joy
but first he suffered pain,
and entered not into glory before he was crucified:
mercifully grant that we, walking in the way of the cross,
may find it none other than the way of life and peace;
through Jesus Christ your Son our Lord,
who is alive and reigns with you,
in the unity of the Holy Spirit,
one God, now and for ever.

 Reflection by **Mark Oakley**

Psalms **56**, 57 *or* **143**, 146
Jeremiah 14
John 8.31-47

Thursday 16 March

Jeremiah 14

'... we are called by your name' (v.9)

The second half of verse 9 is often read at the late night office of Compline. In the stillness, surrounded by encroaching darkness and with a long night ahead, the congregation prays to the Lord who is 'in the midst of us' and asks that he does not forsake them. Similarly, we find in the poetry of today's passage, a people who have become aware of their own sins and who can't breathe in the frightening atmosphere of their own creation. They need God, and now they see that need. They ask that God will not be like some 'stranger' to them.

The reading today begins with the image of drought and thirst. Everyone – including the animals and environment – is thirsty and needs water if hope is to be restored. This is a spiritual metaphor, of course, and yet God alerts Jeremiah to the fact that at a time when people are longing for refreshment, false prophets come along and say everything is all right. At the risk of sounding like some vengeful and capricious deity, God nevertheless has to reveal the severity of the situation before any change is possible. Out of the calamity comes the heartfelt cry from his people, 'remember and do not break your covenant with us'.

COLLECT

Eternal God,
give us insight
to discern your will for us,
to give up what harms us,
and to seek the perfection we are promised
in Jesus Christ our Lord.

Reflection by **Mark Oakley**

Friday 17 March

Psalm **22** *or* 142, **144**
Jeremiah 15.10-end
John 8.48-end

Jeremiah 15.10-end

'... utter what is precious, and not what is worthless' (v.19)

In the Church of England's *Book of Common Prayer*, there is a collect that asks that we might 'inwardly digest' Scripture, God's nutritious word. In Jeremiah's lament, which we read today, he says that he has eaten the language of God, made inseparable from him, so that he can make God's vision known to his contemporaries. The problem is, he continues, this has made him a lonely figure and given him a life of unceasing pain. He audaciously takes God on about this, complaining that God appears to be a deceitful brook that has dried up and stopped giving.

God's reply is to the point. Look at me, keep your eyes on me, speak what is precious – and then people will turn to you for help in their renewed search for me. Some will still not like you, Jeremiah, but you will overcome this with me by your side.

Just as we are told before a plane takes off that, should there be difficulty, we should place the oxygen mask over ourselves before assisting others, we need to breathe if we are to help others survive, so Jeremiah learns that he needs to be spiritually resourced and fortified by God, before he will have any authenticity or plausibility among a distracted and hungry people.

COLLECT

Almighty God,
whose most dear Son went not up to joy
but first he suffered pain,
and entered not into glory before he was crucified:
mercifully grant that we, walking in the way of the cross,
may find it none other than the way of life and peace;
through Jesus Christ your Son our Lord,
who is alive and reigns with you,
in the unity of the Holy Spirit,
one God, now and for ever.

Reflection by **Mark Oakley**

Psalm **31** *or* **147**
Jeremiah 16.10 – 17.4
John 9.1-17

Saturday 18 March

Jeremiah 16.10 – 17.4

'O Lord, my strength and my stronghold' (16.19)

The questions raised in this passage are those that lie at the heart of the book of Jeremiah: What have we done wrong? Why are we suffering? What do we need to do? God's reply to Jeremiah is clear. The people have forsaken him and followed other gods, not keeping his law, and their selfish pursuits have reached the inevitable consequence of leaving them confused and without any compass. There is nothing new in this; they are acting like their ancestors, but they are the more foolish for not having learned a better way than them.

In the middle of all this distress, we find in verses 19 and 20 a voice breaking into the chaos that is loyal and confident. It is a voice of calm and trusting faithfulness, speaking intimately with God as 'strength', 'stronghold' and 'refuge'. The voice acknowledges the lies of the past and the worthless pursuits that have led the generations into barren and desperate places, even, on the way, making gods in the image of themselves.

As we read Jeremiah's pages, with its laments, questions, hurt and loss – both God's and his deported people's – such a voice shows us a pool of light, a relationship that imbues a true sense of identity again, built on renewing trust and instilling peace.

COLLECT

Eternal God,
give us insight
to discern your will for us,
to give up what harms us,
and to seek the perfection we are promised
in Jesus Christ our Lord.

Reflection by **Mark Oakley**

Monday 20 March

Joseph of Nazareth

Psalms 25, 147.1-12
Isaiah 11.1-10
Matthew 13.54-end

Matthew 13.54–end

'... is this not the carpenter's son?' (v.55)

Matthew describes Jesus as 'the carpenter's son'. This visit by Jesus to his home town, Nazareth, is recorded in almost identical words in Mark's Gospel, except there Jesus is called 'the carpenter'.

In his commentary on the New Testament, eminent theologian Anthony Harvey wondered whether this change was significant. Was Matthew revealing a reluctance on the part of the first Christians to acknowledge that Jesus had been a tradesman? It seems unlikely there was much of that sort of class snobbery around in first century Galilee. In any case, being a carpenter was quite respectable. A good carpenter is rarely out of work.

This tangential reference to Joseph (perhaps still alive when Jesus began his ministry) is all the more valuable because otherwise he disappears from the Gospels after the family visit to Jerusalem when Jesus was twelve. We're reminded here that Jesus was part of an ordinary human family for three decades. The names of his brothers – James, Joseph, Simon and Judas – are mentioned. Sometimes we speak of 'the holy family' as if it consisted only of Mary, Joseph and Jesus. It's the very ordinariness of his wider family that makes people think Jesus cannot be the Messiah. This is another reminder that those who witnessed the incarnation were blindest to it, just as we are so frequently unable to see God in the lives of those closest to us. Where may we see him in our life today?

COLLECT

God our Father,
who from the family of your servant David
raised up Joseph the carpenter
to be the guardian of your incarnate Son
and husband of the Blessed Virgin Mary:
give us grace to follow him
in faithful obedience to your commands;
through Jesus Christ your Son our Lord,
who is alive and reigns with you,
in the unity of the Holy Spirit,
one God, now and for ever.

Reflection by **Graham James**

Psalms 54, **79** *or* **5**, 6 (8)
Jeremiah 18.1-12
John 10.1-10

Tuesday 21 March

Jeremiah 18.1-12

'... he reworked it into another vessel' (v.4)

I visited a pottery where I was invited to have a go at the potter's wheel. I showed no natural talent. It took a long time, and a good many reworkings, to produce anything that looked vaguely like a bowl. But the benefit of clay was that I could take what was misshapen, roll it up and start again.

I remember being told to work *with* the clay, and to avoid too much pressure (or too little). Clay may be malleable, but you cannot do just what you please with it. Clay can be resistant to the potter's hands. It definitely was to mine. While the potter determines how the clay is shaped, the character of clay means it's a process in which the good potter respects the clay and its inherent qualities.

In using this image of the potter and the clay, Jeremiah is illustrating the undoubted sovereignty of God. But this is not a God unresponsive to his people, imposing himself without regard for them. This is a God who says he may change his mind and who will remake his people if they amend their ways.

When I watch a potter at work, it is the deep respect for the material that I notice, a tenderness and respect for the recalcitrant clay. That's why this image remains such a powerful and moving reminder of a God who is always prepared to rework us into a better shape.

COLLECT

Merciful Lord,
absolve your people from their offences,
that through your bountiful goodness
we may all be delivered from the chains of those sins
which by our frailty we have committed;
grant this, heavenly Father,
for Jesus Christ's sake, our blessed Lord and Saviour,
who is alive and reigns with you,
in the unity of the Holy Spirit,
one God, now and for ever.

Reflection by **Graham James**

Wednesday 22 March

Psalms 63, **90** *or* **119.1-32**
Jeremiah 18.13-end
John 10.11-21

Jeremiah 18.13-end

'... let us make plots against Jeremiah' (v.18)

Although in our contemporary world, biblical knowledge is not what it was, someone forecasting disaster may still be described as a 'Jeremiah'. Today's reading tells us why. Jeremiah's prophecies of doom for Israel continued for around 30 years, and so his credibility waned. If Jeremiah was really speaking words from the Lord, why did nothing happen? The priests and leading figures among the people of Israel got fed up having their integrity impugned so they plotted to destroy Jeremiah's reputation. Why should he not get a taste of his own medicine?

Jeremiah, aware of the plotting against him, pleads with the Lord to act. God may have his reasons for being patient with his faithless people, but within Jeremiah himself there's a longing that the Lord should not 'forgive their iniquity'.

There are two features of the human condition vividly reflected here. The first is the way in which we long to strike back at those who are our severest critics. Sometimes we know in our hearts that what they say has a measure of truth. That may make us even more angry and resentful. Was that the case with Jeremiah's opponents?

When we are in the right, however, and face opposition, we may want to see our critics face retribution. That's dangerous too since we become judgemental, usurping God's place. Righteousness can morph into self-righteousness. Being resentful or becoming self-righteous. Neither is attractive. Which is the greater danger in our own lives?

COLLECT

Merciful Lord,
absolve your people from their offences,
that through your bountiful goodness
we may all be delivered from the chains of those sins
which by our frailty we have committed;
grant this, heavenly Father,
for Jesus Christ's sake, our blessed Lord and Saviour,
who is alive and reigns with you,
in the unity of the Holy Spirit,
one God, now and for ever.

Reflection by **Graham James**

Psalms 53, **86** *or* 14, **15**, 16
Jeremiah 19.1-13
John 10.22-end

Thursday 23 March

Jeremiah 19.1-13

'... you shall break the jug' (v.10)

Broken pottery litters archaeological sites in the Middle East. Pots were frequently broken and thrown away. But Jeremiah takes a perfectly good jug, and in the presence of the senior priests and elders of the people, smashes it as an acted metaphor that the Lord is going to destroy the faithless people and their city too. Unlike the image used in the previous chapter in which the clay could be reworked, this vessel 'can never be mended'. It's a bleak prospect.

Over a decade ago at a service in Norwich Cathedral, the preacher gave his text, and as people settled in their seats, he took a glazed pot and threw it from the pulpit onto the stone floor in front of the nave altar. The robed clergy in the vicinity looked as shattered as the pot. The preacher was not re-enacting Jeremiah's action but drawing attention to St Paul describing himself and his fellow Christians as no better than 'earthen vessels' (2 Corinthians 4.7, KJV) to contain the treasure of the gospel. Fragile, cracked and misshapen we may be, the preacher said, but God takes, mends and remakes us.

History shows us that societies and civilizations do break apart, never to be mended. But peoples, including the people of Israel, are made and remade. God has a habit of being tender to the broken. What brokenness in us needs to be remade today?

COLLECT

Merciful Lord,
you know our struggle to serve you:
when sin spoils our lives
and overshadows our hearts,
come to our aid
and turn us back to you again;
through Jesus Christ our Lord.

Reflection by **Graham James**

Friday 24 March

Psalm **102** *or* 17, **19**
Jeremiah 19.14 – 20.6
John 11.1-16

Jeremiah 19.14 – 20.6

'The Lord has named you ... "Terror-all-around".' (20.3)

It was after the destruction of the twin towers of the World Trade Center in New York in 2001 and the tragic loss of so many lives that the United States President spoke of a 'war on terror'. Even at the time, some commentators wondered how war could be waged on an abstraction. It soon became clear that it would be a war against terrorists and the nations that harboured, trained or encouraged them. Osama bin Laden himself embodied this terror.

Jeremiah tells us that Pashur was the chief officer in the temple. He would have been in charge of security and expected to keep the peace in the house of the Lord. Jeremiah saw how the temple had become home to foreign cults and wayward teaching. He renames Pashur and calls him 'Terror-all-around'. It's another symbolic action, like the smashing of the jar. Pashur will be enveloped in the terror that's to come upon the people of Judah. He will be at the epicentre of that terror and is now the very embodiment of it.

We don't hear Pashur's side of this story. Pashur may have been simply trying to do his job. He may not have been able to see beyond his situation. Jeremiah is hoping to open his eyes, but even more to warn the people of Judah about the fate that awaited them. How easy it is for us to have our eyes open but fail to see what God demands of us.

COLLECT

Merciful Lord,
absolve your people from their offences,
that through your bountiful goodness
we may all be delivered from the chains of those sins
which by our frailty we have committed;
grant this, heavenly Father,
for Jesus Christ's sake, our blessed Lord and Saviour,
who is alive and reigns with you,
in the unity of the Holy Spirit,
one God, now and for ever.

Reflection by **Graham James**

Psalms 111, 113
1 Samuel 2.1-10
Romans 5.12-end

Saturday 25 March

Annunciation of Our Lord to the Blessed Virgin Mary

Romans 5.12-end

'... grace abounded all the more' (v.20)

It is surprising how often the word 'grace' is used in the English-speaking world today. An actor may be praised for performing with grace; a secretary replying on behalf of the Queen may say she has been 'graciously pleased' to receive a gift; and an invocation before a meal is called grace. Church meetings end frequently with everyone saying the Grace – words adapted from 2 Corinthians 13.13, where Paul refers to 'the grace of the Lord Jesus Christ...' In one dictionary I consulted, there were 16 different definitions of this single word 'grace'.

Apart from when someone is accused of having 'airs and graces', the definitions are positive. Elegance, beauty, goodwill: these are connected with grace. The gracious person is favoured. It's no surprise that the angel hails Mary at the Annunciation by telling her that she is favoured, 'full of grace', as many people throughout the Christian world say every day in their devotions. The Holy Spirit is to come upon Mary and enable her to have the grace (and strength) to give birth to Jesus.

Archbishop William Temple once reflected on the difficulty we experience if we are selfish and want to be unselfish. He said we need more than moral resolution to change. Something has to take hold of us from outside – the gift of grace. Grace 'abounds', as Paul testifies, and may bring God's favour into our lives today.

COLLECT

We beseech you, O Lord,
pour your grace into our hearts,
that as we have known the incarnation of your Son Jesus Christ
by the message of an angel,
so by his cross and passion
we may be brought to the glory of his resurrection;
through Jesus Christ your Son our Lord,
who is alive and reigns with you,
in the unity of the Holy Spirit,
one God, now and for ever.

Reflection by **Graham James**

Monday 27 March

Psalms **73**, 121 *or* 27, **30**
Jeremiah 21.1-10
John 11.28-44

Jeremiah 21.1-10

'... perform a wonderful deed for us' (v.2)

Since Jeremiah had prophesied doom for so long, it's surprising King Zedekiah would want to consult him when faced by Babylonian invaders. The Judean political and religious elite must have been desperate, but they cherished a hope that their God would 'perform a wonderful deed for us, as he has often done'. They remembered what God had done for their ancestors. Surely God would want to protect his name and his people?

Jeremiah also believed in the Lord's ability to do wonderful deeds. The temptation for him to say something pleasing may have been huge. But he had long believed the nation had rebelled so fully against God that its destruction was inevitable. Only this would lead to a radical rebuilding and a renewed trust in God. Jeremiah makes no political or military calculation before he speaks. He holds no brief for the Babylonians. He sees them simply as the instrument God has chosen by which the destruction will happen. Jeremiah speaks without consideration for his own wellbeing.

Some 2600 years separate us from Jeremiah. But ours remains a world in which individual courageous voices are heard in countries where prophetic words are not simply unwelcome but vigorously suppressed. In our everyday lives we know how challenging it is to say something unpopular and unwelcome, especially if we are in a tiny minority. Today, let us give thanks and pray for the prophets of our own age.

COLLECT

Most merciful God,
who by the death and resurrection of your Son Jesus Christ
delivered and saved the world:
grant that by faith in him who suffered on the cross
we may triumph in the power of his victory;
through Jesus Christ your Son our Lord,
who is alive and reigns with you,
in the unity of the Holy Spirit,
one God, now and for ever.

Reflection by **Graham James**

Psalms **35**, 123 *or* 32, **36**
Jeremiah 22.1-5, 13-19
John 11.45-end

Tuesday 28 March

Jeremiah 22.1-5, 13-19

'Act with justice and righteousness ...' (v.3)

The book of Jeremiah is not chronological. In the last chapter we were in King Zedekiah's reign, and now we have gone back in time to his predecessor King Jehoiakim. But there's no distinction between them as far as the force of Jeremiah's condemnation is concerned.

Jeremiah expected a lot of the king of Judah because the nation's faithfulness to God's law and commandments rested upon the shoulders of the Davidic king. The king was to be exemplary in acting with righteousness and justice, protecting the widows and orphans, and those most vulnerable in the land. Jehoiakim had neglected these things and imagined the grandeur of his lavish lifestyle reflected divine approval. His father Josiah had lived well too (as did David himself), but Jeremiah says Josiah gave priority to judging 'the cause of the poor and the needy'. The Davidic monarchy was to be different from that of other nations because it was a living expression of God's covenant with his people.

The expectation of exemplary character in monarchs has lasted to the present day. Many have been far from worthy but the expectation is still there. Even a constitutional monarch with very little political power may be looked upon as the protector of all that is just and right. The monarch is called to be the servant of the people as well as the embodiment of the nation. That's a sacred trust.

COLLECT

Gracious Father,
you gave up your Son
out of love for the world:
lead us to ponder the mysteries of his passion,
that we may know eternal peace
through the shedding of our Saviour's blood,
Jesus Christ our Lord.

Reflection by **Graham James**

Wednesday 29 March

Psalms **55**, 124 *or* **34**
Jeremiah 22.20 – 23.8
John 12.1-11

Jeremiah 22.20 – 23.8

'I ... will gather the remnant of my flock' (23.3)

After so much unremitting condemnation, it comes as a relief that Jeremiah changes his tone. Although he puts no trust in Judah's kings and their heirs, he does point to a day when God will raise up a 'righteous Branch' from the line of David to restore justice and righteousness in a renewed nation.

But there are years of pain to come first. Jeremiah anticipates both the exile of the people in Babylon and their return. He suggests that this return will be so wonderful that it will even displace the exodus from Egypt in the memory of God's people. These exiles will be the ones to build the nation again, not those who remain in Jerusalem living under whatever conditions the Babylonians impose.

The experience of being dispossessed and subjugated in exile will be a school of learning and renewal. Those who suffer the most will learn the most. And from them true shepherds of God's people will be found. When we are burdened and sad, to whom do we go for support? Is it to the brash and self-confident who seem to sail through life? It's unlikely. We go to the person who has suffered themselves, who is attentive and not over-powering, who listens and loves.

Churches rarely ask for the broken and suffering to shepherd them. Yet it is usually the broken and the suffering they get, whoever they've asked for. They make the best shepherds of Christ's flock.

COLLECT

Most merciful God,
who by the death and resurrection of your Son Jesus Christ
delivered and saved the world:
grant that by faith in him who suffered on the cross
we may triumph in the power of his victory;
through Jesus Christ your Son our Lord,
who is alive and reigns with you,
in the unity of the Holy Spirit,
one God, now and for ever.

Reflection by **Graham James**

Psalms **40**, 125 *or* **37***
Jeremiah 23.9-32
John 12.12-19

Thursday 30 March

Jeremiah 23.9-32

'... even in my house I have found their wickedness' (v.11)

When Jeremiah complains that 'the land is full of adulterers', he is not thinking simply of the betrayal of the marriage bed (although there was probably plenty of adultery going on). It's the unfaithfulness of the people and their priests to God that's causing him distress. The worship of Baal with all its associated fertility rites is even found in the temple in Jerusalem – and with the sanction of Judah's religious leaders. What possessed them?

More than a century earlier, the Assyrian king Sennacherib laid siege to Jerusalem but failed to take it and retreated to his own land. The whole event was interpreted as proof that God always protected the temple, his dwelling place on earth. This conviction left a false sense of security. The people of Judah thought they were invincible because God would never let his temple be destroyed. So they partied and sinned, reckless of the consequences.

Nations and individuals may have almost unaccountable experiences of deliverance or liberation – from a threat or illness or some other enemy. The response may be one of gratitude leading to humility or an arrogance derived from a false superiority. Jeremiah hated the arrogance he saw around him. Think of the arrogance of superpowers today, or the conceit of those who think themselves protected by their wealth or power from adversity. By contrast, Jesus blesses the meek and humble of heart. Whom do we resemble?

COLLECT

Gracious Father,
you gave up your Son
out of love for the world:
lead us to ponder the mysteries of his passion,
that we may know eternal peace
through the shedding of our Saviour's blood,
Jesus Christ our Lord.

Reflection by **Graham James**

Friday 31 March

Psalms **22**, 126 *or* **31**
Jeremiah 24
John 12.20-36*a*

Jeremiah 24

'I will give them a heart ...' (v.7)

The heart is the organ of the body with the highest profile in the Bible, with 826 separate references according to a concordance on my bookshelves. Frequently, it is mentioned in conjunction with the mind, as in 'my heart and in my mind' (1 Samuel 2.35). According to the Bible, the heart is where the life force within us is found. It is definitely not merely a pump keeping the blood flowing within our bodies. From the heart flow good desires such as love, obedience and compassion. But the heart can deceive as well. It may generate pride, lust and hatred. 'We have followed too much the devices and desires of our own hearts', as the general confession in the Book of Common Prayer puts it. The metaphor of the heart as both the deepest source of inspiration and guidance as well as folly and deceit, is alive and well in our language today.

Jeremiah expects a renewed nation to be built following the people's exile in Babylon, but will unfaithfulness and disloyalty to God's law emerge in Israel again? The people seem to have been not just unwilling but unable to be obedient. So Jeremiah ponders God giving his people a new heart so that they will be so united with him that they will 'know that I am the Lord'. This will not be obedience through fear but through love. Something new is stirring here that Christians see fully revealed in Jesus Christ.

COLLECT

Most merciful God,
who by the death and resurrection of your Son Jesus Christ
delivered and saved the world:
grant that by faith in him who suffered on the cross
we may triumph in the power of his victory;
through Jesus Christ your Son our Lord,
who is alive and reigns with you,
in the unity of the Holy Spirit,
one God, now and for ever.

 Reflection by **Graham James**

Psalms **23**, 127 *or* 41, **42**, 43
Jeremiah 25.1-14
John 12.36*b*-end

Saturday 1 April

Jeremiah 25.1-14

'King Nebuchadrezzar of Babylon, my servant ...' (v.9)

Through Jeremiah, the Lord is describing a pagan king, Nebuchadrezzar, as 'my servant'. Nebuchadrezzar (it's a variant spelling of Nebuchadnezzar but refers to the same person) is scarcely a model of propriety. Yet he is to be the agent used by the Lord to bring his people's waywardness to an end through defeat and exile, enabling a new opportunity to rebuild a more faithful nation.

Jewish tradition has long seen a later pagan king, Cyrus of Persia, as an agent of God too. He would conquer Babylon and allow the Jewish exiles to return. The idea of an unworthy person being God's agent has been alive in our own time. Some of President Trump's Christian supporters in the United States were well aware that he was scarcely a role model of Christian discipleship. They invoked the example of Cyrus (and could equally have cited Nebuchadrezzar) as someone God used for his good ends. In President Trump's case, they believed his opposition to abortion or his decision to recognize Jerusalem as the capital of Israel were among the things they believed were divinely guided.

The irony in Jeremiah describing Nebuchadrezzar as God's servant is that the king thought he was no-one's servant at all. He believed he was all-masterful. But his empire would be short-lived. Like many dictators or preening powerful people in the world today, his power was an illusion. He would have hated to be regarded as anyone's servant.

COLLECT

Gracious Father,
you gave up your Son
out of love for the world:
lead us to ponder the mysteries of his passion,
that we may know eternal peace
through the shedding of our Saviour's blood,
Jesus Christ our Lord.

Reflection by **Graham James**

Monday 3 April
Monday of Holy Week

Psalm 41
Lamentations 1.1-12*a*
Luke 22.1-23

Luke 22.1-23

'Then Satan entered into Judas called Iscariot' (v.3)

Why do people do the things they do and, particularly, why do they do the awful things they do? The question of why people act in certain ways – especially when what they do has catastrophic consequences – is a question that is hard to avoid as we look around the world in which we live.

It is fascinating, therefore, to notice that the Gospel writers appeared to have asked the same question when they thought about Judas Iscariot – and even more interesting to observe that they seem to give different answers. Mark gives no answer, restricting himself to the simple account that Judas sought to betray Jesus to the chief priests (Mark 14.10). Matthew associates Judas' actions with greed – he asked what they would give him for betraying Jesus – but then reports his remorse and subsequent suicide (Matthew 26.14-16 and 27.3-10). John's Gospel declares it to be the devil who had 'put it into the heart of Judas son of Simon Iscariot to betray him' (John 13.2). Luke's explanation is closest to John's – Satan entered into Judas – but it doesn't go so far as to say it was all Satan's idea.

So why did Judas do what he did? Was it all down to the devil? Was it his own idea, driven by greed? Or are we better not to know why he acted as he did? We face the same questions as we look at the world today – why do people do what they do? As with Judas, we may never know the answer, but asking the question remains important.

COLLECT

Almighty and everlasting God,
who in your tender love towards the human race
sent your Son our Saviour Jesus Christ
to take upon him our flesh
and to suffer death upon the cross:
grant that we may follow the example of his patience and humility,
and also be made partakers of his resurrection;
through Jesus Christ your Son our Lord,
who is alive and reigns with you,
in the unity of the Holy Spirit,
one God, now and for ever.

Reflection by **Paula Gooder**

Psalm 27
Lamentations 3.1-18
Luke 22. [24-38] 39-53

Tuesday 4 April

Tuesday of Holy Week

Luke 22. [24-38] 39-53

'Pray that you may not come into the time of trial' (v.40)

People often comment on the humanity of Jesus that is revealed in this passage. Here we see Jesus vulnerable, scared and suffering, begging his father to remove this cup from him.

It seems to me, however, that Jesus' own humanity is drawn into even sharper relief by another kind of humanity revealed in the actions of his companions. Jesus urges them to pray that they might not come into the time of trial, but instead they fall asleep, oblivious to the looming danger that is about to consume them and change their lives forever. Luke attempts to excuse the disciples on the grounds that they were worn out from grief (something not found in any of the other Gospels), but the contrast remains stark. Jesus, fully aware of what is about to befall him, turns to face it, even though he knows it will bring him untold suffering and pain. The disciples, unable to wrap their minds around the unfolding events, are overwhelmed and fall asleep.

Luke calls on us, the readers, to feel sympathy not just for Jesus, caught in the grip of horror at what was about to happen, but also for the disciples who are napping, completely unaware of what is about to befall them. By observing the grief of the one and the obliviousness of the other, we are drawn into the full tragedy of what is about to happen.

COLLECT

True and humble king,
hailed by the crowd as Messiah:
grant us the faith to know you and love you,
that we may be found beside you
on the way of the cross,
which is the path of glory.

Reflection by **Paula Gooder**

Wednesday 5 April

Wednesday of Holy Week

Psalm 102 [*or* 102.1-18]
Wisdom 1.16 – 2.1; 2.12-22
or Jeremiah 11.18-20
Luke 22.54-end

Luke 22.54-end

'The Lord turned and looked at Peter' (v.61)

Of all of the accounts of Peter's betrayal, Luke's tugs at the heart strings the most. In the other Gospels, after his arrest Jesus was held somewhere inside, while Peter remained outside. This meant that Peter's betrayal took place behind his back. In Luke's Gospel, Jesus is still in the courtyard while Peter denied him and, not only that, turned to look at him as the cock crowed. In other words, Peter denied Jesus almost to his face.

There is something profoundly powerful about this. Whether or not Luke's depiction of the scene is accurate, it packs a bigger emotional punch to have Peter deny Jesus in his presence. It challenges us to reflect on why Peter denied Jesus and, hence also, why we do unfathomable things of a similar nature.

Did Peter imagine that he could deny Jesus without Jesus knowing anything about it because he was elsewhere? Luke says no. Peter knew that Jesus would know that he had denied him and did it anyway. Perhaps he was driven by panic or maybe by anger? Perhaps the emotion of Jesus' arrest threw him off course temporarily? Perhaps his denial revealed something else of which Peter was previously unaware? It isn't even clear if Peter himself knew why he had denied Jesus – he just did. It is this to which Luke draws our attention in this simple phrase, 'The Lord turned and looked at Peter.'

COLLECT

Almighty and everlasting God,
who in your tender love towards the human race
sent your Son our Saviour Jesus Christ
to take upon him our flesh
and to suffer death upon the cross:
grant that we may follow the example of his patience and humility,
and also be made partakers of his resurrection;
through Jesus Christ your Son our Lord,
who is alive and reigns with you,
in the unity of the Holy Spirit,
one God, now and for ever.

Reflection by **Paula Gooder**

Psalms 42, 43
Leviticus 16.2-24
Luke 23.1-25

Thursday 6 April

Maundy Thursday

Luke 23.1-25

'... he sent him off to Herod' (v.7)

In the readings this week, I have been drawing attention to those parts of Luke's narrative that are uniquely Luke. Today's reading is no different.

Luke's Gospel is the only one that reports Jesus being sent to be tried by Herod. The Herod in question was Herod Antipas, son of Herod the Great, on whose death, Herod Antipas began to rule over Galilee and Perea in the north of the kingdom. He also had a palace in Jerusalem. Luke's account envisages that Jesus was sent to the ruler of his home region – Galilee – for a verdict when Pilate found it impossible to decide for himself.

The way that Luke presents his account of Jesus' trial suggests that Pilate was passing the buck. Faced with an impossible choice, of either killing a man he believed to be innocent or aggravating an angry mob, he passed the responsibility on. Herod, Luke notes, promptly passed it back again. The whole episode communicates a sense of profound discomfort and unease. Even Pilate, whose reputation for brutality was so well known that it eventually led to his removal from office, felt so uncomfortable that he tried to force someone else to make the decision for him. Imagine what would have happened if one of them had not dodged the difficult task but taken responsibility and declared Jesus to be as innocent as they knew him to be. Then as now, passing the buck may be tempting, but it never produces the right result.

COLLECT

True and humble king,
hailed by the crowd as Messiah:
grant us the faith to know you and love you,
that we may be found beside you
on the way of the cross,
which is the path of glory.

Reflection by **Paula Gooder**

Friday 7 April

Good Friday

Psalm 69
Genesis 22.1-18
Hebrews 10.1-10

Hebrews 10.1-10

'I have come to do your will' (v.7)

The book of Hebrews can be incredibly hard to understand and this passage is no exception. One of the factors that make it so difficult is its mode of argument, which is very different from how we make a case today.

At the heart of this passage is the author's belief that Jesus is so much the fulfilment of Scripture, that quoting from a Psalm (here Psalm 40.7-9) is effectively quoting the words of Jesus. So the argument in this passage goes: sacrifice for sin was not effective because the priests had to keep on doing it (if it had been effective, sin would have been so wiped out that people no longer sinned). In any case, sacrifice was not what God wanted, as Psalm 40.7-8 makes clear. Christ came to do what God *did* want; in doing so, he abolished what was past and established a new way of being.

The very heart of this passage then is focused in this simple phrase: 'I have come to do your will.' Whatever our view of Hebrews' description of law and sacrifice, this is a beautiful summary of the nature of Christ and worth mulling on today of all days. Christ came to do the will of God and to show us what a life lived entirely focused on God's will can look like.

COLLECT

Almighty Father,
look with mercy on this your family
for which our Lord Jesus Christ was content to be betrayed
and given up into the hands of sinners
and to suffer death upon the cross;
who is alive and glorified with you and the Holy Spirit,
one God, now and for ever.

 Reflection by **Paula Gooder**

Psalm 142
Hosea 6.1-6
John 2.18-22

Saturday 8 April

Easter Eve

John 2.18-22

'I will raise it up' (v.19)

I have always felt a certain sympathy for those who ask questions of the Jesus of John's Gospel. After his responses, it feels as though an awkward silence would fall as those who asked the question in the first place looked at each other trying to work out how on earth his answer related to their original question.

The reference to the temple being under construction for 46 years is a reference to Herod the Great's rebuilding of the second temple. The first iteration of the second temple, built after the exile, was completed in 515 BC but Herod began to expand and rebuild it in 20 BC. This rebuilding continued after his death and would potentially date this conversation, if the dates are correct, to AD 26.

No wonder the Jews were confused, but in the confusion lies a vital strand of Johannine theology. For Jews, the temple was the gateway to heaven, the place where, in the holy of holies, God could come to dwell among God's people and they could, on certain occasions, such as Isaiah's vision in Isaiah 6.1-10, see God seated on the throne in heaven. Jesus is saying here – as he does elsewhere in John – that he, the Word made flesh, was now the gateway to heaven. In him is direct access to God. In him God dwells among us, even as we await his resurrection in the darkness of Holy Saturday.

COLLECT

Grant, Lord,
that we who are baptized into the death
of your Son our Saviour Jesus Christ
may continually put to death our evil desires
and be buried with him;
and that through the grave and gate of death
we may pass to our joyful resurrection;
through his merits,
who died and was buried and rose again for us,
your Son Jesus Christ our Lord.

Reflection by **Paula Gooder**

Monday 10 April

Monday of Easter Week

Psalms **111**, 117, 146
Song of Solomon 1.9 – 2.7
Mark 16.1-8

Song of Solomon 1.9 – 2.7

'... you are beautiful, my beloved' (1.16)

The question of how to interpret the Song of Solomon well is tricky to answer. At face value, it is a book of beautiful – and sometimes surprisingly explicit – love poems spoken alternately by a woman and a man. As a result, it has often been read allegorically as a love poem between God and Israel (in Judaism) or between God and the Church (in Christianity). There are all sorts of questions that arise from reading it like this, but there is no space here to ask them. I will therefore be reading the passages as a general vision of God's love for humanity, while fully aware of the complexities of doing so.

One of the loveliest features of the poems in the Song of Solomon is the extravagant love that each speaker feels for the other. In this Easter week, in which we allow the wonder of the resurrection to sink into our hearts afresh, it is important to tune our ears to God's love song, which has echoed in the world since the dawn of time but never more loudly than in the death and resurrection of Jesus.

The actions of Jesus call to us that we are beautiful, beloved and truly lovely in God's sight. The question for each one of us is whether we can hear this love song and accept the gift it offers.

COLLECT

Lord of all life and power,
who through the mighty resurrection of your Son
overcame the old order of sin and death
to make all things new in him:
grant that we, being dead to sin
and alive to you in Jesus Christ,
may reign with him in glory;
to whom with you and the Holy Spirit
be praise and honour, glory and might,
now and in all eternity.

 Reflection by **Paula Gooder**

Psalms **112**, 147.1-12
Song of Solomon 2.8-end
Luke 24.1-12

Tuesday 11 April

Tuesday of Easter Week

Song of Solomon 2.8-end

'... now the winter is past' (v.11)

One of the feelings that new love brings is a sense of optimism that the future will bring hope and joy; that the days to come will see flowers blooming and birds singing. Spring and new love are intertwined, symbolized by looking forward in hope to hearing the voice of the turtledove once more.

As we are reading this passage in Easter week, it is impossible to avoid drawing a parallel with Jesus' resurrection. Just like with new love, the resurrection holds out a message of hope and new life. But one of the challenges faced by the earliest Christians was how to reconcile all of their hopes about new life with the reality of living in a world in which the Romans were still in control and there was not harmony, prosperity or peace anywhere that they looked. The same is as true today and begs the question of how we celebrate resurrection in a world that feels as though it is riven by pain and despair.

On one level, the answer is in the same way that we celebrate love. Our love for someone else does not make the world any less severe or brutal, but it does change how we feel about it and shows how living in love might transform the way we see the world. In the same way, Jesus' resurrection reminds us to look for the signs of new life all around us. No matter how it feels, the world really has changed forever, bringing hope and joy in its wake.

COLLECT

God of glory,
by the raising of your Son
you have broken the chains of death and hell:
fill your Church with faith and hope;
for a new day has dawned
and the way to life stands open
in our Saviour Jesus Christ.

Reflection by **Paula Gooder**

Wednesday 12 April

Wednesday of Easter Week

Psalms **113**, 147.13-end
Song of Solomon 3
Matthew 28.16-end

Song of Solomon 3

'I will rise now and go about the city' (v.2)

One of the lovely images from chapter 3 is of the woman in the poem, restlessly seeking the one whom she loves, roaming to and fro around the city unable to settle until she has found him.

In this Easter week, it is a vivid image. We are reminded that the love of Jesus was so great that death could not hold him; that he, like the woman in this poem, was driven by that love to rise and seek out those whom he loved. Today, the risen Christ still seeks for us, calling out his endless love as he goes.

Although on one level the passages are very different, this passage brings to mind the encounter between Mary Magdalene and Jesus in the garden near the empty tomb (John 20.11-18). Mary, overwhelmed and incapacitated by grief, was found by Jesus, whose love for her was spoken in a single word, 'Mary'. Unlike in this poem, however, Mary was not able to give in to her response of love for him – holding on to him and never letting go. Mary is told not to cling to Jesus (John 20.17). Jesus' love was not for her alone but for the whole world. For us and for her, it cannot be clung on to but needs to be held lightly and generously, so that it can be shared with everyone we meet.

COLLECT

Lord of all life and power,
who through the mighty resurrection of your Son
overcame the old order of sin and death
to make all things new in him:
grant that we, being dead to sin
and alive to you in Jesus Christ,
may reign with him in glory;
to whom with you and the Holy Spirit
be praise and honour, glory and might,
now and in all eternity.

 Reflection by **Paula Gooder**

Psalms **114**, 148
Song of Solomon 5.2 – 6.3
Luke 7.11-17

Thursday 13 April

Thursday of Easter Week

Song of Solomon 5.2 – 6.3

'I slept, but my heart was awake' (5.2)

One of the challenges that arise when we read the Song of Solomon in Morning Prayer is that its language is like nothing else we use in worship. It evokes imagery that feels a little excessive first thing in the morning. Today's reading is a somewhat explicit dream, in which the female speaker yearns at night for her lover. It is earthy and embodied. It is sexual and vivid.

It is tempting to try to ignore this and find instead a spiritual meaning which some would find less challenging. But Easter week cautions us against this. The story of the resurrection is a story of bodies and embodiment. Jesus' resurrection body may have been different to ours – for example, being able to walk through locked doors – but it *was* an actual body. He ate with his disciples, and walked and talked with them. It is a story of the joy of embodiment.

This is a week to celebrate bodies and embodiment. Jesus whose body suffered agony and death on a cross was raised bodily on Easter day. The Song of Solomon demands that we do not shy politely away from the fact of our embodiment but that we rejoice in our bodies and give thanks for them in all their glory.

COLLECT

God of glory,
by the raising of your Son
you have broken the chains of death and hell:
fill your Church with faith and hope;
for a new day has dawned
and the way to life stands open
in our Saviour Jesus Christ.

Reflection by **Paula Gooder**

Friday 14 April

Friday of Easter Week

Psalms **115**, 149
Song of Solomon 7.10 – 8.4
Luke 8.41-end

Song of Solomon 7.10 – 8.4

'... do not stir up or awaken love until it is ready!' (8.4)

One of the themes running through the Song of Solomon – in 2.7, 3.5 and here in 8.4 – is the importance of not stirring up or awakening love until it is ready. A reading of the Song of Solomon tells you why. Love is all consuming. The poems the book contains talk about how gripped both the unnamed man and unnamed woman are, how they cannot eat or sleep until they are with each other again. It communicates both the pain as well as the joy of love.

If we read these poems as a parable of God's love for the world, we can feel the palpable aching in God's heart for the world God created and loved. For God, love was awoken before the dawn of time and, ever since, God's heart has grieved and yearned for a world that, to quote John 1.10-11, neither knew nor accepted him. No one would ever want to say that God's love was stirred up too early, but this sense of heartache, as God has yearned over thousands and thousands of years for humanity to turn again and be loved, is illustrated by the love expressed in the Song of Songs.

Love brings joy and hope; it also brings pain and despair. Loving deeply and truly requires courage as well as conveying delight. The God of love has loved our broken world for so long and continues to do so no matter how great the cost.

COLLECT

Lord of all life and power,
who through the mighty resurrection of your Son
overcame the old order of sin and death
to make all things new in him:
grant that we, being dead to sin
and alive to you in Jesus Christ,
may reign with him in glory;
to whom with you and the Holy Spirit
be praise and honour, glory and might,
now and in all eternity.

Reflection by **Paula Gooder**

Psalms **116**, 150
Song of Solomon 8.5-7
John 11.17-44

Saturday 15 April
Saturday of Easter Week

Song of Solomon 8.5-7

'... love is strong as death' (v.6)

In so many ways, the love and joy of the Song of Solomon spring from the pages of the text right into our modern world. The descriptions it contains of tenderness and delight, of passion and desire not only resonate with our own experiences of love but also remind us powerfully of God's love. This line from 8.6, however, always makes me want to heckle.

At Easter time, even more than at other times, we celebrate not that love is as strong as death but that it is stronger, far stronger than death. What we celebrate at this time of year is that in the face of God's infinite love for the world, when faced by Christ's passionate dedication, death melted away in impotence.

A few lines later, in 8.7, the sentiment: 'Many waters cannot quench love' feels more to the point; nor can the might of the Roman army defeat it. The single most powerful force in the world is love: death and destruction, fear and hate, despair and hopelessness may seem to be strong, but they dissolve in the face of love. And there has never been greater love shown in the world than the love of God.

At Eastertide, this is the simple message we proclaim – love is stronger than death; many waters cannot quench it, nor floods drown it.

COLLECT

God of glory,
by the raising of your Son
you have broken the chains of death and hell:
fill your Church with faith and hope;
for a new day has dawned
and the way to life stands open
in our Saviour Jesus Christ.

Reflection by **Paula Gooder**

Monday 17 April

Psalms 2, **19** *or* **1**, 2, 3
Deuteronomy 1.3-18
John 20.1-10

John 20.1-10

'They have taken the Lord out of the tomb, and we do not know where they have laid him' (v.2)

Our reading begins in sombre mood. See through Mary's eyes and appreciate the horror she feels. Arriving in darkness, she finds Jesus' tomb open and his body missing, removed by persons unknown. In a state of shock, having witnessed his appalling death, even the rituals of mourning are denied her. The day of resurrection does not begin well.

If we set aside our over-familiarity with the story, we can begin to appreciate the pain, vulnerability and fear of those involved. The journey from the grief of death to resurrection hope is not a simple step. Resurrection hope seeps in incrementally. It is a journey of realization along which some move more quickly than others.

Mary sees an open tomb and a body missing, but can perceive no more. The unnamed disciple sees linen wrappings as he peers into the tomb, blocked from greater understanding until he moves further in. Peter enters the tomb, sees the wrappings and a folded linen headcloth placed to one side, but can perceive nothing further. The unnamed disciple then enters the tomb, sees and believes, but quite what he believes is obscure. Something has shifted within him, but is not yet defined. Then the disciples go home, leaving Mary alone.

As the dawn breaks incrementally, so hope is born. There is something gentle in this movement from horror to hope. Gentle, yet unstoppable as the dawning sun.

COLLECT

Almighty Father,
you have given your only Son to die for our sins
and to rise again for our justification:
grant us so to put away the leaven of malice and wickedness
that we may always serve you
in pureness of living and truth;
through the merits of your Son Jesus Christ our Lord,
who is alive and reigns with you,
in the unity of the Holy Spirit,
one God, now and for ever.

Reflection by **Kate Bruce**

Psalms **8**, 20, 21 *or* **5**, 6 (8)
Deuteronomy 1.19-40
John 20.11-18

Tuesday 18 April

John 20.11-18

'Woman, why are you weeping?' (vv.13 and 15)

As Mary weeps in despair, the light of hope leaks, imperceptible to her, into the darkness. The strange white beings in the tomb – symbols of light and hope – ask why she is weeping, but locked into her grief-filled perspective, she doesn't think to ask who they are or what they are doing there. Grief can lock us into tramline thinking, tears blurring our vision and perspective.

Jesus asks why she weeps, but she simply sees a gardener. Even the very words of the One who *is* Life do not shift the grip of death on her perception, not until he calls her and she hears her name in familiar tones. Now the dawn breaks, rushing in, a tidal wave of light sweeping away the debris of despair. Hope is not a vacuous, empty idea; it is a personal reality.

In her joy she tries to solidify this sense of hope that has poured in, pushing the night aside, by seeking to hold onto him. But hope does not return us to the old state of being; it propels us towards something new. For Mary, there is the task of proclamation: she must run with this beacon of light and let it pierce the darkness of the disciples' despair and disbelief. Hope is comforting, but not comfortable. Mary is not to remain clutching onto the past, but is propelled into this new beginning. Hope turns the page.

COLLECT

Risen Christ,
for whom no door is locked, no entrance barred:
open the doors of our hearts,
that we may seek the good of others
and walk the joyful road of sacrifice and peace,
to the praise of God the Father.

Reflection by **Kate Bruce**

Wednesday 19 April

Psalms 16, **30** *or* **119.1-32**
Deuteronomy 3.18-end
John 20.19-end

John 20.19-end

'Unless I ... put my finger in the mark of the nails and my hand in his side, I will not believe.' (v.25)

Jesus speaks to his frighted followers: 'Peace be with you.' Peace, *shalom*, wholeness be with you. There is a contrast between the wholeness Jesus desires for them and the holes in his resurrected body, yet these wounds are heralds of healing.

Jesus invites Thomas to reach out his hand and put it *into* Jesus' side – not 'on' his side, or 'on' the scar, but 'in' his side. It's startling that the body of the resurrected Jesus still bears scars so deep that they form indentations in his flesh, stamps of suffering. His body is not perfect, smooth and whole with blemishes airbrushed out.

In the resurrection body, suffering is taken up in the Ascension, into the heart of the Godhead. Human suffering is held within God, part of God. The wounded human heart cries to Jesus and is met with compassion and understanding.

Did Thomas reach out to touch the puckered flesh of Jesus' scarred body? I suspect he didn't need to – seeing his resurrected Lord must have been enough to leave him awestruck. We who have come later do not get to see in this direct sense, but we are invited to ponder and perceive, to come to believe as we meditate on the importance of the holes in the body on the One who brings wholeness to our brokenness. In this believing, the scar bearer declares that we are blessed. We are blessed indeed.

COLLECT

Almighty Father,
you have given your only Son to die for our sins
and to rise again for our justification:
grant us so to put away the leaven of malice and wickedness
that we may always serve you
in pureness of living and truth;
through the merits of your Son Jesus Christ our Lord,
who is alive and reigns with you,
in the unity of the Holy Spirit,
one God, now and for ever.

Reflection by **Kate Bruce**

Psalms **28**, 29 *or* 14, **15**, 16
Deuteronomy 4.1-14
John 21.1-14

Thursday 20 April

John 21.1-14

'... but that night they caught nothing' (v.3)

Jesus' death disrupts the disciples' expectations, throwing their lives into confusion. Does his resurrection do anything less? Perhaps Peter wonders: 'I know Jesus lives – I've seen him twice – but things have changed and I don't know what difference any of it makes?' He returns to fishing at night, searching for a bite. The others come with him – back to their old occupation, before Jesus called them. *'That night they caught nothing.'*

Have you ever been there? Major effort for empty nets: perhaps physical labour, or spiritual effort, or psychological work – with nothing to show for it. *'That night they caught nothing.'* There is something achingly painful here. They might have wondered, 'What is the point?'

As they haul in the empty nets, they have no idea that Jesus is about to intervene. The stranger on the shore directs them to cast their nets again and they obey – perhaps remembering the story right at the start of it all, when the strange rabbi gave them fishing tips (Luke 5.1-11).

Suddenly, unexpectedly, the fish are flapping onboard, Jesus is known and a despondent night makes way for a delightful, beachside breakfast with their dear friend. They didn't see that coming. This is a reading for those who know Jesus is alive but have no sense of what that means for them. This is a story for those whose efforts have yielded nothing and who might give up. Don't.

COLLECT

Risen Christ,
for whom no door is locked, no entrance barred:
open the doors of our hearts,
that we may seek the good of others
and walk the joyful road of sacrifice and peace,
to the praise of God the Father.

Reflection by **Kate Bruce**

Friday 21 April

Psalms 57, **61** *or* 17, **19**
Deuteronomy 4.15-31
John 21.15-19

John 21.15-19

'Lord, you know everything; you know that I love you' (v.17)

Three times Jesus asks the same question, which hurts Peter. Why put Peter through this painful questioning? This is a healing story.

Jesus knew that Peter would deny him three times – warning him of this just after Peter's declaration that he would die for him (John 13.36-38). Peter wants to be the loyal hero, but finds he is a fearful man. The denials trip off his tongue three times before the cock crows, after which the synoptics all describe Peter weeping bitter tears. He is bitterly disappointed, bitterly ashamed, and bitterly sorry.

So, the Lord who knows him perfectly undoes the bitterness with the opportunity for threefold restoration, in the declaration of love. Yes, this hurts Peter, but the avoidance of pain is not the primary issue; healing is. Healing is often painful, so maybe, in pain, Peter snaps his response at Jesus, 'Lord, you know everything; you know that I love you.'

Peter needs to hear his own persistent declaration of love, undoing his repeated words of denial. *He* needs to be sure of it, not Jesus – who already knows. Peter, who declared he would lay down his life for his Lord, will be called upon to do just this, and he does – not on the basis of hasty declarations of intention, but on the basis of deep love: his deep love for Jesus – and his Lord's deep love for him, a love that asks painful questions.

COLLECT

Almighty Father,
you have given your only Son to die for our sins
and to rise again for our justification:
grant us so to put away the leaven of malice and wickedness
that we may always serve you
in pureness of living and truth;
through the merits of your Son Jesus Christ our Lord,
who is alive and reigns with you,
in the unity of the Holy Spirit,
one God, now and for ever.

 Reflection by **Kate Bruce**

Psalms 63, **84** *or* 20, 21, **23**
Deuteronomy 4.32-40
John 21.20-end

Saturday 22 April

John 21.20-end

'... what is that to you? Follow me!' (v.22)

There is never any doubt about the humanity of Jesus' followers. Peter has just been through a searing experience, being asked about his love for Jesus in a threefold echo of his denials. This is painful, necessary, healing work. He has been told he will lose independence in old age, and that his desire for a martyr's death will be fulfilled. In this encounter, Jesus' final words to Peter are, 'Follow me'. He is given restoration, destiny and purpose. There is deep divine work afoot.

In the next scene. Peter turns to the disciple described as the 'beloved' and demands to know 'What about him?' Perhaps the sub-question is 'I know my destiny, what about his?' Is there a sense of competition here, curiosity, or maybe even jealousy, of this disciple 'whom Jesus loved', who reclined at his side at table? Whatever the motivation for the question – it's very human.

Jesus' response seems harsh, "If it is my will that he remain until I come, what is that to you? Follow me!" The community interprets this as meaning the beloved disciple won't die. The point is perhaps that Peter needs to attend to his own calling to follow, rather than sticking his nose into Jesus' purposes for another person. The rumour-mongers also need the same lesson. The deep purposes of God for another are not the topic for idle questions or unhelpful rumours. The lesson is: '... what is that to you? Follow me!'

COLLECT

Risen Christ,
for whom no door is locked, no entrance barred:
open the doors of our hearts,
that we may seek the good of others
and walk the joyful road of sacrifice and peace,
to the praise of God the Father.

Reflection by **Kate Bruce**

Monday 24 April

George, martyr,
patron of England

Psalms 5, 146
Joshua 1.1-9
Ephesians 6.10-20

Joshua 1.1-9

'... all the land of the Hittites ... shall be your territory' (v.4)

Today's reading is problematic. How does it sound if you are a Hittite and the territory being promised is the land you till, the place you love, the space where your children play and grow. Are the Hittites occupying the land unimportant? Is their wholesale slaughter just a minor matter? We are on problematic turf. As we read today's passage, we have to recall that the Hittites are created by God, the same God who calls all nations to himself. We need to look to the bigger vision of Scripture which calls us to have the courage to love beyond borders after the pattern of Jesus who loves without limit.

St George's Day, if handled in an insular way, could also be problematic, about limit setting – us and them. However, as we mark this man born in what is now modern-day Turkey, we have an opportunity to celebrate the good of those many countries and cultures who own him as patron: Aragon, Catalonia, Georgia, Portugal, Germany, Lithuania, Palestine, Greece, Moscow, Istanbul, England and Genoa.

Folklore says St George slayed a dragon that was demanding human sacrifices. A fitting celebration of St George's Day in any country should include challenging the dragons of xenophobia, racism, and exclusion – slaying these enemies that dehumanize and devalue the other. It's worth recalling that, following in Jesus' footsteps, St George had a special connection with lepers – those who are outcast. Hittites by any other name?

COLLECT

God of hosts,
who so kindled the flame of love
in the heart of your servant George
that he bore witness to the risen Lord
by his life and by his death:
give us the same faith and power of love
that we who rejoice in his triumphs
may come to share with him the fullness of the resurrection;
through Jesus Christ your Son our Lord,
who is alive and reigns with you,
in the unity of the Holy Spirit,
one God, now and for ever.

Reflection by **Kate Bruce**

Psalms 37.23-end, 148
Isaiah 62.6-10
or Ecclesiasticus 51.13-end
Acts 12.25 – 13.13

Tuesday 25 April
Mark the Evangelist

Isaiah 62.6-10

'... give him no rest until he establishes Jerusalem' (v.7)

Here is a clear biblical injunction to bend God's ear! It almost implies that God might forget his promises to Israel, promises of return and restoration from exile. It speaks beautifully into our human insecurities. We can easily believe that God might forget us, that we might be overlooked. Here Isaiah, speaking with the voice of the Messiah – says 'give him no rest'. You persist. Keep crying out. Refuse to be silenced by despair or disbelief.

This is a call to hope beyond the immediate. It's a hard thing. How many have prayed and prayed and prayed again, and yet it seems heaven's doors are shut. Promises of restoration, of healing and possibility remain unfulfilled. The temptation is to lose faith, to become sullen and silent. The call is clear: 'take no rest, and give him no rest.' Don't lose heart, don't give up. Keep talking to God, open to the God who will not fail to deliver what he has promised. This is a clear call to hope, even when faced by apparent impossibility. Is it foolishness? In human terms, perhaps. But the foolishness of God is wiser than human intellect.

So, today, trust in the God of restoration, whose promises will be fulfilled. This will take effort: 'take no rest, and give him no rest.' There is some gentle humour here: 'If I'm not sleeping, neither are You, God.' Here is a clear biblical injunction to bend God's ear!

COLLECT

Almighty God,
who enlightened your holy Church
through the inspired witness of your evangelist Saint Mark:
grant that we, being firmly grounded in the truth of the gospel,
may be faithful to its teaching both in word and deed;
through Jesus Christ your Son our Lord,
who is alive and reigns with you,
in the unity of the Holy Spirit,
one God, now and for ever.

Reflection by **Kate Bruce**

Wednesday 26 April

Psalm **105** *or* **34**
Deuteronomy 6
Ephesians 2.1-10

Ephesians 2.1-10

'But God, who is rich in mercy ...' (v.4)

Imagine a scene. A throne is elevated on high; sulphur wreathes around it. There is a tawdry allure to this place. The shrieking babble of those clinging to the throne is harsh and grating, appealing to a base desire to please the self above all else. This place pulses with wealth and lust. The stench of deception, corruption and denial is brushed away with clever words. Make no mistake, this is the throne of death. It whispers to the selfish heart, 'Come ascend my steps, sit here and all this is yours.'

All *what*?

Imagine another scene. By a river, with trees either side, people gather, drawn to One rich in welcome, acceptance and love. People arrive in rags and find they are clothed in garments of beauty. People with faces hollowed with hunger are given nourishment. The love-starved are fed. Honest lament is met with open embrace. There is new possibility for all who come with open hands and hearts. A sense of joy weaves through those gathered, shaping a desire to reach out and draw in the hesitant on the edges of the crowd. 'Here is love like we have never known. Here is grace and mercy poured out without end.' There is a kindness in the eyes of the One who welcomes, not a passing, superficial smile, but a deep, knowing, understanding presence. 'Come sit with me. All I am is yours.'

COLLECT

Almighty Father,
who in your great mercy gladdened the disciples
with the sight of the risen Lord:
give us such knowledge of his presence with us,
that we may be strengthened and sustained by his risen life
and serve you continually in righteousness and truth;
through Jesus Christ your Son our Lord,
who is alive and reigns with you,
in the unity of the Holy Spirit,
one God, now and for ever.

 Reflection by **Kate Bruce**

Psalm **136** *or* **37***
Deuteronomy 7.1-11
Ephesians 2.11-end

Thursday 27 April

Ephesians 2.11-end

'... one new humanity in place of the two, thus making peace' (v.15)

Reconciliation involves the re-making of parties once in a state of enmity. When an in-group and an out-group are reconciled, they become more than they were; there is a new creation.

This reconciliation is the work of God in Christ. Paul offers a picture of those who were once insiders and those who were once aliens stepping into a new space, opened by Christ's work, where all are citizens. This movement involves loss and risk. Those of the commonwealth of Israel set aside their old privilege to step into new relationship and possibility, and those who were strangers put aside the old identity to risk new belonging. Paul paints a picture of the household of God growing organically, held together by Christ.

If that seems like a disconnected religious image, remember the power of reconciliation wrought through agencies like the Community of the Cross of Nails. When Coventry Cathedral was bombed in the blitz in 1940, three medieval nails found in the rubble were formed into a cross and this worldwide movement for reconciliation was born. In the ruins of the old cathedral is a statue from the people of Dresden, a sign of reconciliation after such dreadful enmity. Reconciliation is a call into new humanity, wrought by God's intervention and grace, such that old hatreds can be left behind, as new community is born.

Today, what is God calling us to leave behind, let go of and risk for the sake of reconciliation?

COLLECT

Risen Christ,
you filled your disciples with boldness and fresh hope:
strengthen us to proclaim your risen life
and fill us with your peace,
to the glory of God the Father.

Reflection by **Kate Bruce**

Friday 28 April

Psalm **107** or **31**
Deuteronomy 7.12-end
Ephesians 3.1-13

Ephesians 3.1-13

'... news of the boundless riches of Christ' (v.8)

Building on yesterday's theme, we might reflect that sometimes reconciliation seems just a spiritual pipedream for the naïve, an impossibility. We may look at international strife or personal situations, shake our heads and think 'no way', and very often with good reason. Let's acknowledge this, as we also open ourselves to today's reading.

Once Paul pursued followers of Christ, confident in the righteousness of his cause, motivated by murderous zeal. Not a man to mess with. Now listen to him; he speaks of the people he once hated, as 'fellow-heirs, members of the same body, and sharers in the promise in Christ Jesus ...' How has this jaw-dropping transformation happened? Paul tells us, 'grace was given to me to bring to the Gentiles the news of the boundless riches of Christ.'

The shift is utterly astounding. It speaks into our fear and cynicism around the possibility of reconciliation in those relationships and situations we most wrestle with and which can leave us feeling paralysed. Don't despair, don't be afraid, just be open to the unseen movement of God, which is able to 'accomplish abundantly far more than all we can ask or imagine' (Ephesians 3.20). We don't need to crusade into difficult situations, shouldering all responsibility; we just need to be open and responsive to the changes wrought by the grace of God. When the inner cynic sneers and the internal fear clutches, point both to the grace of God, and wait. It is enough.

COLLECT

Almighty Father,
who in your great mercy gladdened the disciples
  with the sight of the risen Lord:
give us such knowledge of his presence with us,
that we may be strengthened and sustained by his risen life
and serve you continually in righteousness and truth;
through Jesus Christ your Son our Lord,
who is alive and reigns with you,
in the unity of the Holy Spirit,
one God, now and for ever.

Reflection by **Kate Bruce**

Psalms 108, **110**, 111 *or* 41, **42**, 43
Deuteronomy 8
Ephesians 3.14-end

Saturday 29 April

Ephesians 3.14-end

'... that you may be filled with all the fullness of God' (v.19)

Imagine describing the colour of gold to someone who can't see it. We might reference warmth, or value, trying to find a way of enabling some comprehension of the colour. Perhaps that individual's perception of gold is analogous to our perception of divine love.

Unaided, we cannot begin to perceive the dimensions of God's love. It 'surpasses knowledge'. It can't be defined since it can't be contained. One of my favourite hymns has this line: 'We make God's love too narrow by false limits of our own.' How can we presume to contain the vast, unfathomable, depth, scope and possibility of the love of God who bowled the planets, lit the stars and sustains the burning of the sun? How can we dare to think we understand the love that submits to the agonies of unfettered evil in order to shatter death's bonds? How can we claim to grasp the limits of this love without borders?

Yet, we are invited to know divine love through experiencing it, as much as our frail humanity can bear. This love longs for us to receive more, yet tempers itself to our capacity for reception, even as God's Spirit seeks to strengthen us that we might know the fullness of the light.

If this seems mere spiritualizing words, look to see how this love transforms us, our daily interactions, our courage and kindness. If we allow it, it always does, in ways far beyond all we can ask or imagine.

COLLECT

Risen Christ,
you filled your disciples with boldness and fresh hope:
strengthen us to proclaim your risen life
and fill us with your peace,
to the glory of God the Father.

Reflection by **Kate Bruce**

Monday 1 May

Philip and James, Apostles

Psalms 139, 146
Proverbs 4.10-18
James 1.1-12

Proverbs 4.10-18

'Hear, my child, and accept my words' (v.10)

St Philip and St James, 'Pip and Jim', are celebrated on the anniversary of the dedication in 560 of the church in Rome that houses their relics. Both were among the Twelve called by Jesus to be apostles. Each is often confused with others – Philip with 'Philip the Evangelist' in Acts, and James, son of Alphaeus and often called 'the Less', with James the Great, brother of John, both sons of Zebedee.

Their roles, as recounted in the Gospels, are small. In John's Gospel, Philip brings Nathanael to Jesus; he is tested at the feeding of the five thousand; and at the Last Supper his request 'show us the Father and we shall be satisfied' catalyses the wonderful teachings of Jesus' farewell discourses. But there's little else.

Yet these two mattered enough to the early Church to be recorded among the Twelve. They heard the call of Jesus; they followed faithfully; they were with him from his early ministry onwards. They were there in the upper room on the evening of the resurrection. The wind and flame of the Holy Spirit descended on them at Pentecost. And it seems they continued in faithfulness.

They heard, accepted and lived by Jesus' words. That mattered. And if at times they did not understand, by raising questions they brought answers that generations since have learned from. May we also hear, accept and walk the long path of righteousness set before us.

COLLECT

Almighty Father,
whom truly to know is eternal life:
teach us to know your Son Jesus Christ
as the way, the truth, and the life;
that we may follow the steps of your holy apostles
Philip and James,
and walk steadfastly in the way that leads to your glory;
through Jesus Christ your Son our Lord,
who is alive and reigns with you,
in the unity of the Holy Spirit,
one God, now and for ever.

Reflection by **Sarah Rowland Jones**

Psalm **139** *or* **48**, 52
Deuteronomy 9.23 – 10.5
Ephesians 4.17-end

Tuesday 2 May

Ephesians 4.17-end

'... be renewed ... clothe yourselves with the new self' (vv.23-24)

Injustice and unfairness are so woven through human experience that it can be all too easy to feel bitterness, anger and even malice. Disagreements within the Church family can at times be particularly vicious.

I wonder if this is because the compassionate, redeeming, healing love of God touches us most profoundly in our deepest wounds and insecurities. If we fear that aspects of our understanding or practice of faith are being challenged, we can feel under threat where we're most vulnerable – and then respond as if attack is the best form of defence.

So when we are thus disturbed, how do we disentangle appropriate anger or upset from a disproportionate response? We should seek the mind of Jesus Christ, by prayerfully asking what in these circumstances causes him anger or grief. We can then find an outlet for our own emotions safely within the godly response – being angry, without sinning, for example. For God's anger at wrong always has within it the seeds of a greater redemptive engagement. We need to connect with this, as we respond to upsetting circumstances.

Being able to grasp this redemptive dynamic at work in whatever has troubled us can also give us courage to ask where we need that healing power to work in our own hurts. How wonderful that by God's grace, the inevitable negative events of life can signpost us to God's redeeming response, through us and in us.

COLLECT

Almighty God,
whose Son Jesus Christ is the resurrection and the life:
raise us, who trust in him,
from the death of sin to the life of righteousness,
that we may seek those things which are above,
where he reigns with you
in the unity of the Holy Spirit,
one God, now and for ever.

Reflection by **Sarah Rowland Jones**

Wednesday 3 May

Psalm **135** *or* **119.57-80**
Deuteronomy 10.12-end
Ephesians 5.1-14

Ephesians 5.1-14

'... live in love, as Christ loved us and gave himself up for us' (v.2)

This letter keeps circling back to the newness of life between Christians that follows from the newness of life we have, individually and together, in Jesus Christ. New unity with God brings unprecedented new unity with others who share that bond, and together we are called into new ways of living. It's more than challenging in our individualistic society to realize that we are called to live in mutuality with each other, both giving and receiving the same quality of love that Jesus has shown us.

What does that mean? There are general instructions, but also the recognition that we will have to do some working out for ourselves what this means, in the particularities of our own circumstances, and in relation to our own personalities and characters. The broad principle is to live as children of light – but we have to work out what, specifically, is pleasing to the Lord.

We have some touchstones for this process of discovery: what leads to long-term thanksgiving and gratitude, instead of short-term gratification – especially when it is at the expense of others, whether through sharp talking or exploitative, greedy action.

As for exposing works of darkness, rather than shoring ourselves up by putting others down, why not turn the spotlight on ourselves? When considering our own words and actions, it can be salutary to ask: 'What will this look like when all is made visible in the light of Christ?'

COLLECT

Almighty God,
whose Son Jesus Christ is the resurrection and the life:
raise us, who trust in him,
from the death of sin to the life of righteousness,
that we may seek those things which are above,
where he reigns with you
in the unity of the Holy Spirit,
one God, now and for ever.

Reflection by **Sarah Rowland Jones**

Psalm **118** *or* 56, **57** (63*)
Deuteronomy 11.8-end
Ephesians 5.15-end

Thursday 4 May

Ephesians 5.15-end

'Be subject to one another out of reverence for Christ' (v.21)

'A text without a context is a pretext' one of my tutors at theological college often used to say. The context of the new life we have together through our new life in Christ is summed up in this phrase of being 'subject to one another', in the love that Christ showed us.

Such subjection is not about being superior or inferior. It is about placing ourselves so that we are individually and together under the influence of redeeming love, which is then active and powerful among us in all our various different relationships. In this way, whoever we are and whatever the dynamic at work between us, these can be relationships of mutuality, interdependence and intimacy, so that everyone is built up in godly love. Every encounter with another in Christ becomes opportunity for mutual, though often differentiated, encouragement and growth.

It's not about competition, and it's not about hierarchy. Whoever I am, in all my uniqueness, I have an opportunity both to be a channel of grace to you, and to receive from you as a channel of grace to me, whoever you are, in all your uniqueness and in the unique dynamic between us. The challenge is to be as generous as I can in my openness towards you, and in my readiness to receive from you. It's the challenge to see every encounter as 'win–win', as we submit together to God's redeeming love.

COLLECT

Risen Christ,
faithful shepherd of your Father's sheep:
teach us to hear your voice
and to follow your command,
that all your people may be gathered into one flock,
to the glory of God the Father.

Reflection by **Sarah Rowland Jones**

Friday 5 May

Psalm **33** *or* **51**, 54
Deuteronomy 12.1-14
Ephesians 6.1-9

Ephesians 6.1-9

'... in the Lord ... of the Lord ... to the Lord ... from the Lord' (vv.1,4,7,8)

This passage is problematic to contemporary ears. Today, we rightly reject all forms of enslavement. But contexts of considerable power imbalance exist in other ways, and it's still worth asking what lessons can be learnt from these words. What can the continuing theme of mutuality say to us in such circumstances?

In my teens, I started exploring the New Testament for myself, and was rocked back on my heels on reading, as one translation puts it, 'parents, do not exasperate your children'. This gave way to gales of laughter. Exasperation so characterized my relationship with my parents, since it was clear to me they persistently got things wrong and utterly failed to recognize this. Now I felt myself heard and understood. It was as if God was on my side, even if he was simultaneously also on my parents' side. He recognized that the evolving child/parent relationship was hard for me, and, I grudgingly accepted, for them also. Through it, he wanted 'the best' for us all: growth in knowledge and love of him, growth in us all, into greater Christlikeness.

Now I find myself in the 'master's' shoes. It's my responsibility to be a good employer, treating employees rightly. There may be differentiation of role, but there's no difference in status, no 'partiality' before God. I must use the opportunities I have, not to exploit others, but to promote mutual flourishing – we're all of equal value.

COLLECT

Almighty God,
whose Son Jesus Christ is the resurrection and the life:
raise us, who trust in him,
from the death of sin to the life of righteousness,
that we may seek those things which are above,
where he reigns with you
in the unity of the Holy Spirit,
one God, now and for ever.

 Reflection by **Sarah Rowland Jones**

Psalm **34** *or* **68**
Deuteronomy 15.1-18
Ephesians 6.10-end

Saturday 6 May

Ephesians 6.10-end

'Peace be to the whole community ...' (v.23)

God's people, bound to God and one another in love with faith, remain at the heart of this letter right through to its final verses. Recognizing this prompted me to re-read the preceding verses through this lens of 'the whole community'. Looking at the original Greek confirmed that the imperatives from 'be strong in the Lord' through to 'pray in the Spirit' and on, are all in the plural. Well, I've probably known that for years, but rather assumed it was an instruction to every one of us, each individually, to put on the whole armour of God.

But today I'm also asking what it means to read these words afresh through the lens of mutuality and unity. First, how can we better help one another put on such armour? There's the challenge too of letting others help us – it's not always easy to admit a need for assistance in our self-sufficient society.

And there's a further dimension to consider. What would it mean for the whole Christian community to stand as one under the protection of God's armour? What if we really saw ourselves as bound together by the one single, shared truth? What if our common mind were protected by the helmet of salvation? What if it were evident to the world that we had shared heart for righteousness? What if we truly prayed as one? What encouragement, and what boldness in the gospel, this might bring us!

COLLECT

Risen Christ,
faithful shepherd of your Father's sheep:
teach us to hear your voice
and to follow your command,
that all your people may be gathered into one flock,
to the glory of God the Father.

Reflection by **Sarah Rowland Jones**

Monday 8 May

Psalm **145** *or* **71**
Deuteronomy 16.1-20
1 Peter 1.1-12

1 Peter 1.1-12

'... when Jesus Christ is revealed' (v.7)

This letter, so overflowing with warmth and affection, is written as an encouragement to those preparing for likely persecution. In the face of probable suffering, it bubbles up with joy and holy optimism – because of the living hope found in Jesus Christ. This brings his strengthening through current circumstances, and his guarantee of the ultimate life of heaven.

Few of us are likely to know such dire physical persecution, though it is real enough for many in our world. Yet the promises of Jesus Christ are for us too, because ours is also the calling to be faithful. Our lives should also be lived in contrast to the prevailing, often alien, culture around us, as we hold fast to genuine Christian distinctiveness. That said, it's not always easy to see clearly what such distinctiveness entails, as our own perspective is inevitably that of our own consumerist culture, with all its temptations to suit ourselves, including through complacency and compromise.

Our touchstone should be Jesus Christ and his resurrection from the dead, which brings living hope now and an imperishable inheritance for eternity. Knowing this helps us to be aware of what he is saying to us: 'This is important! This needs your time, your attention, your resources!' Our response can be to point to our touchstone, and say: No, this is where true importance lies: in Jesus Christ, and when he is revealed, we find what is really praiseworthy, glorious and honourable, our worthy priority above all else.

COLLECT

Almighty God,
who through your only-begotten Son Jesus Christ
have overcome death and opened to us the gate of everlasting life:
grant that, as by your grace going before us
  you put into our minds good desires,
so by your continual help
we may bring them to good effect;
through Jesus Christ our risen Lord,
who is alive and reigns with you,
in the unity of the Holy Spirit,
one God, now and for ever.

Reflection by **Sarah Rowland Jones**

Psalms **19**, 147.1-12 *or* **73**
Deuteronomy 17.8-end
1 Peter 1.13-end

Tuesday 9 May

1 Peter 1.13-end

'Therefore prepare your minds for action ...' (v.13)

It's unclear who first said that 'life is just one damn thing after another', but as far as this epistle is concerned, it's a truism. Being human means living a life of ups and downs, facing challenges and growing through them. These may take many forms, but, as we read yesterday, testing refines, strengthens and matures our faith.

Realistic expectations matter. Indeed, having unrealistic expectations, perhaps shaped by depictions of 'reality' online, can be damaging to our mental wellbeing. It's normal and healthy to feel sad, anxious, nervous and so on, in certain circumstances, and these responses have helped humanity survive the millennia. Life isn't a bed of roses, or if it is, they certainly come with thorns attached!

This letter says that because it's realistic to expect trials of one sort or another to come our way, we should 'prepare our minds for action' in response. Expecting challenges makes them easier to handle. We prepare by fixing our trust on the grace that comes from Christ's revealing, knowing we shall find his purifying presence with us in difficult times.

In other words, when life deals us 'damn things', we should view them with godly hope, knowing that we are being presented with opportunities through which to be purified and to grow in faith. So next time you hit a bump in the road, how might you redefine it as a springboard to hope and holiness?

COLLECT

Risen Christ,
your wounds declare your love for the world
and the wonder of your risen life:
give us compassion and courage
to risk ourselves for those we serve,
to the glory of God the Father.

Reflection by **Sarah Rowland Jones**

Wednesday 10 May

Psalms **30**, 147.13-end *or* **77**
Deuteronomy 18.9-end
1 Peter 2.1-10

1 Peter 2.1-10

'... like living stones, let yourselves be built' (v.5)

When I read Scripture, I'm repeatedly reminded that one of the traps of the English language is the tendency to read the word 'you' as if it is a singular, when more often than not, it is a plural. Generally, we'd be better served if our translators used the Texan 'you-all' in such cases!

Today, though, it is very clear these words of encouragement in times of trial are written to a community. The mercy and grace of God are for them, and us, collectively. It is together that we, God's people, can stand against the trials of life, on the strong foundation of Christ.

Being together is not only for our own wellbeing. It is also for the sake of the gospel. For it is together that we become the 'chosen race, a royal priesthood', whose purpose it is to proclaim 'the mighty acts of him who called you out of darkness into his marvellous light'. Nowadays, there are few places outside of church or other religious gatherings that draw together people of different generations, politics, educational or economic backgrounds, interests and outlooks. Unity in such diversity can certainly be a Christian counter-cultural distinctive

Belonging to a church community matters. It's a powerful witness to the world. Why not spend some time today thanking God for those who are most different to you, in your own Christian group.

COLLECT

Almighty God,
who through your only-begotten Son Jesus Christ
have overcome death and opened to us the gate of everlasting life:
grant that, as by your grace going before us
  you put into our minds good desires,
so by your continual help
we may bring them to good effect;
through Jesus Christ our risen Lord,
who is alive and reigns with you,
in the unity of the Holy Spirit,
one God, now and for ever.

Reflection by **Sarah Rowland Jones**

Psalms **57**, 148 *or* **78.1-39***
Deuteronomy 19
1 Peter 2.11-end

Thursday 11 May

1 Peter 2.11-end

'... aliens and exiles ...' (v.11)

'The time is always right to do what is right' said Martin Luther King Jr, though this begs the question of knowing what is the right thing to do. Today's passage commends a long list of behaviours that seem very conforming in following legal and political power apparently without question. It's hardly the counter-cultural stance that was put before us earlier.

Then comes the difficulty of how to read apparent condoning of slavery. However different the first century's particular context might be from more recent forms of enslavement, this is now abhorrent to us, and rightly so. Does this mean we stand with contemporary culture, against the Bible?

For me, the answer lies in the call to be 'servants of God', and 'live as free people'. This is the freedom to develop our own true identity and self-understanding through the liberating power of the gospel, and freedom to engage with the world on this basis. Such freedom entails knowing our identity does not come from the culture around, nor from its legal and political structures. Instead, we are released from those constraints by being aliens and exiles. As citizens of heaven, we live under the rule of the Servant King, 'whose service is perfect freedom' as the Prayer Book Collect for Peace puts it. This provides us with the integrity to discern and do what is truly right.

COLLECT

Risen Christ,
your wounds declare your love for the world
and the wonder of your risen life:
give us compassion and courage
to risk ourselves for those we serve,
to the glory of God the Father.

Reflection by **Sarah Rowland Jones**

Friday 12 May

Psalms **138**, 149 *or* **55**
Deuteronomy 21.22 – 22.8
1 Peter 3.1-12

1 Peter 3.1-12

'... repay with a blessing' (v.9)

Today's opening sentences may also provoke some tooth-sucking and unease on a first reading. They certainly do with me, and I'm sure my husband would be considerably disconcerted if I started calling him 'lord!' These passages, radical in their own day, challenge us to grapple with how we can live in Christ-like ways in contrast to contemporary assumptions, in our personal relations as well as in our engagement within the public space.

Yesterday's assurance of the freedom we have as the people of God are complemented by the principles set out in verse 8 onwards, of living together in unity of spirit, love, tenderness and mutual humility. Most counter-cultural of all is the call to repay evil and abuse with blessing, and these few words may be the most powerful of the whole letter. For this is of course the same counter-cultural response of Jesus Christ on the cross, who, as we read yesterday 'bore our sins in his body on the cross, so that, free from sins, we might live for righteousness'.

His death and resurrection are what make righteous living possible, which finds expression in repaying good for evil. We become caught up in Christ's redemptive reversal of cycles of evil and abuse, and we both inherit blessing and become vehicles of that blessing spilling over into the world. Dare we hope trying times can provide greater opportunities for such blessing to be shared?

COLLECT

Almighty God,
who through your only-begotten Son Jesus Christ
have overcome death and opened to us the gate of everlasting life:
grant that, as by your grace going before us
    you put into our minds good desires,
so by your continual help
we may bring them to good effect;
through Jesus Christ our risen Lord,
who is alive and reigns with you,
in the unity of the Holy Spirit,
one God, now and for ever.

Reflection by **Sarah Rowland Jones**

Psalms **146**, 150 *or* **76**, 79
Deuteronomy 24.5-end
1 Peter 3.13-end

Saturday 13 May

1 Peter 3.13-end

'... in your hearts sanctify Christ as Lord' (v.15)

From a human perspective, life can often seem inescapably unfair, and sometimes worse. But the choice of how we respond remains with us, whether, like the recipients of this letter, we are confronted by major persecution, or merely face the daily small frustrations of so-called first-world problems.

The advice in today's passage is for all situations: be good, do right, be gentle ... Keeping Jesus Christ at the centre of our lives is the way to achieve this. It's not just that we should follow his teaching, or even his self-sacrificial example – an encouragement to do so though both may be. More than this, he makes it possible, through his suffering, death and resurrection, for us actually to achieve all this. It's not fanciful wishful thinking.

As we sanctify Christ as Lord in our hearts, he sanctifies us. He makes holiness the tone of our lives, shaping into greater Christlikeness all we do and say and are. He strengthens us and bears our sufferings with us, when doing good has hurtful consequences. United with him in baptism, we should expect to find ourselves caught up into his redemptive processes, so that our own dealings with others become infused with his saving power.

The end of this week returns us to our beginning, with the reassurance that in bad times no less than in good times, Christ can be revealed as Saviour and Lord of all. Amen to this!

COLLECT

Risen Christ,
your wounds declare your love for the world
and the wonder of your risen life:
give us compassion and courage
to risk ourselves for those we serve,
to the glory of God the Father.

Reflection by **Sarah Rowland Jones**

Monday 15 May

Matthias the Apostle

Psalms 16, 147.1-12
1 Samuel 2.27-35
Acts 2.37-end

Acts 2.37-end

'... they were cut to the heart' (v.37)

'Nodding off' in sermons is sometimes observed by a preacher, as is the sharing of sweets and efforts to suppress laughter (often induced by a neighbour's acerbic under-the-breath comment). In contrast, Peter's sermon makes a deep impression on his hearers. No nodding off or distraction here: the crowd is 'cut to the heart'. In terms of communication, what is happening that makes the difference?

Earlier in the chapter, Luke describes the divine initiative that brought the Church into being. A multicultural crowd of Jews is overwhelmed by God's sweet and fiery presence. A wonder happens. Each person hears God's goodness told in their own cultural terms. How is it, they ask, 'that we hear, each of us, in our own native language?' (Acts 2.8).

It is Peter who recognizes signs of the Spirit at work, attends to the question raised by it and makes the connections: interpreting what's happening in terms of the fulfilment of prophecy, the story of Jesus and the people in front of him.

Today's reading offers us a pattern to follow as the Church seeks to communicate the good news of God in Christ: discern the action of the Holy Spirit, attend to the questions raised by it (in ourselves or others), and then, in the power of the same Spirit, be courageous in making new connections. Or, put more simply: only connect!

COLLECT

Almighty God,
who in the place of the traitor Judas
chose your faithful servant Matthias
to be of the number of the Twelve:
preserve your Church from false apostles
and, by the ministry of faithful pastors and teachers,
keep us steadfast in your truth;
through Jesus Christ your Son our Lord,
who is alive and reigns with you,
in the unity of the Holy Spirit,
one God, now and for ever.

Reflection by **Jonathan Frost**

Psalms 124, 125, **126**, 127 *or* 87, **89.1-18**
Deuteronomy 28.1-14
1 Peter 4.12-end

Tuesday 16 May

1 Peter 4.12-end

'Beloved, do not be surprised at the fiery ordeal ...' (v.12)

If you've ever rented property, you will know all about coded marketing literature: 'close to the river' (the basement floods); 'at the heart of a vibrant community' (wave goodbye to sleep); or 'long-term lets preferred' (we want this off our books).

Peter's Epistle is different. It is honest and authentic about following Jesus Christ. Christians will suffer for their faith. Indeed, in Peter's day, the empire persecuted Christians. Refusing to deny Christ, many suffered the 'fiery ordeal' of being burned alive as human torches.

The invitation to walk with Christ remains costly. Christians may experience strained, or even broken, relationships with friends, colleagues or family members as the Holy Spirit transforms their lives 'from the inside out'. For others, Christian life means living in fear. So what's going on?

When the Holy Spirit draws a person or community towards Christlikeness, trouble starts, as surely as light dispels darkness. For while life in Christ's friendship brings incomparable joy, peace and purpose, it also throws light on that which sorely needs transformation, in ourselves and in society.

Normal Christian life includes 'fiery ordeals' of different kinds. Some are triggered by foolishness; others are a consequence of the Holy Spirit's refining work within us. Humility and humour are usually the right response to the former. For the rest? Peter calls us to entrust ourselves to 'a faithful Creator', to keep calm... and carry on.

COLLECT

God our redeemer,
you have delivered us from the power of darkness
and brought us into the kingdom of your Son:
grant, that as by his death he has recalled us to life,
so by his continual presence in us he may raise us
to eternal joy;
through Jesus Christ your Son our Lord,
who is alive and reigns with you,
in the unity of the Holy Spirit,
one God, now and for ever.

Reflection by **Jonathan Frost**

Wednesday 17 May

Psalms **132**, 133 *or* **119.105-128**
Deuteronomy 28.58-end
I Peter 5

1 Peter 5

'... clothe yourselves with humility' (v.5)

A teacher of mine would say, as theological or political debate entered fiercely contested ground: 'I suggest we put our tin hats on.' Clothing, actually and metaphorically speaking, plays a part in how we project or protect ourselves in daily life.

Young people can find wearing the 'right' brand an agonizingly precarious element in the struggle to belong. Clothes provide markers of identity; they signal something about ourselves and where we belong (it's instructive to reflect on the wardrobe of an environmental activist or rap artist; of a soldier, football fan or executive). We project or protect ourselves, at least to some degree, through what we wear. Which is what makes Peter's choice of clothing metaphor, so *counter-intuitive* and unexpected in the Epistle's closing chapter.

Writing to encourage a suffering community facing persecution and gross misrepresentation, Peter refuses to commend the way of self-preservation, defensiveness or hitting back. 'Clothe yourselves with humility', he writes. As Jesus Christ is, so are his people called to be in and for the world. Christians signal their true identity when they live in humble trust; in openness and vulnerability to one another, to their neighbour and before the One who raises the dead.

Before reaching for our tin hats today, will you join me in trying on humble trust for size? If we find it too big for us at first, we can always grow into it.

COLLECT

God our redeemer,
you have delivered us from the power of darkness
and brought us into the kingdom of your Son:
grant, that as by his death he has recalled us to life,
so by his continual presence in us he may raise us
to eternal joy;
through Jesus Christ your Son our Lord,
who is alive and reigns with you,
in the unity of the Holy Spirit,
one God, now and for ever.

Reflection by **Jonathan Frost**

Psalms 110, 150
Isaiah 52.7-end
Hebrews 7. [11-25] 26-end

Thursday 18 May
Ascension Day

Hebrews 7. [11-25] 26-end

'... he always lives to make intercession' (v.25)

The dying seconds of the 1966 World Cup Final inspired a memorable moment (readers who believe soccer ranks a poor second to watching paint dry, please suspend judgement!). With seconds to play, two goals to his name, and England clinging to a slender lead, Geoff Hurst hurtled towards the German goal, the ball at his feet, the nation's eyes upon him.

At which point the TV commentator Kenneth Wolstenhome delivered his legendary two-part line: *'They think it's all over ...'* – and then, as Hurst blasted the ball into the German net – *'It is now!'*

Many contemporary football writers believed Hurst was wrongly selected for the final (the popular player discarded for Hurst would, tragically, spend the rest of his days wrestling with bitter disappointment).

On the first Ascension Day, the disciples might well have mistakenly thought or said something similar, as the risen Jesus was lifted up and taken out of their sight: 'It's all over – we're on our own from here.'

Whatever you face today, give thanks for the Ascension and for the outpouring of God's Spirit that will follow, inviting each generation to share Christ's life and leaving no one out. We rejoice because through Christ's ascension – to fill all things, be present in all things and to intercede for us – Christ abides, alive and at large in the world.

All over? Not likely: the celebration's just begun.

COLLECT

Grant, we pray, almighty God,
that as we believe your only-begotten Son
our Lord Jesus Christ
to have ascended into the heavens,
so we in heart and mind may also ascend
and with him continually dwell;
who is alive and reigns with you,
in the unity of the Holy Spirit,
one God, now and for ever.

Reflection by **Jonathan Frost**

Friday 19 May

Psalms 20, **81** *or* **88** (95)
Exodus 35.30 – 36.1
Galatians 5.13-end

Galatians 5.13-end

'Live by the Spirit ...' (v.16)

On February 11 1990, after 27 years in confinement, Nelson Mandela's imminent release was announced by news agencies. In schools, teaching was put on hold. Staff and pupils gathered around television screens. The event's significance was unmistakable for the struggle against apartheid and the cause of human rights the world over. We were witnessing, I felt at the time, a moment in which a glimpse of the coming reign of heaven was visible on earth.

But Mandela's release was only a beginning. It raised urgent questions. How, we waited to see, would Mandela live his freedom? Would he settle scores, deepen hostility and bring simmering dissension to boiling point? To use language drawn from Paul's letter to the churches in Galatia, would Mandela choose the way of the flesh or, against the grain of all reasonable expectation, would he choose the way of the Spirit? The way of self-control, generosity and love of neighbour?

History will surely judge that Mandela, while never a saint and irreducibly complex, chose the way of the Spirit consistently and repeatedly until the end of his life. With grace and dignity, Mandela used his freedom years to work for truth and reconciliation; for the possibility that, in the long-term future of South Africa, those formerly at enmity might eventually flourish as neighbours.

In the opportunities presented by your freedom today, which way will you choose?

COLLECT

Grant, we pray, almighty God,
that as we believe your only-begotten Son
our Lord Jesus Christ
to have ascended into the heavens,
so we in heart and mind may also ascend
and with him continually dwell;
who is alive and reigns with you,
in the unity of the Holy Spirit,
one God, now and for ever.

Reflection by **Jonathan Frost**

Psalms 21, **47** *or* 96, **97**, 100
Numbers 11.16-17, 24-29
1 Corinthians 2

Saturday 20 May

1 Corinthians 2

'... these things God has revealed to us' (v.10)

Over the years, it has been a joy to accompany young people to the Taizé Community in France. Most making the journey have lived formative years within a consumer culture and a competitive educational system. In both, a person's worth, acceptance and value can seem to depend, to an unhealthy degree, upon achievement or the acquisition of possessions.

Surprise is often expressed at what is discovered in Taizé: a counter-cultural community in which love for Jesus Christ and neighbour is being lived through simplicity, mutual acceptance and joyful prayer.

Young people speak in revelatory terms of 'finding home' and of an awareness of God's love (or peace or joy) as they participate in common prayer, simple songs and silence. The importance of simplicity and silence are repeated themes.

The contrast is clear between these kinds of reports and those reaching the ears of St Paul about his beloved Corinthians. In Corinth – like Taizé, a vibrant, Spirit-filled community – what had once been unifying and simple in their faith has become complicated, a source of conflict and competition.

It's possible, in our complex and distracted lives, to lose hold of simple trust in Christ and to forget that Christ holds us. So wherever we are today, a prayer to bring us home:

'Bless us, Christ Jesus; in you alone our hearts find rest and peace.'

COLLECT

Risen Christ,
you have raised our human nature to the throne of heaven:
help us to seek and serve you,
that we may join you at the Father's side,
where you reign with the Spirit in glory,
now and for ever.

Reflection by **Jonathan Frost**

Monday 22 May

Psalms **93**, 96, 97 *or* **98**, 99, 101
Numbers 27.15-end
1 Corinthians 3

1 Corinthians 3

'... are you not merely human?' (v.4)

I live in a vibrant port-city. With no skill in seafaring, I find the sight of ships entering or leaving port a source of wonder. For, humanly speaking, it takes a lot to shift a ship. Reflect on a crew's training or the accumulated wisdom of the pilot, and you'll discern no short cuts. Every safe departure, voyage or arrival is down to investment in teamwork and formation.

In today's reading, we see Paul investing in the formation of the Christian community. The church exasperates him (Paul is so human!). It's taking a lot to shift self-centred attitudes and behaviours towards greater Christlikeness.

Paul compares the Corinthians to infants unready for solid spiritual food. They are immature; swift to fall back into mind-sets and cultural priorities more aligned to their former lives than to their new life in Christ. So we watch as Paul urges them to choose 'the way of the Spirit' and to resist the 'life of the flesh'.

The summons to grow towards greater maturity, for a disciple or Christian community, is unavoidable, cross-shaped and yet also an invitation to life in all its fullness. It involves de-throning the self (no short cuts here) and learning, in and through the company of others, to live more *ec-centrically* – literally, *from a centre* in Jesus Christ. It is the Holy Spirit's work within us. Will you welcome it?

COLLECT

O God the King of glory,
you have exalted your only Son Jesus Christ
with great triumph to your kingdom in heaven:
we beseech you, leave us not comfortless,
but send your Holy Spirit to strengthen us
and exalt us to the place where our Saviour Christ is gone before,
who is alive and reigns with you,
in the unity of the Holy Spirit,
one God, now and for ever.

 Reflection by **Jonathan Frost**

Psalms 98, **99**, 100 or **106*** (*or* 103)
1 Samuel 10.1-10
1 Corinthians 12.1-13

Tuesday 23 May

1 Corinthians 12.1-13

'To each is given the manifestation of the Spirit for the common good' (v.7)

From the touchline we could hear only parts of the post-match talk. Our boys' football team had lost their match. Amongst them the process of identifying the guilty and apportioning blame had begun. The coach gathered his team.

From where we stood, some distance away, we caught snippets as he drew out some positive elements (an object lesson in creative pastoral imagination). We caught the constructive tone, if not all the words. But then, in sudden exasperation and crisply audible across the field, came the words: 'Tommo, it's not all about *you*!'

Whether the context is Corinthian first or twenty-first century Christian community, playground or politics, workplace or home, learning that it's not all about me remains, for most of us, a work in progress. It's why the vision of Christian community in cultures enthralled by individualism is so *counter-cultural*: for the Holy Spirit calls us, with all our gifts and foibles, into community with Christ and one another, to shared joys, sufferings and an abundance of life unimagined by those determined to go it alone.

St Benedict described Christian community as 'a school for love'. For here, painfully yet liberatingly, we learn that it's not all about 'me' (however valued and gifted we are) but about an invitation to life together in Christ, a life lived in and for the world.

Risen, ascended Lord,
as we rejoice at your triumph,
fill your Church on earth with power and compassion,
that all who are estranged by sin
may find forgiveness and know your peace,
to the glory of God the Father.

COLLECT

Reflection by **Jonathan Frost**

Wednesday 24 May

Psalms 2, **29** *or* 110, **111**, 112
1 Kings 19.1-18
Matthew 3.13-end

Matthew 3.13-end

'I need to be baptized by you, and do you come to me?' (v.14)

After my sixth birthday I was taken to watch football regularly (although often finding beef tea and the crowd more interesting than the game). In our household, foul language was frowned upon. So football matches were a revelation.

One fan always stood (and shouted) nearby. When I hear of Jesus being baptized by John, I think of that man. Over 90 minutes, he'd work through a hip flask and a packet of cigarettes. But, strangely, it would be hard to imagine a fan who seemed to loathe his team more than he did. Why ever did he buy a ticket? Surely, there are cheaper ways to have a rotten time! From the safety of the stand he would diagnose the failings of every player: 'Useless the lot of them!'

It doesn't require great therapeutic insight to guess he may have been unhappy. Perhaps he'd drunk deeply from the cup of life's sadness. I will never know. But I'd love him to hear, and know, the story of Jesus being baptized.

Because, for me, it's about a God who leaves the safety of the stands, to stand with us. The humble and gentle God, Mary's child, who loves the lost and calms our fears. God with us, on the pitch, not in the stands. Until the final whistle.

That's something to be cheered about.

COLLECT

O God the King of glory,
you have exalted your only Son Jesus Christ
with great triumph to your kingdom in heaven:
we beseech you, leave us not comfortless,
but send your Holy Spirit to strengthen us
and exalt us to the place where our Saviour Christ is gone before,
who is alive and reigns with you,
in the unity of the Holy Spirit,
one God, now and for ever.

 Reflection by **Jonathan Frost**

Psalms **24**, 72 *or* 113, **115**
Ezekiel 11.14-20
Matthew 9.35 – 10.20

Thursday 25 May

Matthew 9.35 – 10.20

'When he saw the crowds, he had compassion for them ...' (9.36)

We were hiking across exposed, open ground. Moving downhill, wind and torrential rain battered us from behind.

It was then that a child, no more than seven years old, appeared in front of us, walking uphill and struggling against the wind. She had passed us before we registered her vulnerability. We stopped and turned around. A teacher in our group reacted first and ran to join the girl.

Tearful, lost and afraid, she had become detached from her parents' hiking group (now visible, through driving rain, more than half a mile away). The rest of us watched, resting tired feet, as our friend accompanied the child to her parents and safekeeping.

Today's reading may provide a foundation for an integrated and holistic theology of mission. But it's what Matthew notices, and my friend practised, that forms mission's beating heart: *compassion*.

For the mission of the Church, in and for the world, begins, continues and ends here, with the overflowing and abundant love of a compassionate God. In Jesus Christ, God joins us where we are – distressed, lost or wrestling with fear – restores our humanity from the inside and, through the gift of the life-giving Spirit, invites us to reflect his compassion in the world.

Or, as St John will put it in another place: 'we love because he first loved us' (1 John 4.19).

COLLECT

Risen, ascended Lord,
as we rejoice at your triumph,
fill your Church on earth with power and compassion,
that all who are estranged by sin
may find forgiveness and know your peace,
to the glory of God the Father.

Reflection by **Jonathan Frost**

Friday 26 May

Psalms **28**, 30 *or* **139**
Ezekiel 36.22-28
Matthew 12.22-32

Matthew 12.22-32

'Can this be the Son of David?' (v.23)

Although a scientific consensus about humankind's role in global warming has been established for some years, I suspect it is lived experience that has shifted the deniers and prised open previously closed minds. For more frequent high winds and floods possess a devastating eloquence: connecting life and science, reshaping perception and requiring urgent action.

To persist with a closed mind, in denial of experience and evidence, is always to place ourselves in grave danger. For when we refuse to adjust our stance, we risk cutting ourselves off from the truth of our situation and from sources of hope, change and renewal within it.

We see the impact of closed minds in today's reading. A demon-possessed man, unable to see or to speak, is liberated through encounter with Jesus. For those with open minds, evidence of the Holy Spirit's action in Jesus raises the question of his true identity: 'Can this be the Son of David?' they ask. By contrast, the Pharisees have already made up their minds about Jesus.

Nothing will shift them; not even the presence of a man, blind and mute seconds before, who now speaks of what he sees. Blinded by cynicism, the Pharisees interpret the good act of God's Spirit as a work of the evil one and so cut themselves off from the life Jesus offers to them.

Will you pray with me, today, for openness to God's Spirit?

COLLECT

O God the King of glory,
you have exalted your only Son Jesus Christ
with great triumph to your kingdom in heaven:
we beseech you, leave us not comfortless,
but send your Holy Spirit to strengthen us
and exalt us to the place where our Saviour Christ is gone before,
who is alive and reigns with you,
in the unity of the Holy Spirit,
one God, now and for ever.

Reflection by **Jonathan Frost**

Psalms 42, **43** *or* 120, **121**, 122
Micah 3.1-8
Ephesians 6.10-20

Saturday 27 May

Ephesians 6.10-20

'... our struggle is not against enemies of blood and flesh' (v.12)

Few of us will forget the shock of watching Russia's invasion of Ukraine unfold. It recalled the evils of the Second World War as Ukranians were displaced by an act of premeditated state violence.

Led by its President, the Ukrainian people responded with courage and resourcefulness. The nation's leader remained with his people, refused offers of safe haven and broadcast inspiring messages of unimpeachable integrity. Mothers met in city parks to make Molotov cocktails as men and women volunteered to take up arms against their aggressor.

But St Paul reminds us that struggle in this world is never struggle on the human level alone. For in Christian understanding, the created order of earth and heaven is far more complex, multi-dimensional and mysterious than allowed for in secular interpretation. For this is a moral universe in which sinful human beings are also capable of scaling the moral and emotional heights of love. It's not only matter that matters in this world, but also concern for the flourishing of our neighbour and planet.

St Paul stretches us yet further, in a way that challenges our secular western assumptions; for 'in, with and under' the ways of the world he discerns other powers at work, 'spiritual forces of evil in heavenly places'. Against these powers, it is humble prayer and trust in the One who raises the dead that will see right prevail, however long the wait or bitter the struggle.

COLLECT

Risen, ascended Lord,
as we rejoice at your triumph,
fill your Church on earth with power and compassion,
that all who are estranged by sin
may find forgiveness and know your peace,
to the glory of God the Father.

Reflection by **Jonathan Frost**

Monday 29 May

Psalms 123, 124, 125, **126**
2 Chronicles 17.1-12
Romans 1.1-17

2 Chronicles 17.1-12

'His heart was courageous in the ways of the Lord' (v.6)

The Chronicler's view of Jehoshaphat is overwhelmingly positive, as summed up in the unusual statement that 'his heart was courageous in the ways of the Lord'. The word translated here 'courageous' literally means 'lifted up', and that alerts us to the unique force of the Chronicler's assessment. Usually in the Bible, for somebody's heart to be 'lifted up' is a sign of hubris, and of likely forthcoming disaster – particularly when, like Jehoshaphat, the person in question is also possessed of wealth and honour. Pride, riches and power tend to make their owner forgetful of their primary allegiance and duty to God, as happens repeatedly in the Chronicler's account of the kings of Judah.

Not so with Jehoshaphat, it would seem: he somehow manages to keep his pride centred in the 'ways of the Lord', his courage derived from God's grace rather than his own strength. For this he is held up as an exemplar in Chronicles, equal only to the great David himself.

The challenges and choices presented to us are likely to be very different from those that faced a ninth-century BC Middle Eastern monarch. But a sense of self-sufficiency and pride can be just as much a temptation to us, drawing us into disregard or forgetfulness of God. Paul wrote of the need to boast (if boast we must) only in the Lord; like Jehoshaphat, we need to discipline ourselves so that we exalt our hearts in God alone.

COLLECT

O Lord, from whom all good things come:
grant to us your humble servants,
that by your holy inspiration
we may think those things that are good,
and by your merciful guiding may perform the same;
through our Lord Jesus Christ,
who is alive and reigns with you,
in the unity of the Holy Spirit,
one God, now and for ever.

Reflection by **Michael Ipgrave**

Psalms **132**, 133
2 Chronicles 18.1-27
Romans 1.18-end

Tuesday 30 May

2 Chronicles 18.1-27

'A lying spirit in the mouth of these your prophets' (v.22)

Micaiah son of Imlah stands out as a uniquely truthful and courageous figure among the prophets who throng the court of Ahaz of Israel. Always the messenger of unwelcome news, he has grown to be odious to the king, who is dismayed by his consistently gloomy messages. In the extraordinary scene that unfolds in this strange narrative, Micaiah lives up to his reputation, presenting Ahaz with a strikingly bleak image of Israel scattered and leaderless on the mountain.

The story does not stop here, though. Other prophets challenge Micaiah with more upbeat messages. Remarkably, Micaiah claims that these prophets have been misled by a spirit of falsehood sent by the Lord himself. This is a difficult claim to place within the overall biblical emphasis on the trustworthiness of God, and it is not clear whether Micaiah intends it to be taken literally or ironically.

What is clear, though, is that the discernment of truth in messages from prophets, or from anybody else for that matter, is not straightforward. This is our own experience in trying to work out what God is saying to us through others in the choices we have to make in our own lives. Like Ahaz, we are always inclined to turn against the messenger of bad news. But we should not take Micaiah's suggestion of a lying spirit from God as normative; we can and we must have confidence that our God is truthful and wishes to lead us into the truth.

COLLECT

O Lord, from whom all good things come:
grant to us your humble servants,
that by your holy inspiration
we may think those things that are good,
and by your merciful guiding may perform the same;
through our Lord Jesus Christ,
who is alive and reigns with you,
in the unity of the Holy Spirit,
one God, now and for ever.

Reflection by **Michael Ipgrave**

Wednesday 31 May

Visit of the Blessed Virgin Mary to Elizabeth

Psalms 85, 150
1 Samuel 2.1-10
Mark 3.31-end

1 Samuel 2.1-10

'My heart exults in the Lord' (v.1)

This reading is refracted in Luke's account of Mary's visitation to Elizabeth in two ways. Mary's Magnificat echoes Hannah's exultant song. But it is Elizabeth whose experience mirrors Hannah's: the unexpected gift of a child to one deemed incapable of conception.

Childlessness is a difficult experience for many. It still carries a stigma in some cultures, and even in a society like our own, which emphasises freedom of choice in lifestyles, it can be the cause of real sadness, with a sense of loss and sometimes of shame. In the Israel of both Hannah's and Elizabeth's time, childlessness also brought with it economic and social disadvantage. For Hannah at least, to this was added insult and mockery, which the well-intended attempts of her husband to offer comfort did little to alleviate.

Indeed, in both of these stories, the men – Elkanah, Zechariah, Joseph – are peripheral to the narrative. By contrast, in Hannah, Elizabeth and Mary, we see three women who all encounter a dramatic change in their lives through unexpected motherhood. For the first two, this is longed for but unanticipated; for Mary it is unlooked for, but nonetheless graciously accepted. For each, this intensely personal experience opens up a universal horizon of the God whose Spirit breaks into the world radically to invert the settled order. Whether parents or not, all can exult with Hannah, Elizabeth and Mary at the new life that God brings into our world; all can take comfort in the solace this brings to the afflicted; all can share in the radical newness of the kingdom.

COLLECT

Mighty God,
by whose grace Elizabeth rejoiced with Mary
and greeted her as the mother of the Lord:
look with favour on your lowly servants
that, with Mary, we may magnify your holy name
and rejoice to acclaim her Son our Saviour,
who is alive and reigns with you,
in the unity of the Holy Spirit,
one God, now and for ever.

Reflection by **Michael Ipgrave**

Psalms **143**, 146
2 Chronicles 20.1-23
Romans 2.17-end

Thursday 1 June

2 Chronicles 20.1-23

'... all Judah stood before the Lord' (v.13)

Jehoshaphat and his people face a serious concerted attack by an alliance of nations. A military response would be the obvious answer, and elsewhere it is clear that this king is usually ready to fight against his enemies. Here, though, the picture is less clear. It is not his army whom Jehoshaphat addresses but the whole 'assembly of Judah and Jerusalem'. The Chronicler makes clear that this gathering includes women and children as well as those capable of bearing arms. The specific reference to the people as 'standing' probably implies that this was a gathering for prayer: the central prayer of later Jewish liturgy is called the *Amidah*, meaning, simply 'standing', as the people do here.

So it is a religious, not a military, assembly that faces this existential threat, and the divine message delivered to Jahaziel explains why this is so: 'the battle is not yours but God's'. It transpires that Jehoshaphat's forces have no active fighting to do; through divine agency, their enemies turn on and destroy one another.

Jehoshaphat's attitude in this crisis may strike us as one of extreme passivity: 'We do not know what to do', he says forlornly at one point. This may seem like a rabbit caught in the headlights, but the text goes on to show that actually his gaze is fixed elsewhere: 'Our eyes are on you', that is, on God. In this case at least, non-action and trust in divine protection prove to be the right answer. Sometimes that can be true for us in the crises we face.

COLLECT

O Lord, from whom all good things come:
grant to us your humble servants,
that by your holy inspiration
we may think those things that are good,
and by your merciful guiding may perform the same;
through our Lord Jesus Christ,
who is alive and reigns with you,
in the unity of the Holy Spirit,
one God, now and for ever.

Reflection by **Michael Ipgrave**

Friday 2 June

Psalms 142, **144**
2 Chronicles 22.10 – end of 23
Romans 3.1-20

2 Chronicles 22.10 – end of 23

'Treason! Treason!' (23.13)

Athaliah is introduced into the story of the royal house of Judah as a murderer and a usurper, who yet manages to exercise rule over the kingdom for six years. She was a younger contemporary (possibly a daughter) of Jezebel, the Queen of Israel, and the Bible's antipathy to both women rests on religious as well as political grounds.

Nevertheless, it is difficult not to feel some sympathy with Athaliah when her violent end comes, in a meticulously planned palace coup led by the priest Jehoiada. The queen, apparently unaware up to that point of the plot against her, is portrayed as totally isolated, abandoned by her defenders. Her cries of 'Treason! Treason!' are inaudible above the joyful music of singers and trumpeters, and so she is led away to her ignominious execution.

The Chronicler is in no doubt that this shows the purpose of God being acted out in human history, and he also emphasizes that the revolution has the support of the people, who proceed to make with their new king a covenant that they should be the Lord's people. Having seen how easy it is to find religious or ideological justifications for regime change, modern-day readers of this text may feel less confident in assigning one side of a revolution so clearly to God and the other side to his enemies. This once strong woman's cry of 'Treason!' haunts us down the centuries, as do the cries of those she herself murdered.

COLLECT

O Lord, from whom all good things come:
grant to us your humble servants,
that by your holy inspiration
we may think those things that are good,
and by your merciful guiding may perform the same;
through our Lord Jesus Christ,
who is alive and reigns with you,
in the unity of the Holy Spirit,
one God, now and for ever.

Reflection by **Michael Ipgrave**

Psalm **147**
2 Chronicles 24.1-22
Romans 3.21-end

Saturday 3 June

2 Chronicles 24.1-22

'They stoned him to death in the court of the house of the Lord!' (v.21)

This passage follows the previous chapter's description of a conspiracy, organized by the priest Jehoiada, resulting in the death of Athaliah. Now the tables are turned as a new conspiracy leads to the death of Jehoiada's son Zechariah. Unlike Athaliah's murder, the Chronicler sees this as a shocking transgression. Its terrible character is heightened by the fact that Zechariah is killed in the court of the Lord's house itself (Jehoiada had insisted that Athaliah's death take place outside the temple). To the death of a righteous person is therefore added the defilement of the sanctuary.

The murder of Zechariah was counted in later Jewish tradition as one of the sins leading eventually to the destruction of the temple. It may also be the event that Jesus in the Gospels couples with the murder of Abel as egregious instances of the shedding of innocent blood that will incur judgement.

Some might argue that it makes little difference whether a killing takes place within or outside a sacred site. On a lesser level, similar arguments are applied to arrests in or deportations from churches or other holy places. It is true that ecclesiastical immunity is no longer recognized in law as a source of protection, but the idea of sanctuary remains a powerful and compelling one in our society, and its violation continues to shock us. Zechariah's death reminds us in our own age of turbulence and persecution to take seriously the divine protection afforded to those who seek refuge with God.

COLLECT

O Lord, from whom all good things come:
grant to us your humble servants,
that by your holy inspiration
we may think those things that are good,
and by your merciful guiding may perform the same;
through our Lord Jesus Christ,
who is alive and reigns with you,
in the unity of the Holy Spirit,
one God, now and for ever.

Reflection by **Michael Ipgrave**

Monday 5 June

Psalms 1, 2, 3
2 Chronicles 26.1-21
Romans 4.1-12

2 Chronicles 26.1-21

'... he loved the soil' (v.10)

As we read the account of Uzziah in our age of ecological awareness, we are likely to take in a positive sense the unusual comment of the Chronicler that 'he loved the soil'. Following Uzziah's promotion of irrigation, herding and viticulture, this seems a due acknowledgement of the king's environmental and economic enthusiasms, and perhaps a welcome counter-balance to his military activities.

However, as the narrative moves on, Uzziah appears in a less favourable light, and Jewish commentators found a connection between this and his agricultural enthusiasms. They pointed out that the Bible identifies three figures as particularly attached to the soil, each of whom met with disgrace or punishment: Cain, the tiller of crops, who was indelibly marked on his forehead as the first murderer; Noah, planter of a vineyard, who suffered the shame of public drunkenness; and Uzziah, whose pride led him to rash actions resulting in leprosy.

Except perhaps in the case of Noah, the connecting links between these three men's ecological passions and their subsequent fates are not easy to trace. And surely, we may think, in our own time of environmental crisis to be a 'lover of the soil' must be in itself an admirable quality. Nevertheless, the story of Uzziah (as of Cain and Noah) reminds us that ecological commitment is not in itself a sufficient mark of holiness for God's people. We are to love and reverence the earth because it is God's creation; we go astray if the creation takes the place of the Creator in our allegiance.

COLLECT

Almighty and everlasting God,
you have given us your servants grace,
by the confession of a true faith,
to acknowledge the glory of the eternal Trinity
and in the power of the divine majesty to worship the Unity:
keep us steadfast in this faith,
that we may evermore be defended from all adversities;
through Jesus Christ your Son our Lord,
who is alive and reigns with you,
in the unity of the Holy Spirit,
one God, now and for ever.

Reflection by **Michael Ipgrave**

Psalms **5**, 6 (8)
2 Chronicles 28
Romans 4.13-end

Tuesday 6 June

2 Chronicles 28

'... they clothed all that were naked' (v.15)

A conflict between north and south results in the capture of a large number of Judaeans by the Israelites, and an argument breaks out over how they should be treated. The debate is conducted entirely by those operationally involved on the ground, without reference to the kings of either Israel or Judah.

There are two factors that decisively influence the Israelite commanders. One is awareness of the guilt in which they already stand before God from having fought against the Judaeans, killed some and captured others; they are anxious not to exacerbate their sin through further ill-treatment. At the same time, the detail with which the text lists their caring actions – clothing, giving sandals, providing food and drink, anointing, carrying the infirm on donkeys, reuniting the prisoners with their compatriots – also shows a deep humanitarian concern for those recognized as kindred.

The Chronicler makes clear that these actions of kindness take place on a level beyond that of political machinations between the two monarchs. In his view of history, this episode reveals the fundamental unity between the northern Israelites and the southern Judaeans, and is a proper expression of the kinship binding them together. Yet we may go further, seeing here a touching and hopeful sign of the common humanity we all share. Indeed, as Christians it is impossible to read this story without calling to mind Jesus' parable of the Samaritan (northerner) who rescues a distressed Jew (southerner), on a road near Jericho. The message is clear: those we meet in distress are our neighbours and kindred, deserving our practical care.

COLLECT

Holy God,
faithful and unchanging:
enlarge our minds with the knowledge of your truth,
and draw us more deeply into the mystery of your love,
that we may truly worship you,
Father, Son and Holy Spirit,
one God, now and for ever.

Reflection by **Michael Ipgrave**

Wednesday 7 June

Psalm **119.1-32**
2 Chronicles 29.1-19
Romans 5.1-11

2 Chronicles 29.1-19

'... he opened the doors of the house of the Lord' (v.3)

The Bible is uniformly positive about Hezekiah, and the Chronicler underlines this by emphasizing that at the outset of his reign the king orders the re-opening and strengthening of the temple gates, and the cleansing and re-hallowing of the temple itself.

We can read this against the political and religious struggles of the time, as a sign of Hezekiah's determination to restore the worship of the Lord in the heart of Jerusalem following the aberrations of his father Ahaz. Archaeology shows Hezekiah's reign to be a time of renewed activity and rebuilding, matching with his reform agenda.

But it is not difficult also for us to relate to the re-opening of the temple doors at a more personal level. Having experienced during the COVID pandemic the enforced closure of churches and other places of worship, many of us came to a more profound appreciation of the place of buildings in the life of faith. I remember vividly the day when Lichfield Cathedral was re-opened for private prayer after several months' closure. It felt as if I was able almost physically to breathe in the atmosphere of prayer in that holy place; my spirit sang as I was glad to go into the house of the Lord.

For Christians and Jews alike, the worship of the temple in Jerusalem is no longer operative, so in a sense the doors that Hezekiah opened are closed again. But there still persists the sense of the holiness of those places where God chooses to dwell with his people, and we are right to value that.

COLLECT

Almighty and everlasting God,
you have given us your servants grace,
by the confession of a true faith,
to acknowledge the glory of the eternal Trinity
and in the power of the divine majesty to worship the Unity:
keep us steadfast in this faith,
that we may evermore be defended from all adversities;
through Jesus Christ your Son our Lord,
who is alive and reigns with you,
in the unity of the Holy Spirit,
one God, now and for ever.

Reflection by **Michael Ipgrave**

Psalm 147
Deuteronomy 8.2-16
1 Corinthians 10.1-17

Thursday 8 June

Day of Thanksgiving for the Institution of Holy Communion (Corpus Christi)

1 Corinthians 10.1-17

'... all ate the same spiritual food' (v.3)

Paul tells the story of the people of Israel, given food and drink by God in the wilderness, to teach the Corinthian church about the Lord's Supper. Why does he call this food and drink 'spiritual'? The manna the Israelites ate, the water they drank, were physical substances nourishing their bodies: 'spiritual' does not imply 'unreal'. The same is true of the Eucharist, which is prefigured in the wilderness: we eat real bread, drink real wine, at the Lord's table.

'Spiritual' refers rather to the world of meaning: just as the Israelites ate and drank from signs provided by the presence of the God who shared their journey, so in the Blessed Sacrament the physical elements of bread and wine are charged for us by the Spirit's work to become the body and blood of the Christ whose pilgrim people we are.

This work of the Spirit has both horizontal and vertical dimensions. Horizontally, as Paul emphasizes throughout this passage, the supper brings us into communion with one another in eating the reality of the same spiritual food. It is through sharing in one bread that we become one Body. At the same time, in the vertical dimension the Spirit gives a gift of God like the manna from above: it is the bread of heaven, the Body of the Risen Lord, on which we feed in this meal. Horizontal and vertical belong together: in receiving the Body we become the Body, and so in this wonderful sacrament we perceive, know among ourselves and show forth the fruits of redemption.

COLLECT

Lord Jesus Christ,
we thank you that in this wonderful sacrament
you have given us the memorial of your passion:
grant us so to reverence the sacred mysteries
of your body and blood
that we may know within ourselves
and show forth in our lives
the fruits of your redemption;
for you are alive and reign with the Father
in the unity of the Holy Spirit,
one God, now and for ever.

Reflection by **Michael Ipgrave**

Friday 9 June

Psalms 17, **19**
2 Chronicles 30
Romans 6.1-14

2 Chronicles 30

'... to keep the passover in the second month' (v.2)

The precise dating of religious festivals is a concern for all faith communities, including Christianity. Disputes over Easter have deeply divided the churches. In England the choice between Irish and Roman customs was resolved at the Synod of Whitby (664) essentially by settling of the method used for Paschal dating.

It is remarkable then to read Hezekiah's proposal to postpone the date of the Passover celebration from the first to the second month. It is true that Numbers 9 allows individuals to keep Passover a month later, but this is a concession to particular circumstances; what is envisaged here is a total redating of the festival as a corporate event. This is a radical step indeed, and it is not surprising that Hezekiah's plans met with opposition.

As far as we know, the postponement of this Passover festival was a one-off occasion. It is likely that Hezekiah's experiment was an attempt to draw northern Israelites into the southern Judaean celebration in Jerusalem, as is made clear by the message of his emissaries. Hezekiah was prepared to override the instructions of Torah in the interests of political expediency.

From time to time in our own society, it is proposed that the date of Easter be fixed, to be more convenient for our economic, educational and leisure life of the country. Such proposals present us again with something like the dilemma that Hezekiah faced; his choice was never repeated by the people of God.

COLLECT

Almighty and everlasting God,
you have given us your servants grace,
by the confession of a true faith,
to acknowledge the glory of the eternal Trinity
and in the power of the divine majesty to worship the Unity:
keep us steadfast in this faith,
that we may evermore be defended from all adversities;
through Jesus Christ your Son our Lord,
who is alive and reigns with you,
in the unity of the Holy Spirit,
one God, now and for ever.

Reflection by **Michael Ipgrave**

Psalms 20, 21, **23**
2 Chronicles 32.1-22
Romans 6.15-end

Saturday 10 June

2 Chronicles 32.1-22

'... and the prophet Isaiah son of Amoz' (v.20)

The attack on Jerusalem planned by Sennacherib, king of Assyria, is probably better known to us through the account in 2 Kings 18-19. Hezekiah's foes are miraculously destroyed by the angel of the Lord, as described poetically by Lord Byron:

The Assyrian came down like the wolf on the fold,
And his cohorts were gleaming in purple and gold ...

The Angel of Death spread his wings on the blast,
And breathed in the face of the foe as he passed ...
And the might of the Gentile, unsmote by the sword,
Hath melted like snow in the glance of the Lord!

The Chronicler reproduces the story of miraculous angelic deliverance, but differs noticeably from 2 Kings. In that account, the prophet Isaiah plays a major role, strengthening his king's resolve, giving a promise of salvation, and delivering an oracle against Sennacherib.

In Chronicles, by contrast, the prophetic figure is withdrawn from the limelight. There is one short reference to him 'praying with' the king and 'crying to heaven' in response to Sennacherib's arrogant demands. This account emphasizes the direct action of God, rather than the intermediary role of the prophet. Perhaps these dramatic events seemed so wonderful to the Chronicler looking back on the city's divine deliverance that he did not wish any human agency to be given prominence. Perhaps he was in general wary of giving too much profile to prophets or prophecy. In any case, for Christians, who so often read the Old Testament through a prophet-focused lens, it is salutary to see even Isaiah almost dropping out of the plot.

COLLECT

Holy God,
faithful and unchanging:
enlarge our minds with the knowledge of your truth,
and draw us more deeply into the mystery of your love,
that we may truly worship you,
Father, Son and Holy Spirit,
one God, now and for ever.

Reflection by **Michael Ipgrave**

Monday 12 June

Psalms 27, **30**
2 Chronicles 33.1-13
Romans 7.1-6

2 Chronicles 33.1-13

'Then Manasseh knew that the Lord indeed was God' (v.13)

The story of Manasseh is told twice in the Old Testament, and here the Chronicler shows him in a better light than the author of 2 Kings 21. While vv. 1-9 follow closely the account in 2 Kings, the Chronicler adds an account of Manasseh's repentance while a prisoner in Assyria and his restoration by the Lord. Manasseh's name appears in Assyrian inscriptions as a vassal king, which adds weight to this account.

However, the puzzle remains that, if Manasseh indeed repented at the end of his life, why does 2 Kings not record this? Did that writer not have all the evidence, or did he omit it because of a different theological purpose? It is a reminder perhaps that all of us make judgements about other people without necessarily knowing all the facts.

This story is also a wonderful testimony to the grace and mercy of God. God doesn't give up on us, even if sometimes he has to take us into times of distress in order that we might listen to his voice. If God can see something worth redeeming in the life of King Manasseh, who had done such evil, then there is great comfort for each one of us, that we are not beyond redemption, however far we might have fallen.

And there is also great challenge. If God could see the potential for good in Manasseh, how dare I presume to write off another person and say, 'They'll never change'.

COLLECT

O God,
the strength of all those who put their trust in you,
mercifully accept our prayers
and, because through the weakness of our mortal nature
we can do no good thing without you,
grant us the help of your grace,
that in the keeping of your commandments
we may please you both in will and deed;
through Jesus Christ your Son our Lord,
who is alive and reigns with you,
in the unity of the Holy Spirit,
one God, now and for ever.

Reflection by **Mark Ireland**

Psalms 32, **36**
2 Chronicles 34.1-18
Romans 7.7-end

Tuesday 13 June

2 Chronicles 34.1-18

'... while he was still a boy, he began to seek the God of his ancestor David' (v.3)

The Chronicler has a different order in telling this story to the author of 2 Kings, for whom the discovery of the Book of the Law was the trigger for Josiah's reformation.

Josiah would have been about 15 or 16 years old when he began to seek after God, an age at which not many teenagers are in church today. But Josiah's upbringing wouldn't have included much guidance in the ways of God either – the temple had fallen into disuse, the book of the covenant had been lost and forgotten about, and his father's brief reign had reverted to Manasseh's earlier idol worship. Yet Josiah began to seek after God – perhaps he had heard something of the conversion of his grandfather Manasseh, who died when he was six.

This passage encourages me to take very seriously the searching questions of teenagers in secondary schools, many of whom may not have had a religious upbringing, but are often searching for meaning and with a strong sense of justice, inclusion and care for creation. As I pause to pray today for teenagers I know, I pray that one day some of them might find a dusty copy of God's word hidden in the chaos of their bedroom, perhaps given by a parent or godparent many years ago.

And having found this ancient book, Lord, may they read it and be changed by it.

COLLECT

God of truth,
help us to keep your law of love
and to walk in ways of wisdom,
that we may find true life
in Jesus Christ your Son.

Reflection by **Mark Ireland**

Wednesday 14 June

Psalm **34**
2 Chronicles 34.19-end
Romans 8.1-11

2 Chronicles 34.19-end

'... he read in their hearing all the words of the book of the covenant' (v.30)

Josiah's response to hearing the words of the book of the covenant is striking. First he is moved to deep repentance and seeks guidance from the prophet Huldah. Josiah tears his clothes and humbles himself with tears. When did I last allow the Scriptures to challenge me in this deeply personal way, to the point of weeping over my own sins and those of people around me?

Second, Josiah gathers everyone together in the temple and personally reads out the book of the covenant to them. If reading the Scriptures is something I find so helpful in my own discipleship, whom could I encourage to read the Bible? Is there someone I could offer to read the Bible with once a week, to help them learn the habit?

And third, Josiah made a covenant on behalf of the people, and made them commit themselves publicly to keeping the commands in the book. In the United Kingdom and Commonwealth, we have seen the positive influence of a sovereign who has made Bible reading and prayer an integral part of her life and has commended her faith to others in many broadcast Christmas messages.

Let us pause to pray for our national leaders today, that God would raise to the fore godly women and men whose example of faith can influence our nation.

COLLECT

O God,
the strength of all those who put their trust in you,
mercifully accept our prayers
and, because through the weakness of our mortal nature
we can do no good thing without you,
grant us the help of your grace,
that in the keeping of your commandments
we may please you both in will and deed;
through Jesus Christ your Son our Lord,
who is alive and reigns with you,
in the unity of the Holy Spirit,
one God, now and for ever.

Reflection by **Mark Ireland**

Psalm **37***
2 Chronicles 35.1-19
Romans 8.12-17

Thursday 15 June

2 Chronicles 35.1-19

'Josiah contributed to the people, as passover offerings for all ...' (v.7)

A lot of churches worry these days about how to inspire and encourage people to give more generously. Rather than announcing how much it costs to pay the gas bill or meet the parish share, today's reading would encourage us to focus on two things – discipleship and example.

It is interesting how Josiah's massive gift of his own flocks and herds comes immediately after the public reading of Scripture and the renewal of the covenant, which we read about yesterday. Generous giving flows out of a growth in personal discipleship. The more our lives are shaped by solid habits of Bible reading and prayer, the more we want to give money to God's work, out of thankfulness for God's mercies, out of love for God and out of a yearning to see more of God's kingdom break into his world.

We grow as disciples through the inspiring examples of other believers. In this chapter, King Josiah leads by example, and his example inspires his officials to great generosity also. King David also knew the importance of leading by example in the area of giving, as he collected gifts for the building of the temple (1 Chronicles 29.1-9).

Jesus of course warns us of the spiritual dangers of wanting our giving to be seen by others, but he also says the same about prayer in Matthew 6. We know that prayer is often best taught by example – is that true of giving also?

COLLECT

God of truth,
help us to keep your law of love
and to walk in ways of wisdom,
that we may find true life
in Jesus Christ your Son.

Reflection by **Mark Ireland**

Friday 16 June

Psalm **31**
2 Chronicles 35.20 – 36.10
Romans 8.18-30

2 Chronicles 35.20 – 36.10

'He did not listen to the words of Neco from the mouth of God ...' (35.22)

I have discovered over my years as a parish priest that God has a slightly annoying habit – when he wants to speak a word to the congregation, he doesn't necessarily go through the vicar. Sometimes he speaks through the irritating person who sits behind a pillar at the early service, or a local councillor who never darkens the door.

Yesterday, we were at the high water-mark of Josiah's reign; he had led the people in a major reformation against idolatry, sealed with a great Passover celebration the like of which had not been seen for generations. The sad warning from today's passage is that we are never so vulnerable spiritually as when we have just achieved a great victory for God's kingdom.

Josiah's downfall and death came because he did not listen to a word from God that came from an unlikely source. In this case, from the king of Egypt, who was seeking a safe passage through his kingdom to take on the king of Babylon. In other places, God speaks through leaders outside of his chosen people – such as Jethro who gives Moses good advice (Exodus 18) and Cyrus who lets the exiles go (2 Chronicles 36.23).

Lord, please protect me from fighting unnecessary battles, and make me ready to hear you speak to me today, even through an unexpected person.

COLLECT

O God,
the strength of all those who put their trust in you,
mercifully accept our prayers
and, because through the weakness of our mortal nature
we can do no good thing without you,
grant us the help of your grace,
that in the keeping of your commandments
we may please you both in will and deed;
through Jesus Christ your Son our Lord,
who is alive and reigns with you,
in the unity of the Holy Spirit,
one God, now and for ever.

Reflection by **Mark Ireland**

Psalms 41, **42**, 43
2 Chronicles 36.11-end
Romans 8.31-end

Saturday 17 June

2 Chronicles 36.11-end

'All the days that it lay desolate it kept sabbath ...' (v.21)

Today's reading marks the conclusion of the Hebrew Bible. It is a story that ends in utter defeat and exile, but with a note of hope in the last few verses repeated in Ezra 1.

Tucked away at the end of the account of the destruction of the temple and the forced exile of the people, the Chronicler records a sabbath rest for the land. The seventy years of sabbaths allowed the land to rest after all the bloodshed, idolatry and injustice associated with the last four reigns of the kings of Judah.

The Israelites had failed to observe the rest for the land, one year in seven, required by the Law (Leviticus 25.1-7), and so now the enforced period of exile is seen as giving the land its long-overdue rest before the purposes of God resume with the return from exile.

We live today in a time when the earth has been exploited and damaged and given no rest, resulting in soil degradation and climate change. The effect of lockdowns around the world has been to give a temporary rest to creation, while nations wrestle with the difficult changes needed to secure the long-term future of the planet.

When the airports and roads fell strangely quiet, were we able to hear the cry of the earth for rest? And if so, what changes are we making in our behaviour, that we may be bringers of hope to creation?

COLLECT

God of truth,
help us to keep your law of love
and to walk in ways of wisdom,
that we may find true life
in Jesus Christ your Son.

Reflection by **Mark Ireland**

Monday 19 June

Psalm **44**
Ezra 1
Romans 9.1-18

Ezra 1

'The Lord ... has charged me to build him a house at Jerusalem in Judah' (v.2)

The ruined temple in Jerusalem was not the only temple King Cyrus sought to restore. We know from ancient inscriptions that Cyrus restored a number of such buildings in cities he had conquered. As a polytheist, this may have been a pragmatic strategy to try to keep local deities on board as his empire expanded.

Whatever his motive, God is able to use Cyrus' edict to open the door for his people to return from exile to the promised land. And yet once permission is given, the people do not come running. In fact, the exiles return very gradually, in three or four waves, over the next century. And the building project initiated by Cyrus is still unfinished in the time of the prophet Haggai, who has to challenge the people to resume work on the temple.

It seems that life in Babylon was not so bad after all. Many of the exiles managed quite well, and some even gained positions of influence in government service, like Daniel. The exile was also a time of spiritual growth and renewal, when people learned they could sing the Lord's song in a strange land, and when the writing-down of their story became an important part of worship.

Is there a calamity you are dreading today? Perhaps in the future, you may be able to look back and see how God was at work and brought good out of it.

COLLECT

Lord, you have taught us
that all our doings without love are nothing worth:
send your Holy Spirit
and pour into our hearts that most excellent gift of love,
the true bond of peace and of all virtues,
without which whoever lives is counted dead before you.
Grant this for your only Son Jesus Christ's sake,
who is alive and reigns with you,
in the unity of the Holy Spirit,
one God, now and for ever.

Reflection by **Mark Ireland**

Psalms **48**, 52
Ezra 3
Romans 9.19-end

Tuesday 20 June

Ezra 3

'... the people responded with a great shout when they praised the Lord' (v.11)

Building sites are usually noisy places, but this one must have been especially so, with the singing, the sound of trumpets and cymbals, and shouts of joy and cries of weeping. It's not clear from the text whether the cries of weeping from the older members was the release of pent-up grief at their earlier loss or a sense of disappointment at how the new structure compared with their memories of the previous temple.

Why was it all so noisy? The clue is to be found in verse 3, 'Despite their fear of the peoples around them...' (NIV). Praise and worship is a great antidote to fear, which is why it was particularly hard not to be able to sing together during the Covid pandemic. Noisy and lively worship gave the returning exiles courage to proceed with rebuilding the temple, despite the menacing opposition of the peoples around them. The first thing they built was the altar, so that sacrificial worship could resume while the building work continued.

When I am feeling afraid, but know I need to take a stand on some matter, I find singing some full-throated praise shifts the focus of my thoughts from my weakness to God's all-sufficient power and love. Sadly I'm rarely in tune, but God doesn't seem to mind!

Next time you are in need of courage to do the right thing, might giving voice to some full-throated praise help you too?

Faithful Creator,
whose mercy never fails:
deepen our faithfulness to you
and to your living Word,
Jesus Christ our Lord.

COLLECT

Reflection by **Mark Ireland**

Wednesday 21 June

Psalm **119.57-80**
Ezra 4.1-5
Romans 10.1-10

Ezra 4.1-5

'Let us help you' (v.2, NIV)

I have learnt over many years in parish life that not every offer of help is what it appears. Sometimes it is a coded criticism of how I'm doing things; sometimes there is a subtle bid for power; sometimes the 'helper' wants to change the project out of all recognition; sometimes the person offering simply doesn't have the gifts needed for the task. And yet turning down an offer of help can sow seeds of disappointment and resentment that may turn a potential friend into a frustrating foe.

Which of these dynamics is present in this passage? Those who were described neutrally as 'the neighbouring peoples' in 3.3 are now referred to as 'the adversaries' (4.1). The returning exiles clearly struggled with people of other races who were imported into the land under Babylonian rule, even though the incomers had done their best to worship the God of Israel. But the subsequent behaviour of those whose offer of help was rejected (vv.4-5) raises a question about their initial sincerity.

Offers of help from those outside the community of faith call for prayerful discernment today, as they did in the days of Ezra. When might it be right to accept someone's offer (having done appropriate checks) and perhaps find we are helping them on their journey to faith? And when might the right course be to turn down their offer, even though we risk pushing them further away?

COLLECT

Lord, you have taught us
that all our doings without love are nothing worth:
send your Holy Spirit
and pour into our hearts that most excellent gift of love,
the true bond of peace and of all virtues,
without which whoever lives is counted dead before you.
Grant this for your only Son Jesus Christ's sake,
who is alive and reigns with you,
in the unity of the Holy Spirit,
one God, now and for ever.

 Reflection by **Mark Ireland**

Psalms 56, **57** (63*)
Ezra 4.7-end
Romans 10.11-end

Thursday 22 June

Ezra 4.7-end

'... and by force and power made them cease' (v.23)

There is quite a time jump here, to further opposition that occurred a century after Cyrus, long after the temple was finally completed in the time of the prophets Haggai and Zechariah. Here, we have opposition to the rebuilding of the walls of the city in the time of Nehemiah, in the twentieth year of King Artaxerxes (Nehemiah 2.1).

The link seems to be the theme of opposition to God's work. The full story, and the eventual completion of the walls, is told vividly in the book of Nehemiah. Here, the focus is on the enforced stopping of the work of rebuilding the walls, after the matter had been referred up to King Artaxerxes by the local officials on the ground. The author is keen for readers to learn the lesson from both stories that human force cannot stop the work of God from triumphing.

The switch from temple to city walls is not such a big leap as it may appear to the modern reader. The holiness of the temple extended to make the whole city holy, as it is described in Nehemiah 11.1. In the Songs of Zion in the Psalter, temple and capital city are described as a single sacred complex – see for example Psalm 48. And so rebuilding the walls makes the whole city holy.

In what ways does your church extend its influence beyond its walls to bless your local community and make it holy?

COLLECT

Faithful Creator,
whose mercy never fails:
deepen our faithfulness to you
and to your living Word,
Jesus Christ our Lord.

Reflection by **Mark Ireland**

Friday 23 June

Psalms **51**, 54
Ezra 5
Romans 11.1-12

Ezra 5

'... have a search made in the royal archives' (v.17)

We do not value the gift of administration and good record-keeping as we should. I remember someone commenting on reading a tribute paid to a retiring bishop: 'If it says he was a good administrator, you know they were struggling for something else to say.' Yet this part of Ezra shows the importance and value of written reports and record-keeping.

Inspired by Haggai and Zechariah, work has restarted on rebuilding the temple, after a gap of twenty years. Tattenai, the governor, is told they were given permission by Cyrus, and requests the new king Darius to check the records of his predecessor Cyrus to see if this story stacks up. The next chapter tells how a diligent search of the archives reveals a written decree and so work on the temple is allowed to continue, with the royal seal of approval and at public expense. The Israelites had cause to be thankful for Persian efficiency.

Interestingly, St Paul lists 'administration' as one of the gifts of the Holy Spirit, alongside healing, helping and speaking in tongues (1 Corinthians 12.28, ESV). I hate filing papers or reports as much as the next person, and so today's reading is a challenge to me to see administration and good record-keeping as a gift from God that can be a blessing to others – not least my successors.

COLLECT

Lord, you have taught us
that all our doings without love are nothing worth:
send your Holy Spirit
and pour into our hearts that most excellent gift of love,
the true bond of peace and of all virtues,
without which whoever lives is counted dead before you.
Grant this for your only Son Jesus Christ's sake,
who is alive and reigns with you,
in the unity of the Holy Spirit,
one God, now and for ever.

Reflection by **Mark Ireland**

Psalms 50, 149
Ecclesiasticus 48.1-10
or Malachi 3.1-6
Luke 3.1-17

Saturday 24 June
Birth of John the Baptist

Malachi 3.1-6

'See, I am sending my messenger to prepare the way' (v.1)

Nothing is known about the person of Malachi. His name simply means 'my messenger', and may be a reference to this verse. Yet his message provides a vital link from the Old Testament to the New. Jesus quotes this verse and applies it to the person of John the Baptist in Matthew 11.10. Jesus also identifies John with the figure of Elijah, who in Malachi 4.5 is promised to come 'before the great and terrible day of the Lord comes' (Matthew 11.14).

John the Baptist is an uncomfortable figure, like Malachi's messenger who is described as a refiner's fire. Fuller's soap may refer to a bleach used by launderers or to lye used in the second stage of the smelting process to separate the gold or silver from the dross. Malachi cares passionately about corruption in the priesthood, which is preventing the offering of right sacrifices, and so the role of the messenger is to purify the Levites until they are able to present offerings to the Lord in righteousness.

Both the messenger and John the Baptist point us to the uncomfortable truth that the promised Day of the Lord is a day of judgement as well as a day of salvation. However, both point us also to the comforting knowledge that the One who will judge is precisely the One who has already suffered in our place. He who is judge is also saviour.

COLLECT

Almighty God,
by whose providence your servant John the Baptist
was wonderfully born,
and sent to prepare the way of your Son our Saviour
by the preaching of repentance:
lead us to repent according to his preaching
and, after his example,
constantly to speak the truth, boldly to rebuke vice,
and patiently to suffer for the truth's sake;
through Jesus Christ your Son our Lord,
who is alive and reigns with you,
in the unity of the Holy Spirit,
one God, now and for ever.

Reflection by **Mark Ireland**

Monday 26 June

Psalm **71**
Ezra 7
Romans 11.25-end

Ezra 7

'... scribe of the law of the God of heaven' (v.12)

From verse 12 onwards, this chapter of Ezra is not in Hebrew but in Aramaic. That would indeed have been the language of a letter like that issued to Ezra. Whether or not the text is an accurate transcript of an official document, it shows Ezra's place in the Persian bureaucratic world, as one invested with significant juridical and religious authority.

Ezra is described as both 'priest' and 'scribe'. The former is a specifically Hebrew term, referring to his role in restoring worship in Jerusalem. By contrast, 'scribe of the law of the God of heaven' is a more universal term, designating one who is learned and authorized in religious matters generally. The Persian state recognized the Jerusalem temple worship as a particular local cult, and gave Ezra authorization to reform the judicial system so as to support that cult.

In this period after the exile, the people of Israel had to live out their particular faith in their One God among peoples who worshipped multitudes of gods. They did so with markedly ambivalent attitudes towards the Persian kings. Here, Artaxerxes appears as a benefactor and guardian of the Jews, but by the end of Ezra's long prayer in Nehemiah 9 the monarchs are described as oppressors enslaving God's people in their own land. In an age where we are constantly having to rethink our own position in relation to secular authority, and where we can sometimes feel like exiles in our own country, the changing and nimble story of Ezra, priest and scribe, can teach us much wisdom.

COLLECT

Almighty God,
you have broken the tyranny of sin
and have sent the Spirit of your Son into our hearts
whereby we call you Father:
give us grace to dedicate our freedom to your service,
that we and all creation may be brought
to the glorious liberty of the children of God;
through Jesus Christ your Son our Lord,
who is alive and reigns with you,
in the unity of the Holy Spirit,
one God, now and for ever.

Reflection by **Michael Ipgrave**

Psalm **73**
Ezra 8.15-end
Romans 12.1-8

Tuesday 27 June

Ezra 8.15-end

'I proclaimed a fast ... at the river Ahava' (v.21)

It might seem imprudent and illogical for Ezra to call for a fast as he and his company are about to set out on a long, arduous and dangerous journey. Surely, one might think, this should be the time to ensure that the travellers are all well replenished; an army proverbially cannot march on an empty stomach.

But Ezra's spiritual logic reaches deeper than matters of dietary well-being. The point of fasting is to place him and his companions in a position symbolically close to death, a point of extreme self-abasement that will in turn invoke the saving power of God, on whom alone the travellers rely. In this sense, the decision to fast goes hand in hand with Ezra's refusal to seek an armed escort from the king: the logic of mortification through fasting implies an exclusive trust in divine protection.

Fasting remains an important spiritual practice in contemporary Christianity and in many other religions. It is even making something of a comeback in the contemporary Western Church. However, it is often justified by essentially didactic arguments: that it reminds us of the reality of global poverty; or that it helps us to establish control of our lives; or even that it is good for our health. In other cultures and other faiths, fasting has never lost its deep-seated meaning as a casting of ourselves, in face of challenge and danger, onto divine mercy and protection. Maybe we cannot rationalize the argument for Ezra's fast, but we can experience the spiritual force of its appeal to God.

COLLECT

God our saviour,
look on this wounded world
in pity and in power;
hold us fast to your promises of peace
won for us by your Son,
our Saviour Jesus Christ.

Reflection by **Michael Ipgrave**

Wednesday 28 June

Psalm **77**
Ezra 9
Romans 12.9-end

Ezra 9

'... the holy seed has mixed itself with the peoples of the lands' (v.2)

Most of us will feel distinctly uncomfortable reading Ezra's reaction to the intermarriage of Jews and foreigners. That feeling will grow sharper as the next chapter describes the harsh measures that Ezra enacts. The exclusivism, xenophobia and sexism in these passages offend our instincts of inclusion and equality. It is important to acknowledge these feelings as we read the texts.

It is also true that Ezra's is not the only type of response to 'foreign marriages' in the Old Testament. The book of Ruth, for example, famously presents a very different attitude in its story of Ruth, a Moabite (one of the nations on Ezra's 'prohibited' list), acclaimed as ancestor of both David and Jesus. The question of intermarriage is one on which the biblical authors take a variety of views, and Ezra's position is one end of a spectrum.

Ezra's particular concern is not with racial purity as such, but with preserving the integrity of worship; it is the danger of Israelites being led into worship of other gods that lies at the heart of his warnings. The catalogue of peoples whom Ezra lists does not in fact describe the demography of the Judaean lands of his time. Rather, it is based largely on the ancient list of foreign nations against whom Israel was enjoined to fight. So there is something formulaic about his protest here. There is also an understandable anxiety about the survival of the small community of returned exiles. Perhaps we can understand that, however shocking we find his language and actions.

COLLECT

Almighty God,
you have broken the tyranny of sin
and have sent the Spirit of your Son into our hearts
whereby we call you Father:
give us grace to dedicate our freedom to your service,
that we and all creation may be brought
to the glorious liberty of the children of God;
through Jesus Christ your Son our Lord,
who is alive and reigns with you,
in the unity of the Holy Spirit,
one God, now and for ever.

Reflection by **Michael Ipgrave**

Psalms 71, 113
Isaiah 49.1-6
Acts 11.1-18

Thursday 29 June

Peter the Apostle

Isaiah 49.1-6

'... too light a thing' (v.6)

Our text announces the extension of the mission of God's chosen servant, from Israel alone to all nations. To the onerous task of restoring one chosen people, ironically described as 'too light a task', is added the further burden of gentile enlightenment. That may strike us as a natural development, but in first Jewish and then Christian history, the task of holding together these two dimensions has proved complex and taxing, as the two apostles commemorated today remind us.

There is in the New Testament a tension between Peter and Paul, which sometimes breaks out into open conflict. Paul describes one such incident at Antioch, where it was Jewish-gentile relations that set the apostles against one another: 'I opposed him (Peter) to his face'. Paul has a formula that should have avoided trouble: 'I had been entrusted with the gospel for the uncircumcised, just as Peter ... for the circumcised' (Galatians 2.7).

The reality was not so neat as this simple demarcation might suggest. Peter witnessed to gentiles more than once, and Paul continued to have a passionate concern for his fellow Israelites. What the prophecy described as 'too light a task' has remained an unresolved challenge throughout the ages – within the Church the contested relation between gentile and Jewish believers in Jesus, and beyond that the still deeper and bitter division between Christians and Jews. Yet for all their disagreements, Peter and Paul both met martyrs' deaths at the hand of pagan authorities. May their differing yet united witness point the way to reconciliation of the people of God.

COLLECT

Almighty God,
who inspired your apostle Saint Peter
to confess Jesus as Christ and Son of the living God:
build up your Church upon this rock,
that in unity and peace it may proclaim one truth
and follow one Lord, your Son our Saviour Christ,
who is alive and reigns with you,
in the unity of the Holy Spirit,
one God, now and for ever.

Reflection by **Michael Ipgrave**

Friday 30 June

Psalm **55**
Nehemiah 1
Romans 13.8-end

Nehemiah 1

'... this man' (v.11)

In his prayer for success in the grand project he is formulating to restore Jerusalem, Nehemiah abruptly refers to his royal master Artaxerxes as 'this man'. The language he uses when praying is brusque, even rude, and it is in striking contrast to the respectfully honorific way in which Nehemiah addresses the king in person.

To some extent, we all think of people, or we talk about them to our intimate acquaintances, in ways that are different from those in which we speak of them in public or to their face. The tension is particularly acute for those who have to deal on a daily basis with persons of exalted degree, as Nehemiah clearly has to do in his office of royal cupbearer. Is he then guilty of a kind of hypocrisy, saying one thing to the king's face and another behind his back?

Rather than that, surely Nehemiah's abruptly concise expression 'this man' demonstrates the honesty and transparency with which he engages in prayer. In the presence of God, even the most exalted king is just another human being, one who might help either to fulfil or to impede the divine purpose. Praying in a stressful situation, or in a power imbalance, or in a moment of crisis, we hold our fellow men and women before God and we realize that in the divine presence there is always a radical equality of creatures. That realization can give us confidence and can strengthen our faith, as it did Nehemiah's.

COLLECT

Almighty God,
you have broken the tyranny of sin
and have sent the Spirit of your Son into our hearts
whereby we call you Father:
give us grace to dedicate our freedom to your service,
that we and all creation may be brought
to the glorious liberty of the children of God;
through Jesus Christ your Son our Lord,
who is alive and reigns with you,
in the unity of the Holy Spirit,
one God, now and for ever.

Reflection by **Michael Ipgrave**

Psalms **76**, 79
Nehemiah 2
Romans 14.1-12

Saturday 1 July

Nehemiah 2

'... the city of my ancestors' graves' (v.5)

My rabbi friend and I were looking out towards the Mount of Olives, its slopes covered by cemeteries glistening in the bright Jerusalem sunlight. 'Over there are my parents' graves', he said, 'and next to them is reserved the place for my own grave'. I felt privileged to be part of such a deeply personal conversation.

As Nehemiah performs his official duties, the mask of respectful cheerfulness slips, and he reveals to the king his deep attachment to 'the city of my ancestors' graves'. This profoundly personal exchange proves a turning point in the narrative, as Nehemiah sets out with royal blessing on his mission to rebuild Jerusalem, and another chapter unfolds in the long story of Jewish attachment to the city.

There is a message here for us too. Human beings from the beginning have treated with special care the places where their ancestors are buried. For many of us, a plot in a churchyard or garden of remembrance is a place of special significance where our loved ones are laid to rest. These are places of remembrance, but the Mount of Olives points to a different dimension too. In traditional Jewish belief, this is the place where resurrection will begin when the Messiah comes. In the same way, our churchyards point not only to memory of the past but also to expectation for the future. As the early Moravian communities said, they are 'God's acre', sown with the bodies of the faithful awaiting the harvest of resurrection. May the place of our ancestors' graves be a place of hope for us.

COLLECT

God our saviour,
look on this wounded world
in pity and in power;
hold us fast to your promises of peace
won for us by your Son,
our Saviour Jesus Christ.

Reflection by **Michael Ipgrave**

Monday 3 July
Thomas the Apostle

Psalms 92, 146
2 Samuel 15.17-21
or Ecclesiasticus 2
John 11.1-16

2 Samuel 15.17-21

'... there also your servant will be' (v.21)

Often remembered as 'the doubter', this text points to a different side of Thomas, linking him to one who is an embodiment of unflagging loyalty. As King David dejectedly sets out into exile in face of a rebellion, he encounters Ittai the Gittite, and expects him too to abandon him; after all, Ittai is a foreigner, with no cause to stay in face of imminent danger.

Ittai's commitment, though, is not to a nation, a system or an idea; it is to a person. He will not turn aside from the one he serves to save himself. Just so, when the disciples are anxious about the fate awaiting their Lord, it is Thomas who rallies them with a heartfelt expression of loyalty: 'Let us also go, that we may die with him' (John 11.16).

Neither Ittai nor Thomas display dramatically heroic behaviour; but both know that, in the moment of testing, they cannot abandon the one they serve. In the 1930s, the Scottish teacher Jane Haining was assigned by her church to teach at a Jewish girls' school in Budapest. When war broke out, she was asked by the Church of Scotland to return home for her safety. Knowing that her place was with the girls she served, Jane stayed put, and was deported with them to Auschwitz-Birkenau, where she died in 1944. Counted as 'Righteous among the Nations', Jane in her own time witnessed to the same constancy that is central to discipleship throughout the ages. Pray that we may do the same in our own times of testing.

COLLECT

Almighty and eternal God,
who, for the firmer foundation of our faith,
allowed your holy apostle Thomas
to doubt the resurrection of your Son
till word and sight convinced him:
grant to us, who have not seen, that we also may believe
and so confess Christ as our Lord and our God;
who is alive and reigns with you,
in the unity of the Holy Spirit,
one God, now and for ever.

Reflection by **Michael Ipgrave**

Psalms 87, **89.1-18**
Nehemiah 5
Romans 15.1-13

Tuesday 4 July

Nehemiah 5

'Remember for my good ... all that I have done' (v.19)

Nehemiah's assertions, here and elsewhere, of the good he has done can rather grate on us. In fact, this problem has long been recognized: Jewish commentators censured him for his pride, and for his disparagement of others. Despite his popularity as a role model for many fervent Christians, Nehemiah does not present as a winsome personality.

But we should remember the context of Nehemiah's remarks, which are set within a 'memoir' recording his actions. The memoir is a recognized genre of literature in the Ancient Near East, written not for human readers, but to set an individual's record straight before his God. In that context, Nehemiah's repeated assertions of righteous dealing are not so much boasting as a defence of his integrity in the only arena that matters, that of divine judgement.

The theme of vindication of righteousness is familiar from the psalms. I can often feel uncomfortable as I read some of the psalmist's assertions of innocence, because I know full well that my own hands are not clean; my heart is not pure; if I am tried and tested, I am a mess. One way Christians deal with this is to recognize that in psalmody and prayer we are joining ourselves with Christ our sinless head: it is his righteousness that we plead, not our own. Nevertheless, the duty of self-examination remains for us, as does the striving for integrity before our God. If, as is likely, we cannot in good conscience make Nehemiah's prayer our own, at least we ought to know why, and strive to do better.

COLLECT

O God, the protector of all who trust in you,
without whom nothing is strong, nothing is holy:
increase and multiply upon us your mercy;
that with you as our ruler and guide
we may so pass through things temporal
that we lose not our hold on things eternal;
grant this, heavenly Father,
for our Lord Jesus Christ's sake,
who is alive and reigns with you,
in the unity of the Holy Spirit,
one God, now and for ever.

Reflection by **Michael Ipgrave**

Wednesday 5 July

Psalm **119.105-128**
Nehemiah 6.1 – 7.4
Romans 15.14-21

Nehemiah 6.1 – 7.4

'... they all wanted to frighten us' (6.9)

There is a growing air of menace and intimidation in this passage, as Nehemiah's opponents resort to exaggeration, rumour and lies to present his actions in the worst possible light. Their intention is to stir up opposition to him, to create conditions in which he will not be able to bring his project to completion; but we can sense that they are also seeking internally to undermine his confidence, to cause him to doubt or abandon his sense of his own credibility.

However, his enemies have underestimated their man. Whatever weaknesses Nehemiah may have, self-doubt is not one of them; he first exposes the conspiracy theories being woven around him and then stakes out his own course with renewed confidence. The gift he particularly takes into his own hands here is that of courage – so often associated in the Hebrew Scriptures with a firm adherence to the cause of God.

In our age of social media, the ability to generate conspiracy theories, to blacken the reputation of individuals, has increased immeasurably compared to the days of Sanballat and Geshem. Sometimes people do this out of malice, sometimes out of ignorance, sometimes because of the shrill intensity of their own narrowly held agendas. Whatever the motive, a social media pile-on can be an intimidating experience, and the mere threat of it can deter people from pursuing a course that they know to be right. At such times, we should pray for Nehemiah's courageous integrity, for all in public life as for ourselves.

COLLECT

O God, the protector of all who trust in you,
without whom nothing is strong, nothing is holy:
increase and multiply upon us your mercy;
that with you as our ruler and guide
we may so pass through things temporal
that we lose not our hold on things eternal;
grant this, heavenly Father,
for our Lord Jesus Christ's sake,
who is alive and reigns with you,
in the unity of the Holy Spirit,
one God, now and for ever.

Reflection by **Michael Ipgrave**

Psalms 90, **92**
Nehemiah 7.73*b* – end of 8
Romans 15.22-end

Thursday 6 July

Nehemiah 7.73*b* – end of 8

'Ezra the priest and scribe' (8.9)

The focus in this passage is very much on Ezra (the passing mention of Nehemiah is probably a later addition). He is here described as fulfilling two of the great roles of Jewish religious leadership: he is both priest and scribe.

As scribe, Ezra's role, with the assistance of the Levites, is to read and explain the law of Moses to the people. This is an early reference in the Bible to public recitation of the Torah. The people's initial reaction is understandable: they weep as they realize how far short they have fallen from the standards laid before them for their life.

However, as priest, as leader of the assembly, Ezra cannot leave his people plunged in sorrow. He reminds them that they are celebrating a festival to their God, and he encourages them to feast and exult. There is a note of joy in this gathering that can take us by surprise, given the overall solemnity of the setting.

The roles of scribe and priest, of teacher of the Scriptures and convenor of the assembly respectively, are complementary in the life of the people of God. They are close to one another, and at different times have been merged into one ideal; yet there is perhaps a difference in emphasis. The close knowledge of Scripture that the scribe brings confronts us with the reality of our fallen situation in the presence of our holy God. But the assurance of divine forgiveness that the priest celebrates fills us with joy and hope. We need both in the life of the Church today.

COLLECT

Gracious Father,
by the obedience of Jesus
you brought salvation to our wayward world:
draw us into harmony with your will,
that we may find all things restored in him,
our Saviour Jesus Christ.

Reflection by **Michael Ipgrave**

Friday 7 July

Psalms **88** (95)
Nehemiah 9.1-23
Romans 16.1-16

Nehemiah 9.1-23

'You gave your good spirit' (v.20)

Ezra's long prayer is recited only on behalf of those of Israelite descent, who at this point separate themselves from 'all foreigners', because their history is different from that of others. The prayer recalls the formative story of Israel's deliverance, the giving of the law, the wandering in the wilderness, the repeated impulses to return to slavery. The constant and unchanging theme is that of God's loving guidance for his people.

There is necessarily repetition in all this – for example, the pillars of cloud by day and fire by night appear both before and after the encounter with God at Sinai. What cannot be repeated, though, is the heart of that encounter: the giving of the law through Moses. So, in order to keep that gift fresh for the people after Sinai, Ezra needs some extended divine provision. He speaks of this as God's 'good spirit'. Later in the prayer, we learn that the same spirit speaks warning through the prophets.

Christians sometimes speak as if the gift of the spirit in the Old Testament is only an occasional and extraordinary occurrence, dispensed through particular individuals for limited periods of time. There are examples of such phenomena, but this prayer speaks of a continuing gift of guidance and encouragement from God to his people. The God who in Jesus Christ walks with his people and anoints them with the blessings of the Holy Spirit is the same God who travelled with Israel through the years of wilderness and restoration and shared with them the gift of his good spirit.

COLLECT

O God, the protector of all who trust in you,
without whom nothing is strong, nothing is holy:
increase and multiply upon us your mercy;
that with you as our ruler and guide
we may so pass through things temporal
that we lose not our hold on things eternal;
grant this, heavenly Father,
for our Lord Jesus Christ's sake,
who is alive and reigns with you,
in the unity of the Holy Spirit,
one God, now and for ever.

Reflection by **Michael Ipgrave**

Psalms 96, **97**, 100
Nehemiah 9.24-end
Romans 16.17-end

Saturday 8 July

Nehemiah 9.24-end

'... and we are in great distress' (v.37)

Ezra's long prayer has been an emotional roller-coaster, leading his people on a journey that acknowledges their rebelliousness and failings, yet which is also shot through with the conviction of divine presence, guidance and mercy. Now, though, he ends on a bleak and seemingly hopeless note: 'we are in great distress'. Indeed, in one sense the position of the Israelites at the end of the prayer is worse than at the beginning: then they were slaves in a foreign land, but now they are effectively enslaved in their own country, their lives and livelihoods under the exacting dominion of the Persian kings.

So the prayer finishes with a stark statement of lament. Whether or not a hope for political transformation may be implicit in the reference to the kings who hold God's people in thrall, there is no explicit petition for deliverance. During the COVID pandemic and its aftermath, we learned again the twofold importance of lament as a form of honest and heartfelt prayer.

On one hand, lament is a realistic expression of who and where we are, a critical self-reflection on our own situation and the failings that have brought us to this point. To make an unvarnished and searing self-appraisal in the presence of God is indeed to be in an authentic place of prayer.

On the other hand, precisely by not making any request of God, lament safeguards a space of freedom in which the divine action, whatever that may be, can take place. As Ezra knew, lament opens a way for us to receive God's undisclosed future afresh.

COLLECT

Gracious Father,
by the obedience of Jesus
you brought salvation to our wayward world:
draw us into harmony with your will,
that we may find all things restored in him,
our Saviour Jesus Christ.

Reflection by **Michael Ipgrave**

Monday 10 July

Psalms **98**, 99, 101
Nehemiah 12.27-47
2 Corinthians 1.1-14

Nehemiah 12.27-47

'The joy of Jerusalem was heard far away' (v.43)

At last, the day has come. The wall is complete, the enemies and scoffers are silent – at least for the moment – and it is time to celebrate. As with everything that Nehemiah does, the day is planned in minute detail, carefully researched and designed.

The day resonates with echoes of the heroic traditions of Israel's past: singers with cymbals, harps and lyres, as in the days of David and Solomon; it ensures the continuing loyalty of significant leaders and donors, who head up processions and are mentioned by name; it gives everyone a chance to see the completed works, as they 'beat the bounds' of the restored walls; and the great crowds of ordinary people get a chance to be part of something colourful, joyful, full of movement, music and laughter. And the goal and heart of the celebration is to give thanks in the house of God.

This feels like an insight into the workings of Nehemiah's mind and soul. He longs for the restoration of Israel, with a deep and obsessive nostalgia, but he is no dreamer: what he longs for, he works for. And although it is his dream, it is not about himself, but about the whole people, because that is what restoration means: not just bricks but the nation. Just for now, it has all paid off: the attention to detail, the painstaking building up of trust, learning names and families, identifying leaders. Just for now, Nehemiah can relax.

COLLECT

Almighty and everlasting God,
by whose Spirit the whole body of the Church
    is governed and sanctified:
hear our prayer which we offer for all your faithful people,
that in their vocation and ministry
they may serve you in holiness and truth
to the glory of your name;
through our Lord and Saviour Jesus Christ,
who is alive and reigns with you,
in the unity of the Holy Spirit,
one God, now and for ever.

Reflection by **Jane Williams**

Psalm **106*** (*or* 103)
Nehemiah 13.1-14
2 Corinthians 1.15 – 2.4

Tuesday 11 July

Nehemiah 13.1-14

'Why is the house of God forsaken?' (v.11)

Nehemiah is getting an insight into how difficult it is to radically transform hearts and minds. After a day of glorious, joyful celebration of the completion of the rebuilding of Jerusalem, Nehemiah thinks it is safe to pay an important courtesy call to Babylon and to King Artaxerxes, whose patronage and permission-giving have been vital to the whole enterprise. He has appointed good leaders, and the people seem to be starting to take responsibility for their own religious revival, as they hear the book of Moses and put into practice the separation of the people of Israel from the foreigners.

But the minute Nehemiah's back is turned, two most fundamental characteristics reassert themselves: the desire to keep in with the powerful, and the desire to hang onto one's own possessions.

Eliashib tries to ingratiate himself with Tobiah by giving him the best room in the house of God. Tobiah has been a constant thorn in the flesh to Nehemiah and his plans, working against him, mocking him, threatening him. Everything that has been achieved has been in the teeth of Tobiah, but now he expects to benefit; he has mocked Nehemiah and Nehemiah's God, but now expects the best room in the house.

Meanwhile, the people have conveniently 'forgotten' that they promised to maintain the Levites and the singers, so that they could continue to praise in God's house.

Nehemiah comes back to find the House of God double scorned: by the presence of Tobiah and the absence of praise.

COLLECT

Almighty God,
send down upon your Church
the riches of your Spirit,
and kindle in all who minister the gospel
your countless gifts of grace;
through Jesus Christ our Lord.

Reflection by **Jane Williams**

Wednesday 12 July

Psalms 110, **111**, 112
Nehemiah 13.15-end
2 Corinthians 2.5-end

Nehemiah 13.15-end

'Remember this also in my favour, O my God, and spare me' (v.22)

It is perhaps unsurprising that the people should have forgotten so much about their old ways of life: they would never have known a time before exile and defeat; unlike Nehemiah, many of them would not have pored over the old days of glory, the old ways of faith. In today's reading, Nehemiah is at work with his usual ferocious attention to every detail, on two areas that he saw as vital to the restoration of Israel as the people of God. With one we can perhaps identify, but the other is harder.

First of all, Nehemiah is determined to restore the Sabbath. The habit of commerce has crept into every day of the week, for these people, as for us. Typically, Nehemiah does not attempt a theological or psychological account of the importance of Sabbath: he just enforces it. Next, Nehemiah turns his attention to what he sees as the undermining effects of intermarriage and families who have different traditions of language and faith.

All through the book, we have seen Nehemiah's strengths, which have led to such success. But here we perhaps see the weakness of his methods. Could there have been a better way to draw these mixed families into the people of God?

But the ending of the book is disarming. 'Remember me, O my God, for good', he begs. He has tried to honour God in all things, which is not necessarily the mainspring of all of our own actions.

COLLECT

Almighty and everlasting God,
by whose Spirit the whole body of the Church
is governed and sanctified:
hear our prayer which we offer for all your faithful people,
that in their vocation and ministry
they may serve you in holiness and truth
to the glory of your name;
through our Lord and Saviour Jesus Christ,
who is alive and reigns with you,
in the unity of the Holy Spirit,
one God, now and for ever.

Reflection by **Jane Williams**

Psalms 113, **115**
Esther 1
2 Corinthians 3

Thursday 13 July

Esther 1

'... he sent letters to all the royal provinces ... declaring that every man should be master in his own house' (v.22)

God does not make an open appearance in the Book of Esther, but that does not mean that God is absent or inactive. It is the art of the storyteller to shape our theological imaginations, and the book does that with great subtlety. God works, as in the Wisdom literature, through virtuous, wise, courageous and loving individuals, changing the world slowly but certainly, and drawing us to admire discerningly, and see the values that abide.

In the first chapter, we are invited into the luxurious palace of the king; but we cannot help noticing that the proud owner of all this wealth is an idiot, easily manipulated by his officials. We are not told what Queen Vashti has done to annoy the officials, but we see their vicious revenge. When the Queen refuses to come and entertain the King's guests, they make sure that the King sees his personal hurt as a damage to the whole kingdom, and never let him see Vashti again.

How will our heroes fare in such corrupt company? All around them are superficial, venial and faithless people, interested only in wealth and power. As the Queen refuses to humour her husband, and as the King dismisses her in a fit of pique, the storyteller is introducing us to the sad, empty world of those who do not follow God's wisdom.

Soon, we will meet Esther and Mordecai, exiled and bereaved, yet rich in love and courage. We are being prepared to value what they – and God – do.

COLLECT

Almighty God,
send down upon your Church
the riches of your Spirit,
and kindle in all who minister the gospel
your countless gifts of grace;
through Jesus Christ our Lord.

Reflection by **Jane Williams**

Friday 14 July

Psalm **139**
Esther 2
2 Corinthians 4

Esther 2

'Mordecai adopted her as his own daughter' (v.7)

The storyteller continues to show the king as a weak man, surrounded by unscrupulous courtiers. As soon as the king begins to regret what he has done to Vashti, the courtiers find a distraction, and one that will create potential money-making schemes for them and their cronies. Officials are to be sent all over the kingdom to pick up pretty women, all of whom are to be brought to the palace, provided with cosmetics, gifts, board and lodging, and paraded in front of the king so that Vashti never enters his head again.

Among the women is Esther, the adopted daughter of Mordecai, a Jewish exile. As in any good story, Esther is not only beautiful but also universally loved. She makes friends in all the right places, and captivates the king. What's more, with the help of Mordecai, she foils an assassination attempt against the king.

The themes of human wisdom, human ingenuity in seizing chances offered, are beginning to come through. Where Vashti alienated the dangerous men around her, Esther placates them; when Mordecai overhears the remarkably naïve plotters chatting openly about their plans, he makes sure that it is Esther who tells the king.

The storyteller does not seem to feel any discomfort about Esther's virtual prostitution, or Mordecai's willingness to send the plotters to death for his own advantage. This is, of course, just a story. The plot devices should not distract us from the unseen hand of God, moving to save God's people.

COLLECT

Almighty and everlasting God,
by whose Spirit the whole body of the Church
is governed and sanctified:
hear our prayer which we offer for all your faithful people,
that in their vocation and ministry
they may serve you in holiness and truth
to the glory of your name;
through our Lord and Saviour Jesus Christ,
who is alive and reigns with you,
in the unity of the Holy Spirit,
one God, now and for ever.

Reflection by **Jane Williams**

Psalms 120, **121**, 122
Esther 3
2 Corinthians 5

Saturday 15 July

Esther 3

'Mordecai did not bow down and do obeisance' (v.2)

Yet again, the king shows himself naïve and incompetent, caught up in a power struggle that brings him no advantage. And yet again, his officials persuade him that this is not a personal issue but a national one. Just as with the dismissal of Vashti, when the king was told he was saving the reputation of every man in his kingdom, so now, Haman's personal grudge against Mordecai is portrayed as dealing with a threat to the whole nation.

Although Haman focuses on the fact that Mordecai is a Jew, it is not clear that Mordecai is actually being persecuted for this faith. He refuses to bow to Haman, but whereas in Daniel, what brings Daniel's death sentence is his persistence in praying to God, there are no obvious religious overtones to Mordecai's refusal to show honour to Haman. It is almost as if Mordecai is deliberately provoking Haman, deliberately drawing attention to the presence of this race of people all through the kingdom. It may be a calculated risk, but it is a very dangerous one. Mordecai's people have been living inconspicuously, rubbing along with their neighbours, apparently able to follow most of their own laws. They are not exactly assimilated, but they are not obviously different, either. Mordecai's great gamble will either lead to their annihilation or to their chance to be recognized and live freely as a distinctive people.

'The city of Susa was thrown into confusion', we are told. Mordecai's plan starts to take effect.

COLLECT

Almighty God,
send down upon your Church
the riches of your Spirit,
and kindle in all who minister the gospel
your countless gifts of grace;
through Jesus Christ our Lord.

Reflection by **Jane Williams**

Monday 17 July

Psalms 123, 124, 125, **126**
Esther 4
2 Corinthians 6.1 – 7.1

Esther 4

'... there was great mourning among the Jews' (v.3)

Mordecai's people, the Jews, are now unmistakable. Where they had been living peacefully, keeping their heads down, making necessary compromises but being allowed to get on with their lives, now they are under the spotlight of the king's lethal decree, the whole people weeping and wearing sackcloth and ashes and unmistakably separate from the rest of the nation.

Despite his apparent danger, and the fact that he cannot come to court dressed in his mourning garb, Mordecai is still remarkably well-informed. He is able to get a copy of the king's decree for Esther and, even more strikingly, is able to tell Esther that there is a lot of money changing hands in this conflict.

He is as ruthless with Esther as he is with his fellow-countrymen. Esther, too, must risk her life for the sake of her people; she cannot escape her heritage. Mordecai does not mention God, but he does appeal to a providence at work through apparently unconnected actions. 'Perhaps you have come to royal dignity for just such a time as this', he says. Here are Mordecai and God, hand in glove, engineering Esther's role, forcing both Esther and the Jewish people throughout the land to acknowledge who they are. The plan is coming to fruition. Already, Mordecai's people are united in mourning; already Queen Esther turns to her religious family to support her with prayer and fasting at this critical juncture. All of them have only two choices: death or religious freedom.

COLLECT

Merciful God,
you have prepared for those who love you
such good things as pass our understanding:
pour into our hearts such love toward you
that we, loving you in all things and above all things,
may obtain your promises,
which exceed all that we can desire;
through Jesus Christ your Son our Lord,
who is alive and reigns with you,
in the unity of the Holy Spirit,
one God, now and for ever.

Reflection by **Jane Williams**

Psalms **132**, 133
Esther 5
2 Corinthians 7.2-end

Tuesday 18 July

Esther 5

'So the king and Haman came to the banquet that Esther had prepared' (v.5)

So far, we have seen Mordecai as the cunning one, weighing the risks, setting up the desired confrontation. But now the plot passes into Esther's hands, and she shows herself just as capable of working with the designs of providence as Mordecai is. Shamelessly, Esther uses her beauty, her femininity, to draw the King and Haman into her toils. It does not occur to either man that Esther is a threat. Haman sees her simply as part of a successful strategy to keep the king occupied and complaisant, so that he will not question Haman's doings. The King sees her as a pretty plaything, one who is always adoring and grateful.

Both men leave their dinner feeling very pleased with themselves: the King has offered Esther half his kingdom, but she seems only to want his company; while Haman goes home to boast about his own possessions and success, and determine to rid himself of the one fly in the ointment, the one persistent irritant that keeps suggesting he might not be as powerful as he believes. The time has come, Haman decides, to get rid of Mordecai, the one person who will not show him proper deference.

Although Mordecai and Esther have deliberately kept their relationship a secret, nonetheless, it is a serious failure of political intelligence that Haman has not bothered to find out more about the Queen. Mordecai is far better informed about Haman than Haman is about Mordecai.

COLLECT

Creator God,
you made us all in your image:
may we discern you in all that we see,
and serve you in all that we do;
through Jesus Christ our Lord.

Reflection by **Jane Williams**

Wednesday 19 July

Psalm **119.153-end**
Esther 6.1-13
2 Corinthians 8.1-15

Esther 6.1-13

'If Mordecai ... is of the Jewish people, you will not prevail against him' (v.13)

Here is a perfect example of the implicit theology of the Book of Esther, and guidance for times when God does not seem to intervene or work miracles. Here is a quiet confidence that the purposes of God work out for the good of God's people, in the interaction between human ingenuity, courage, stupidity and apparent coincidence. Discerning God's ways sometimes asks of us the disciplines of trust and patience.

At this critical juncture, while Haman is building a gallows from which to hang Mordecai, the King suddenly cannot sleep and decides to read the Annals instead; and where should his eye fall but on the account of the time when Mordecai saved him from assassination. Instead of hanging Mordecai, Haman is instructed to load him with exactly the wealth and honour that Haman was confidently expecting to be his. It is a scene heavy with irony and humour, as Haman preens himself on the King's favour, and then realises it is not for him but for his mortal enemy.

It is Haman's wife who points out the theological truth: 'If Mordecai ... is of the Jewish people, you will not prevail against him.' Haman cannot hope to plot better than the God of Israel; he relied on his own cunning and the stupidity of the King, but they were of no avail against the wit and trust of Esther and Mordecai. The world is tilting around him, and he has no idea why or how to stop it.

COLLECT

Merciful God,
you have prepared for those who love you
such good things as pass our understanding:
pour into our hearts such love toward you
that we, loving you in all things and above all things,
may obtain your promises,
which exceed all that we can desire;
through Jesus Christ your Son our Lord,
who is alive and reigns with you,
in the unity of the Holy Spirit,
one God, now and for ever.

Reflection by **Jane Williams**

Psalms **143, 146**
Esther 6.14 – end of 7
2 Corinthians 8.16 – 9.5

Thursday 20 July

Esther 6.14 – end of 7

'So they hanged Haman on the gallows that he had prepared for Mordecai' (7.10)

When Haman last went to a banquet given by Esther, in chapter 5, he was powerful, wealthy and looking to a bright future, one in which he could get rid of anyone who failed to give him proper respect, like Mordecai. Once again, the storyteller's values operate with subtle understatement. Haman wants power for himself alone, while Esther is putting her life in danger for the sake of her people, rather than using her privilege as queen to ensure her own safety and comfort. She could have left Mordecai and her community to die, as Haman certainly would have done in her place, while she herself lived in luxury. This, the story implies, is why providence will work for Esther and not for Haman.

With sly humour, Esther adopts Haman's own tactics to use against him. Haman had argued that the King needed to get rid of the Jewish people to uphold his own position (see 3.8). Now Esther puts forward the same argument: the King's own status will be damaged by the destruction of so many of his subjects: 'no enemy can compensate for this damage to the king', she says. Esther's tone is perfect: she is humble, deferential, demurely pointing out that the king has been misled by Haman, who has been an enemy all along.

Haman is hanged on the gallows that he built for Mordecai. Providence is very thrifty.

COLLECT

Creator God,
you made us all in your image:
may we discern you in all that we see,
and serve you in all that we do;
through Jesus Christ our Lord.

Reflection by **Jane Williams**

Friday 21 July

Psalms 142, **144**
Esther 8
2 Corinthians 9.6-end

Esther 8

'... how can I bear to see the destruction of my kindred?' (v.6)

At last, Esther is able to be herself in front of the king. She is able to acknowledge her relationship to Mordecai and her whole community.

King Ahasuerus has not come out of this story looking particularly intelligent or forceful; he has been vain and easily manipulated throughout, but that proves to be part of the gentle, mocking theology of this book. The king has no hesitations about reversing an order that he has so recently given; he allows Mordecai to send messages throughout the kingdom, basically saying, 'Oops, I made a mistake, signed, the King'.

The picture suddenly pans out to show all Esther's people as the shadow of death is lifted from them. They are free to defend themselves and their possessions against their enemies, free to live in 'light and gladness, joy and honour', their position not just restored to former times but greatly enhanced. With a gentle nudge, the story tells us that others even converted to Judaism, 'because the fear of the Jews had fallen upon them'. Perhaps that fear was just a response to the fact that the Jews now have powerful friends at court; but perhaps it is also a covert acknowledgement that there is more than earthly power on the side of the Jewish people.

God's work through Esther is to be of benefit to more than one people: God the creator cares about the other nations, too, and brings them into the family.

COLLECT

Merciful God,
you have prepared for those who love you
such good things as pass our understanding:
pour into our hearts such love toward you
that we, loving you in all things and above all things,
may obtain your promises,
which exceed all that we can desire;
through Jesus Christ your Son our Lord,
who is alive and reigns with you,
in the unity of the Holy Spirit,
one God, now and for ever.

Reflection by **Jane Williams**

Psalms 30, 32, 150
1 Samuel 16.14-end
Luke 8.1-3

Saturday 22 July
Mary Magdalene

Luke 8.1-3

'The twelve were with him, as well as some women who had been cured of evil spirits and infirmities' (vv.1-2)

These three verses of Luke's Gospel are hugely significant in what they take for granted. Almost in passing, Luke shows us the people who accompanied Jesus on his travels 'through cities and villages', hearing and sharing in Jesus' mission. The Twelve are there, of course, but so are a number of women, whom Luke expects the early Christian community to have heard of; he does not explain or excuse, he simply states: Jesus had women disciples, too, and without them, he could not have pursued his mission.

More than funding the work, the women are also living proof of the good news, the liberating power of Jesus. The women can tell their own stories of healing and restored dignity, transformed lives, all that Jesus offers to the people he meets along the way.

It is possible for the modern reader almost to miss the importance of these verses, but Luke's first readers must have been as amazed by them as were the people who met Jesus and his strange friends. The sight of women and men working together, travelling together, preaching together must have been wholly unexpected.

Mary Magdalene had a testimony of great power to offer. She had been freed from 'seven demons', a number indicating the totality of what had been controlling her life before she met Jesus. Now she walked with him and his companions, free and generous, living the good news.

COLLECT

Almighty God,
whose Son restored Mary Magdalene to health of mind and body
and called her to be a witness to his resurrection:
forgive our sins and heal us by your grace,
that we may serve you in the power of his risen life;
who is alive and reigns with you,
in the unity of the Holy Spirit,
one God, now and for ever.

Reflection by **Jane Williams**

Monday 24 July

Psalms **1**, 2, 3
Jeremiah 26
2 Corinthians 11.1-15

2 Corinthians 11.1-15

'I may be untrained in speech ...' (v.6)

We've got the evidence that Paul was a great letter writer. The New Testament would be a good deal shorter if that had not been the case. But Paul did not claim for himself any great ability as a speaker and preacher. He refers here to a lack of training in oratory. He has already said his speech was 'contemptible' (2 Corinthians 10.10). By contrast, the Corinthians have been very impressed by the eloquence of those Paul describes, a little petulantly, as 'super-apostles'. We don't know what they were preaching, but Paul believes they are leading the Corinthian Christians astray, no matter how articulate they may be.

One of the weakest and most hesitant preachers I've ever known was a priest, now long retired, whose sermons never lasted more than five minutes. He was so stumbling in the pulpit that his homilies felt much longer. Nevertheless, for many years he led a large congregation with rarely less than 200 people of all ages at the main Sunday Eucharist. He was untrained in speech but a superb pastor. People learned the faith from him in other ways. Being eloquent with words is not the only way of preaching Christ crucified and risen. It was 'the truth of Christ in me' that Paul relied on.

Has it been great preaching or fine oratory that has most influenced you, or someone conveying the truth of Christ in them through all that they are?

COLLECT

Lord of all power and might,
the author and giver of all good things:
graft in our hearts the love of your name,
increase in us true religion,
nourish us with all goodness,
and of your great mercy keep us in the same;
through Jesus Christ your Son our Lord,
who is alive and reigns with you,
in the unity of the Holy Spirit,
one God, now and for ever.

 Reflection by **Graham James**

Psalms 7, 29, 117
2 Kings 1.9-15
Luke 9.46-56

Tuesday 25 July
James the Apostle

Luke 9.46-56

'... they entered a village of the Samaritans' (v.52)

The brothers James and John are not always presented in a good light in the Gospels. They asked for the best seats at the heavenly banquet (Mark 10.37), so could be quite pushy. It would be surprising if they were not leaders in the discussion among the disciples about which of them is the greatest. Jesus gives James and John a nickname – 'boarneges (sons of thunder)' (Mark 3.17) – because of their fiery and explosive character. It's definitely on display in today's reading. When a Samaritan village prevents Jesus and his disciples from passing through, James and John suggest calling fire down from heaven to consume the inhospitable people.

Jews and Samaritans may have had much in common in their religion, but the rift between them was deep. It went back to the time of exile in Babylon. The Samaritans did not go into exile and became particularly resentful of the people of Jerusalem after the exile was over. Since Jesus was on his way there, they had no desire to help him.

Jesus is frequently shown to be unusually charitable to Samaritans, whether in his teaching (the parable of the Good Samaritan) or in his encounters (with the woman of Samaria at the well), as well as here. He cools tempers, and rebukes James and John. It's a lesson in reducing tensions, refusing to be provoked, bringing peace. What opportunities do we have to do that today?

COLLECT

Merciful God,
whose holy apostle Saint James,
leaving his father and all that he had,
was obedient to the calling of your Son Jesus Christ
and followed him even to death:
help us, forsaking the false attractions of the world,
to be ready at all times to answer your call without delay;
through Jesus Christ your Son our Lord,
who is alive and reigns with you,
in the unity of the Holy Spirit,
one God, now and for ever.

Reflection by **Graham James**

Wednesday 26 July

Psalm **119.1-32**
Jeremiah 29.1-14
2 Corinthians 12

2 Corinthians 12

'... a thorn was given to me in the flesh' (v.7)

Paul says he does not want to boast of spiritual experiences but refers to 'a person in Christ' who 'fourteen years ago was caught up to the third heaven'. He is speaking of himself, if obliquely, and to a deep mystical experience, a sign of the authenticity of his calling. But even 'the exceptional character' of that event is insignificant compared to the suffering he has endured. It's the 'insults, hardships, persecutions, and calamities' that speak more about Christ in Paul than any transports of spiritual delight.

Above all, he has been given 'a thorn ... in the flesh' to stop him getting carried away by his extraordinary spiritual experience. This 'thorn' may have been a physical disability – perhaps a speech impediment which could have been one of the reasons for his poor speaking. Or it may have been a form of depression or spiritual ennui that would sometimes overcome him. Whatever it was, it was deeply personal to Paul, so much so that he does not, or cannot, share it.

Church congregations everywhere seem to have a high proportion of people who have 'a thorn in the flesh', whether physical, mental or spiritual. Clergy frequently long for a few strong and uncomplicated characters to join their congregations but discover that Christ appears to call the weak and needy more easily. Perhaps the strong and self-sufficient are less likely to acknowledge their need of God. Like Paul, we may need our thorns to keep us grounded.

COLLECT

Lord of all power and might,
the author and giver of all good things:
graft in our hearts the love of your name,
increase in us true religion,
nourish us with all goodness,
and of your great mercy keep us in the same;
through Jesus Christ your Son our Lord,
who is alive and reigns with you,
in the unity of the Holy Spirit,
one God, now and for ever.

Reflection by **Graham James**

Psalms 14, **15**, 16
Jeremiah 30.1-11
2 Corinthians 13

Thursday 27 July

2 Corinthians 13

'Greet one another with a holy kiss' (v.12)

At the conclusion to his letter to the Romans, Paul refers to 'the kiss of peace' or 'holy kiss' (Romans 16.16). We know it was part of Christian liturgy by the mid second century, but it seems to have become customary much earlier. It seems likely that Paul's letter would have been read to the Corinthians when they were gathered for worship. Then, as instructed in his concluding sentences, the kiss of peace would have been shared, followed by the invocation before the Lord's Supper was celebrated.

Two millennia ago, people in the Graeco-Roman world would have frequently greeted each other with a kiss, whether on the cheek, or even the hands or forehead. This 'holy kiss' was not simply a greeting but a sign of shared communion with one another in the love of Christ. Although Paul has had some harsh things to say to the Corinthians, he finishes with a message of love for them, urging them to love each other too.

Covid meant that the sharing of the Peace in church services was reduced to a liturgical nod or a wave. While some were relieved by this, others found this tangible reminder of our physical distance from each other in the community of faith a sadness. A few, including me, found we valued the Peace more than we ever thought we did. What do you make of Paul's instruction?

COLLECT

Generous God,
you give us gifts and make them grow:
though our faith is small as mustard seed,
make it grow to your glory
and the flourishing of your kingdom;
through Jesus Christ our Lord.

Reflection by **Graham James**

Friday 28 July

Psalms 17, **19**
Jeremiah 30.12-22
James 1.1-11

James 1.1-11

'James, a servant of God and of the Lord Jesus Christ' (v.1)

The Hebrew name 'Jacob' is James in Greek. It was a very common name in New Testament times, one borne by two of Christ's disciples (James, the son of Zebedee, and James, the son of Alphaeus). But this James is thought to be the brother of Jesus (mentioned in Mark 6.3). He became the leader of the Church in Jerusalem, a man revered because of his parentage, but more because of his faith and wisdom. Paul tells us that he was a pillar of the Church in Jerusalem (Galatians 2.9) whom he consulted, and clearly respected. The Jewish historian Josephus informs us that James was stoned to death in AD 62.

The Gospels tell us that the immediate family of Jesus were not initially very impressed by his teaching ministry. They try to persuade him to come home (Mark 3.21) since they thought he was 'out of his mind'. We are even explicitly told that his brothers did not believe in him (John 7.5).

Clearly, James changed his mind about Jesus. Perhaps it happened when the risen Christ appeared to him. Paul mentions such an appearance (1 Corinthians 15.7). There was certainly a conversion of some sort.

None of this should surprise us. We sometimes fail to see the qualities of those closest to us, and need our eyes to be opened. Is there anyone among your family or close friends you have failed to appreciate and understand? What might you learn from them?

COLLECT

Lord of all power and might,
the author and giver of all good things:
graft in our hearts the love of your name,
increase in us true religion,
nourish us with all goodness,
and of your great mercy keep us in the same;
through Jesus Christ your Son our Lord,
who is alive and reigns with you,
in the unity of the Holy Spirit,
one God, now and for ever.

Reflection by **Graham James**

Psalms 20, 21, **23**
Jeremiah 31.1-22
James 1.12-end

Saturday 29 July

James 1.12-end

'Religion that is pure and undefiled ...' (v.27)

In contemporary secular Western society, it's frequently claimed that religion is a source of war and division, even a cradle of hypocrisy or the resort of the feeble minded. With such a public reputation, it's not surprising that some people pride themselves on being 'spiritual but not religious'.

'Religion' is a rare word in the New Testament, found only three times, and in each case, it refers primarily to ceremonial rites and duties. In both Judaism and the pagan cults of the Roman empire, religion was woven into every aspect of everyday life since all were expected to participate. Religion was not a matter of private conviction but of public and civic duty. The core meaning of the word religion is 'to bind together'.

Modern critics of religion may be surprised to find that James, like them, has little time for a religion of ceremonial rituals alone. Yet he does not dismiss religion itself. 'Pure and undefiled' religion shows its fruit in care for widows and orphans, those most needy in the ancient world since they had no means of support without a husband or father. James believed Christians should be 'doers of the word, and not merely hearers'. Religion – like secularism – is not good in itself. But you can see its good results. 'By their fruits you shall know them' (Matthew 7.20) was how Jesus put it.

COLLECT

Generous God,
you give us gifts and make them grow:
though our faith is small as mustard seed,
make it grow to your glory
and the flourishing of your kingdom;
through Jesus Christ our Lord.

Reflection by **Graham James**

Monday 31 July

Psalms 27, **30**
Jeremiah 31.23-25, 27-37
James 2.1-13

James 2.1-13

'... have you not made distinctions among yourselves?' (v.4)

Jesus criticized the scribes for wanting the best seats in the synagogue (Mark 12.39), and yet it seems that the early Christian communities quickly developed their own problems with seating arrangements. James tells us the well-dressed and well-to-do were given preferential treatment over the poor when the assembly gathered. The rich were used to wielding power and influence in society. Yet God chose 'the poor in the world to be rich in faith and to be heirs of the kingdom'. This reversal of the social order, so clearly believed to be part of the core message of Jesus, sustained the faith of the first Christians, the majority of whom were far from wealthy.

Creating distinctions in church regarding social importance thus undermined the teaching of Christ. Even so, the history of the Church is one in which this mistake has been repeated again and again in different ways. Think of pew rents, once commonplace, with varying payments depending on the desirability of the location, and free sittings for the poor at the back or somewhere out of sight. The custom of reserving seats in cathedrals and churches nowadays may be necessary at big services but invariably benefits the privileged more than the poor.

Were James to observe the practices of our churches today, what do you think he would say? What distinctions do you notice, and what changes should there be?

COLLECT

Almighty Lord and everlasting God,
we beseech you to direct, sanctify and govern
both our hearts and bodies
in the ways of your laws
and the works of your commandments;
that through your most mighty protection, both here and ever,
we may be preserved in body and soul;
through our Lord and Saviour Jesus Christ,
who is alive and reigns with you,
in the unity of the Holy Spirit,
one God, now and for ever.

 Reflection by **Graham James**

Psalms 32, **36**
Jeremiah 32.1-15
James 2.14-end

Tuesday 1 August

James 2.14-end

'... a person is justified by works and not by faith alone' (v.24)

Martin Luther famously called the letter of James 'an epistle of straw'. Since Luther proclaimed 'justification by faith alone' as expressed in Paul's letters as the central message of the Christian faith, he was unlikely to be happy with what James says here.

Paul did believe that it was by faith in Christ alone, and not through good works, however admirable they may be, that God counted people as righteous. But Paul was adamant that this did not mean that believers in Christ had no need to uphold the moral law. Justification by faith alone was not commended by immorality. What James may be arguing against here is a version of Paul's theology that suggested that, as long as you had faith in Christ, you could do as you liked. Sometimes Paul himself had to argue against such ideas (Romans 6.1-2).

This issue does not simply belong to the distant past of Christian history. It's sometimes claimed nowadays that the gospel is 'all about Jesus' and faith in him. Apart from a Trinitarian deficit in such theology, there's a lurking danger that the assurance of salvation, without any mention of the necessity of good works flowing from them, may become morally insidious. It could be why so many tele-evangelists and big-personality preachers have gone off the rails. It's when we do not even see this danger that we may be most likely to be trapped by it.

COLLECT

Lord God,
your Son left the riches of heaven
and became poor for our sake:
when we prosper save us from pride,
when we are needy save us from despair,
that we may trust in you alone;
through Jesus Christ our Lord.

Reflection by **Graham James**

Wednesday 2 August

Psalm **34**
Jeremiah 33.1-13
James 3

James 3

'And the tongue is a fire' (v.6)

Problems with hate speech predate social media. James says, 'no-one can tame the tongue'. It is unruly. Curses as well as blessings come from it.

It's easy to blurt things out in a moment of passion, things we may later regret. When we write things down in a letter, the very act of writing gives us time to weigh our words more carefully. But such letter writing is in serious decline. One of the challenges of our age is that social networking, Twitter especially, gives us the means to blurt things out to an audience much larger than those who would be listening otherwise to our spoken conversation. When James describes the tongue as a fire, he could hardly have imagined the incendiary character of the controversies in the Twittersphere.

The way we put words together, and how we marshal our knowledge and communicate it, influences both our own lives and those around us. Someone who is careless about what they say or write, and tells lies easily, soon becomes untrusted. We know that the fibber has no depth or wisdom. 'You cannot rely on their word' is what we say.

Although this chapter is particularly directed at teachers in the Church, modern communications have made us all teachers of one another. James believes we all have the capability to curb our tongues and be 'peaceable, gentle ... full of mercy'. How will I control my tongue today?

COLLECT

Almighty Lord and everlasting God,
we beseech you to direct, sanctify and govern
both our hearts and bodies
in the ways of your laws
and the works of your commandments;
that through your most mighty protection, both here and ever,
we may be preserved in body and soul;
through our Lord and Saviour Jesus Christ,
who is alive and reigns with you,
in the unity of the Holy Spirit,
one God, now and for ever.

 Reflection by **Graham James**

Psalm **37***
Jeremiah 33.14-end
James 4.1-12

Thursday 3 August

James 4.1-12

'... who are you to judge your neighbour?' (v.12)

In Britain in the 1960s, when laws liberalizing divorce, abortion and censorship were all passed, it was claimed that 'the permissive society is the civilized society'. I was a teenager at the time and recall that being 'judgemental' was a serious social sin among my peers. Despite this, there were marches against the Vietnam War and many of my contemporaries wanted to ban nuclear weapons. We did make judgements, sometimes very strong ones.

In his letter, James is not against robust opinions (he has plenty of them) or making judgements on the issues of the day, but it is the condemnation of other people, especially fellow believers, that appals him. It's noticeable that he nowhere mentions by name or denigrates any of his opponents in the whole of his epistle. Although there was clear division over doctrine in these early Church communities, the admonition of Jesus not to judge lest you be judged (Mathew 7.1) was remembered.

Sometimes, the enmities today within our churches over doctrine or behaviour can become deeply personal. There are many purportedly Christian websites where the comments would prompt James to righteous anger. When we condemn someone, and question their salvation, we are putting ourselves in God's place, usurping his authority in our life. The growth of cancel culture in wider society would be in James' sights too. Are we careful to avoid such judgement of others?

COLLECT

Lord God,
your Son left the riches of heaven
and became poor for our sake:
when we prosper save us from pride,
when we are needy save us from despair,
that we may trust in you alone;
through Jesus Christ our Lord.

Reflection by **Graham James**

Friday 4 August

Psalm **31**
Jeremiah 35
James 4.13 – 5.6

James 4.13 – 5.6

'Come now, you rich people, weep and wail ...' (5.1)

Back in 1935, Frank Capra's classic film *You Can't Take It With You* was released. James Stewart played the successful businessman Mr Kirby. He's told 'stop trying to be so desperate about making money ... you can't take it with you, Mr Kirby. So what good is it?'

James suggests much the same thing in his letter. What's the point of 'doing business and making money' when 'you are a mist' that will vanish? But James goes further. His excoriating language about the rich seems to condemn and judge them, the very thing he has been warning his readers against a few sentences earlier. While some scholars have contended that James is aiming his remarks at the rich outside the Church who have persecuted or defrauded believers, it seems more likely that it is the wealthy within the churches whom James has in mind. It's their failure to share their wealth and assist their poorer brothers and sisters that appals him. He's offering a strong call to repentance, a last chance, the more urgent since James believed the end of all things was not to be long delayed.

The Church has rarely handled disparities of wealth well and these verses of Scripture are not frequently read in public worship. Why? If you knew you were to die soon, what changes would you make in your life, including with your money?

COLLECT

Almighty Lord and everlasting God,
we beseech you to direct, sanctify and govern
both our hearts and bodies
in the ways of your laws
and the works of your commandments;
that through your most mighty protection, both here and ever,
we may be preserved in body and soul;
through our Lord and Saviour Jesus Christ,
who is alive and reigns with you,
in the unity of the Holy Spirit,
one God, now and for ever.

Reflection by **Graham James**

Psalms 41, **42**, 43
Jeremiah 36.1-18
James 5.7-end

Saturday 5 August

James 5.7-end

'Be patient, therefore, beloved ...' (v.7)

Patience is a virtue that does not seem to be much in fashion. Perhaps it's because life has speeded up. We are in instant communication through text, email and social media. 24-hour news is voracious and treats almost everything as urgent. Many organizations have a 'Rapid Response Unit' or something of the sort to put right whatever has gone wrong. A '*Slow* Response Unit' might do a better job since there would be longer and more purposeful reflection about solutions. But no one would dare establish something so countercultural. We have made speed a yardstick of virtue. We are rarely content to wait for anything. Hence patience is unpopular.

It was Augustine who said that 'patience is the companion of wisdom', while Gregory the Great claimed that 'patience is the root and guardian of all the virtues'. It's no surprise that, as he concludes his letter, James urges patience, not simply in waiting for the coming of the kingdom of God, but in the dealings brothers and sisters in Christ have with one another. Being patient with each other paves the way towards mutual forgiveness and living in unity. The patient person does not usually grumble (a pet hate of James) but shows endurance when tested.

What would a Christian Church that cherished patience before the Lord look like? What change would the cultivation of greater patience make in our lives?

COLLECT

Lord God,
your Son left the riches of heaven
and became poor for our sake:
when we prosper save us from pride,
when we are needy save us from despair,
that we may trust in you alone;
through Jesus Christ our Lord.

Reflection by **Graham James**

Monday 7 August

Psalm **44**
Jeremiah 36.19-end
Mark 1.1-13

Mark 1.1-13

'The beginning of the good news of Jesus Christ, the Son of God' (v.1)

If Mark's Gospel were an athletics event, it would consist of 100 metres at a sprint, with a steady-to-slow marathon pace towards the end. Mark is in such a hurry that he starts his narrative with a bold announcement of 'beginning'. There is no word for 'the' in the original Greek. While these verses aren't much help for a Christmas nativity play, Mark gives us some important information about who Jesus is, and why this is good news. In so doing, Mark creates a new genre of document: a gospel, a word that means 'good news'. While Mark explicitly references the prophecy of Isaiah, this passage also refers even further back to another 'beginning': Genesis. Mark's focus on Jesus' identity invites us to consider the totality of God's deeds in creation.

While Mark is intent on letting his community know about Jesus, there's another dynamic at work here that invites us to reflect on more contemporary modes of communication. Most mornings, I take a look at the scanned front pages of the national newspapers. You can tell a lot about what sorts of agendas are being set, despite the apparent attempts at media neutrality. Mark's Gospel demands our attention, speaking as it does into the headline-grabbing world of the Roman Empire. This is an announcement to take note of.

If I had to get someone's attention today about who Jesus is, I wonder what my headline would be?

COLLECT

Almighty God,
who sent your Holy Spirit
to be the life and light of your Church:
open our hearts to the riches of your grace,
that we may bring forth the fruit of the Spirit
in love and joy and peace;
through Jesus Christ your Son our Lord,
who is alive and reigns with you,
in the unity of the Holy Spirit,
one God, now and for ever.

Reflection by **Helen-Ann Hartley**

Psalms **48**, 52
Jeremiah 37
Mark 1.14-20

Tuesday 8 August

Mark 1.14-20

'And immediately they left their nets and followed him' (v.18)

A few years ago, when we moved to live and work in New Zealand, I was often asked why. My answer today is the same as it was back then: because we had a clear sense of God's call that we could not ignore. While the journey didn't become the expected one (I went there to do one job and ended up being called to consider another role altogether, which rather changed our lives), God was in it all.

When I read the narrative of the call of Jesus' first disciples, I try and imagine between the lines what might have been going on in the disciples' own minds. Did they have *any* questions? What did their families make of this apparently sudden change in direction?

Mark seems to be a great fan of the word 'immediately'; it occurs many times in his narrative. This still gives me pause for wondering, however, whether there are degrees of immediacy.

The other issue up for consideration is what it was about Jesus that clearly inspired such confidence and certainty. Mark wants us to consider who Jesus is, and this narrative of call-and-response leads us to conclude that whoever Jesus was at this point to the first disciples, he must have conveyed complete confidence in God's presence. God calls us, and we must respond.

COLLECT

Gracious Father,
revive your Church in our day,
and make her holy, strong and faithful,
for your glory's sake
in Jesus Christ our Lord.

Reflection by **Helen-Ann Hartley**

Wednesday 9 August

Psalm **119.57-80**
Jeremiah 38.1-13
Mark 1.21-28

Mark 1.21-28

'They were astounded at his teaching, for he taught them as one having authority, and not as the scribes' (v.22)

Today's reading is all about impact, with a focus on Jesus' surprising authority. Here's another theme Mark is interested in, and in what follows we get a clear idea of the measure of Jesus' own authority: over unclean spirits and in the recognition of those who witnessed what was happening. It is significant that the man who is healed identifies Jesus as 'the Holy One of God'. This is a bold assertion of Jesus' power within the kingdom of God, a power that also extends beyond to obliterate the forces of evil. Such a compelling vision confronts us with the reality of who Jesus is.

Perhaps you can recall a time when you heard someone speak and what they said astonished you, and remained with you? One thing that strikes me in Mark's often concise narratives is that the texts give more than they actually state. Light on detail, yet searching in implication, at the end of this passage we just get one brief sentence about Jesus' fame spreading across the region. The 'what happened next' invites us to join the drama and consider where and how we might respond.

It is significant, too, that Mark clearly presents Jesus' words and actions as both having authority and action. What we say matters, but it's also about what we can do as a result. At times this drive to action can be exhausting, but being a disciple is about an intentionality balanced by prayer. How can I respond afresh to these challenges today?

COLLECT

Almighty God,
who sent your Holy Spirit
to be the life and light of your Church:
open our hearts to the riches of your grace,
that we may bring forth the fruit of the Spirit
in love and joy and peace;
through Jesus Christ your Son our Lord,
who is alive and reigns with you,
in the unity of the Holy Spirit,
one God, now and for ever.

Reflection by **Helen-Ann Hartley**

Psalms 56, **57** (63*)
Jeremiah 38.14-end
Mark 1.29-end

Thursday 10 August

Mark 1.29-end

'In the morning, while it was still very dark, he got up and went out to a deserted place, and there he prayed' (v.35)

I am definitely more of an early bird than a night owl. There's something special about getting up early, and going out for a run. This is prayer time, as I run the streets thinking of all who live and work in the local community; across the market-square as traders are setting up their stalls. In the midst of a busy day, I try to recall that early morning space and peace, and through it exercise patience and a prayerful approach.

This is an important aspect of who Jesus is that Mark wants to convey: Jesus needed to pray. The second aspect should not surprise: Jesus also needed space! There's a contemporary ring to the narrative here, as we have just heard about Jesus' fame spreading, and the crowds pressing in on him, literally hunting him down. Jesus' response is to withdraw, regroup and resource himself with energy for the tasks ahead. This glimpse of Jesus' humanity is thoroughly relatable. God knows and understands the busyness of our lives, but God can't make us slow down; only we can choose to do that.

Another key point in this passage is in the healing of Simon's mother-in-law. Note the physicality of these verses as Jesus takes the woman by her hand and lifts her up. Given Mark's careful use of language, there must be significance in the imagery of serving; this is used later in the Gospel by Jesus to describe his own ministry. This is the work of being a disciple, and here, so early on in the Gospel, it is perfectly exemplified by this one woman.

COLLECT

Gracious Father,
revive your Church in our day,
and make her holy, strong and faithful,
for your glory's sake
in Jesus Christ our Lord.

Reflection by **Helen-Ann Hartley**

Friday 11 August

Psalms **51**, 54
Jeremiah 39
Mark 2.1-12

Mark 2.1-12

'I say to you, stand up, take your mat and go to your home' (v.11)

One of the many things I like about Mark's Gospel is the opportunity it gives me to be a bystander, imagining myself in the midst of the crowd and watching as the drama unfolds.

Jesus' command to the man is bold, and we know what happens next: the man does as he is told, and further amazement abounds. The key point here is that the resultant praise is directed towards God. Jesus' identity is bound up in God's very being, and it is to God that wonder is directed. Jesus is God, and God is Jesus.

Again, the debate centres around Jesus' authority, and the discontent resides with the scribes and the particular issue of the forgiveness of sins. There is no mistaking where Jesus' authority derives from, however, but we know this won't be the end of the matter.

In our contemporary lives, I have in mind those who provide prophetic voice to key issues of our age, such as climate change, and how movements can grow and spread. There will always be those who cast doubt, it seems, but for all the negativity that can sometimes overwhelm, the truth can be edgy and uncomfortable.

Jesus' disciples might have been swept along by the drama, and if we dare to follow along too, we might find ourselves brought into unexpected scenes, with surprising results.

COLLECT

Almighty God,
who sent your Holy Spirit
to be the life and light of your Church:
open our hearts to the riches of your grace,
that we may bring forth the fruit of the Spirit
in love and joy and peace;
through Jesus Christ your Son our Lord,
who is alive and reigns with you,
in the unity of the Holy Spirit,
one God, now and for ever.

Reflection by **Helen-Ann Hartley**

Psalm **68**
Jeremiah 40
Mark 2.13-22

Saturday 12 August

Mark 2.13-22

'Why does he eat with tax-collectors and sinners?' (v.16)

On Christmas Day, I usually spend the morning in a prison near to where we live. I remember someone asking me: 'Why would you do that?' I was surprised at the question because I thought the answer was pretty obvious. I found myself quoting the verse mentioned above, and that seemed to satisfy the curiosity of the person who had quizzed me.

Jesus kept company with people others wouldn't give a second thought to, or who evoked a high level of suspicion. Tax-collectors weren't popular – and as for sinners, well enough said there. I do wonder how you would tell if someone was a sinner or not? The point is that declarations of righteousness don't cut it with the complexity and messiness of the world God entered into through Jesus. That's an encouragement to us, but also a salutary warning: the good news of Jesus is for all people, and everyone should have access to sitting at the table of God's hospitality.

What I find remarkable in my Christmas Day visit to the prison, is the welcome extended to me by the community there. As we sing carols about Jesus' birth in the prison chapel, fresh clarity illumines my own journey as a disciple. The question I ask myself as well as the people I encounter in that place is this: 'What does it mean to say happy Christmas here?' The searing reality of new birth and hope is the answer.

COLLECT

Gracious Father,
revive your Church in our day,
and make her holy, strong and faithful,
for your glory's sake
in Jesus Christ our Lord.

Reflection by **Helen-Ann Hartley**

Monday 14 August

Psalm **71**
Jeremiah 41
Mark 2.23 – 3.6

Mark 2.23 – 3.6

'The Pharisees said to him, "Look, why are they doing what is not lawful on the sabbath?"' (v.24)

It is a source of constant bemusement when someone says to me 'Sunday, that must be your busy day', or the reflection that Christmas and Easter must also see me busily occupied with Church endeavours. On the one hand, it's encouraging that there is still something perceived to be important about Sunday, and the major festivals of the Church (and commercial) year. On the other hand, I do wonder what people think I do the rest of the week?

In today's passage, we get a glimpse of a topic of debate in the first century that focused around work and rest. Jesus' disciples are, in the eyes of some, breaking strict rules concerning no work on the Sabbath by doing a bit of harvesting. Jesus, however, points out that when basic needs of life and health are at stake, that principle overrides the religious laws around labour and rest.

There is a point to this, as it indicates something deeper around rhythms of life and care of creation: you can't timetable hunger, or the need to save a life. By acknowledging that God is over all, and in all, that provides the foundational motivation for action. It doesn't mean that rest isn't important; it is. What it helps us understand is how we look out for those around us, and enable our faith to heal rather than to harm.

COLLECT

Let your merciful ears, O Lord,
be open to the prayers of your humble servants;
and that they may obtain their petitions
make them to ask such things as shall please you;
through Jesus Christ your Son our Lord,
who is alive and reigns with you,
in the unity of the Holy Spirit,
one God, now and for ever.

 Reflection by **Helen-Ann Hartley**

Psalms 98, 138, 147.1-12
Isaiah 7.10-15
Luke 11.27-28

Tuesday 15 August
The Blessed Virgin Mary

Isaiah 7.10-15

'Look, the young woman is with child and shall bear a son, and shall name him Immanuel' (v.14)

The connection between this verse and today's feast day is obvious, but it is important to be clear on what basis this is made. It also raises some challenging issues about the nature of prophecy and its interpretation. In the context in which it was written, Isaiah's prophecy must refer to something contemporary, and one commentator even suggests it conveys a sense of 'any young woman'. When this particular word is translated into Greek and thereby appears in its New Testament context, the meaning is changed to mean 'virgin'. It then becomes a staple in the suite of Christmas readings. There's nothing wrong of course with this, as long as we know that our response to this reading seeks to view this Isaiah passage in relationship to Mary and her giving birth to Jesus.

The most striking aspect of these verses is the assertion that God is with us (the meaning of the word 'Immanuel'). As we remember Mary's vocation to be the God-bearer, we hold the particular human experience of pregnancy and birth in mind. God experiences the fullness of our lives that we might share in God's vision for a redeemed creation. Mary's 'yes' becomes our 'why': the reason for our journey as disciples in this age and in the ages to come.

Let this day be a day to reflect on the 'with', and seek connections between heaven and earth in fresh and inspiring ways.

COLLECT

Almighty God,
who looked upon the lowliness of the Blessed Virgin Mary
and chose her to be the mother of your only Son:
grant that we who are redeemed by his blood
may share with her in the glory of your eternal kingdom;
through Jesus Christ your Son our Lord,
who is alive and reigns with you,
in the unity of the Holy Spirit,
one God, now and for ever.

Reflection by **Helen-Ann Hartley**

Wednesday 16 August

Psalm **77**
Jeremiah 43
Mark 3.19*b*-end

Mark 3.19*b*-end

'When his family heard it, they went out to restrain him, for people were saying, "He has gone out of his mind".' (v.21)

Mark's carefully-shaped narrative focuses attention on the question: who is Jesus? Related to this is the question, identified by a former colleague of mine, the New Testament scholar Nicholas King: 'Why must Jesus die?' If we hold these two questions in mind when we read Mark, it helps us navigate the drama that unfolds and it challenges us to reflect on our own journey as disciples in the different contexts we inhabit from day to day.

Today's passage gives us a glimpse into the challenges that Jesus' family must have faced when his public ministry became increasingly one of conflict. I imagine their desire was to protect Jesus, but there would also have been a fear of Jesus bringing shame upon his family by his controversial words and actions. This reminder of Jesus' wider family helps us understand the networks of support and challenge that Jesus was part of.

Mark's narrative style is so vivid, it's easy to picture the attempt to restrain Jesus. It's an uncomfortable scene, and deliberately so. We know that Jesus' ministry led to his death, and that, in turn, led to resurrection. The path to salvation is not an easy one, but it is not one that Jesus bore solely on his own. We too share in God's unfolding plan.

COLLECT

Let your merciful ears, O Lord,
be open to the prayers of your humble servants;
and that they may obtain their petitions
make them to ask such things as shall please you;
through Jesus Christ your Son our Lord,
who is alive and reigns with you,
in the unity of the Holy Spirit,
one God, now and for ever.

 Reflection by **Helen-Ann Hartley**

Psalm **78.1-39***
Jeremiah 44.1-14
Mark 4.1-20

Thursday 17 August

Mark 4.1-20

'Listen! A sower went out to sow' (v.3)

Living and working in a rural context, Jesus' parables come to life on an almost daily basis. As I drive past fields, I notice the turn of the seasons as the rhythm of the year passes by. Farmers provide our food, care for the land, and remind us of the fundamentals of life and death, as creation renews itself in good times and in bad. Surrounded by another rural landscape, it's not surprising that Jesus draws on this to provide illustrations of God's kingdom. Jesus as teacher is certainly one important aspect that Mark wants us to understand. The command to 'listen' invites us not just to hear what Jesus is saying, but to consider it at a deeper level. What can this story of a sower and the haphazard sowing technique tell us about the success or otherwise of communicating God's word?

We do more than just observe the unfolding scene; Jesus asks us to consider how we ourselves are affected by what we hear. Are we willing to let change take place within ourselves, so as to enable fresh growth?

One of the challenges of this passage is that Jesus explains the meaning of the parable to the disciples, and not it seems to the large crowd who had gathered to listen to him. Why is that? One reason is that the crowd are left to reflect on the teaching and discern its meaning in their daily life. Kingdom growth needs to be worked at, bit by bit.

COLLECT

Lord of heaven and earth,
as Jesus taught his disciples to be persistent in prayer,
give us patience and courage never to lose hope,
but always to bring our prayers before you;
through Jesus Christ our Lord.

Reflection by **Helen-Ann Hartley**

Friday 18 August

Psalm **55**
Jeremiah 44.15-end
Mark 4.21-34

Mark 4.21-34

'It is like a mustard seed, which, when sown upon the ground, is the smallest of all the seeds on earth' (v.31)

I'll never forget some wise words of a friend and colleague who told me never to forget the disruptive potential of the mustard seed. I have a jar of these seeds on my desk, so I am always reminded of this parable. Many of our local church communities are small, and it's easy to fall into the narrative of 'small means failing'. Growth is important, but it is important to remember that growth isn't always immediately apparent. Numbers are one thing, but the growth within a person or within a community can be less visible, or seen in ways that can surprise and delight. Think of individuals like Malala, and Greta Thunberg, who despite the odds have managed to inspire, and effect change in our world. Their prophetic cry has captured the imagination of millions of people, and in turn fostered movements of transformation and advocacy. It's easy to feel cynical at times, even annoyed by the disruption that such movements entail, yet this is where God is at work.

The mustard seed that Jesus talks about grows into the largest of trees, offering a home for the birds to make their nests. One seed, one tree, for the flourishing of many. Perhaps today is an opportunity to ask yourself the question: what can I do that will make a difference in God's world?

COLLECT

Let your merciful ears, O Lord,
be open to the prayers of your humble servants;
and that they may obtain their petitions
make them to ask such things as shall please you;
through Jesus Christ your Son our Lord,
who is alive and reigns with you,
in the unity of the Holy Spirit,
one God, now and for ever.

 Reflection by **Helen-Ann Hartley**

Psalms **76**, 79
Jeremiah 45
Mark 4.35-end

Saturday 19 August

Mark 4.35-end

'A great gale arose, and the waves beat into the boat, so that the boat was already being swamped' (v.37)

When I took on a new leadership role, I was offered some wise words of advice from an elder: leadership is a bit like climbing a mountain, the higher you go the better the views, but the more likely you are to encounter complex weather-systems. How true this has proved to be! Once, when I found myself in a particularly difficult situation, I had an unexpected gift of grace. During a service one morning, a child came up to me and presented me with a sticker. It said this: 'Be strong, do not fear', quoting the Old Testament book of Joshua. I put the sticker on, and after the service had finished I carefully removed it and transferred it to my iPad, so I now see it several times in the day.

The disciples end this passage in awe of Jesus. The Greek here is more accurately translated with the understanding that the disciples 'feared a great fear'. This is the usual response to a revelation of God's presence. Jesus calms the storm, but doesn't take away the challenges that come our way. The more we are challenged, the more curious we become about how God uses the difficulty to enable us to grow.

Note how the disciples wonder among themselves, rather than on their own. Discernment through community engagement can help us come to terms with difficult events to glimpse God's light and peace into the future.

COLLECT

Lord of heaven and earth,
as Jesus taught his disciples to be persistent in prayer,
give us patience and courage never to lose hope,
but always to bring our prayers before you;
through Jesus Christ our Lord.

Reflection by **Helen-Ann Hartley**

Monday 21 August

Psalms **80**, 82
Micah 1.1-9
Mark 5.1-20

Mark 5.1-20

'What have you to do with me, Jesus...?' (v.7)

The question comes from a conflicted human being. He is violent, abusive and not in control of himself, but he recognizes Jesus, talks to him and bows down before him.

Nothing deterred Jesus from acting decisively and with compassion. The man who questions is gentile, but Jesus has already ventured into the gentile territory of Gerasenes. The man is socially outcast, cut off from other human beings, homeless and mentally ill: a man stripped off every shred of humanity. A respectable Jewish teacher would not have anything to do with him.

The deliverance here is multi-faceted. The man is delivered from his illness, social isolation and the evil powers that dominate him. At the same time, Gerasa works well as a symbol of Roman violence and Jewish resistance, because the town rebelled in the Jewish revolt of the late 60s. This story would have symbolically satisfied the desire to drive Roman legions into the sea like pigs. God's liberation also addresses structural enslavements and the experience of the people who are dominated by unwelcome forces.

Healing in Christ breaks down boundaries, so that those formally excluded from the community are included. Jesus asks the man to stay in his own community, throwing down a challenge to the community; rather than giving them the easy option of tolerating the presence of a mad man outside the boundaries of the town, he confronts them with a healed man testifying to the transforming power of God.

COLLECT

O God, you declare your almighty power
most chiefly in showing mercy and pity:
mercifully grant to us such a measure of your grace,
that we, running the way of your commandments,
may receive your gracious promises,
and be made partakers of your heavenly treasure;
through Jesus Christ your Son our Lord,
who is alive and reigns with you,
in the unity of the Holy Spirit,
one God, now and for ever.

Reflection by **John Perumbalath**

Psalms 87, **89.1-18**
Micah 2
Mark 5.21-34

Tuesday 22 August

Mark 5.21-34

'Who touched my clothes?' (v.30)

Jesus' disciples did not think it was a question worth asking, but Jesus's interrogation plays a crucial role in this story. Jesus is providing an opportunity for the woman to see that not only is she worthy of healing, but also that she offers the crowd a witness of deep faith, persistence and courage.

Jesus is on his way to heal the daughter of a prominent community leader. There is a dramatic contrast between Jairus and this woman. He is named; she is not. He is a respected leader; she has no official status. He speaks; she is silent until Jesus calls her out. He has wealth and social support; she has lost all her wealth and support. She is the least likely recipient of attention, yet Jesus stops his journey to listen to her story.

It is not just Jesus who transgresses society's invisible boundaries. The woman's faith has already made her bold enough to overcome social and religious obstacles. Her condition had made her 'impure' and, therefore, she had to overcome ritual and social boundaries to approach Jesus. Her faith provided her with hope – a bold, persistent and expectant hope.

The woman moves from fear and trembling to courage. Fear is identified with lack of faith in Mark's Gospel. The disciples and the crowd are seen to respond in fear on various occasions. In all these instances of fear, only this unnamed woman manages to overcome fear by faith.

COLLECT

God of glory,
the end of our searching,
help us to lay aside
all that prevents us from seeking your kingdom,
and to give all that we have
to gain the pearl beyond all price,
through our Saviour Jesus Christ.

Reflection by **John Perumbalath**

Wednesday 23 August

Psalm **119.105-128**
Micah 3
Mark 5.35-end

Mark 5.35-end

'Why trouble the teacher any further?' (v.35)

People who came from Jairus' house to report the girl's death do not find any point in troubling Jesus anymore. Associates and friends continue to provide an obstacle to Jesus' healing work. But Jesus carries on, continuing to the house. Jesus is already bothered, and his journey of healing will continue despite the fact that the people around have concluded that there is no hope anymore.

There are several parallels between the woman in yesterday's episode and the dying girl in today's passage. Both stories are about women and feature 'twelve years', 'daughter', a life-threatening illness, and healing through Jesus' touch. After twelve years of childhood or illness, they have been deprived of their creative and life-giving potential. Jesus grants them both a renewed life. Jesus also includes the child's mother in the small group allowed to witness the miracle, unlike in many Old Testament examples of selected witnesses where women were excluded.

Jesus would have got to Jairus' home before the girl's death had he not been interrupted by a desperate woman. Even then, he could have carried on without stopping, knowing that the woman was already healed. Just imagine the desperate impatience of Jairus!

The story reveals Jesus' way of dealing with interruptions. His sensitivity makes us patient, and his powerful care makes us whole, working through our faith. We may feel frustrated that our work is regularly interrupted until we realize that our interruptions are our work.

COLLECT

O God, you declare your almighty power
most chiefly in showing mercy and pity:
mercifully grant to us such a measure of your grace,
that we, running the way of your commandments,
may receive your gracious promises,
and be made partakers of your heavenly treasure;
through Jesus Christ your Son our Lord,
who is alive and reigns with you,
in the unity of the Holy Spirit,
one God, now and for ever.

Reflection by **John Perumbalath**

Psalms 86, 117
Genesis 28.10-17
John 1.43-end

Thursday 24 August
Bartholomew the Apostle

John 1.43-end

'Can anything good come out of Nazareth?' (v.46)

Bartholomew has been identified traditionally as the Nathanael of this episode, although many modern scholars disagree.

Nathanael's question to Philip reveals some of his prejudices. Philip – and presumably Nathanael too – was from Bethsaida, which was a fairly cosmopolitan town. Nazareth was a small, somewhat isolated village. Can anything good come out of it? After all, Nazareth is never mentioned in the Scriptures as the place from where the Messiah will come.

But Nathanael is willing to investigate. He asks questions, and he listens to the answers. Then when he hears things that don't fit with his prior assumptions, he is willing to change his thinking, letting some new truth in. When he throws in his lot with Jesus, he will find that he is on a journey that will require him to change a lot of inherited categories.

There was a gracious invitation that enabled this inquiry and growth: 'Come and see.' For any restless seeker in this and every time, a welcoming invitation like this as offered by Philip is required. They need space to experience it for themselves but guided by some concrete suggestions based on the host's experience about how and where they may meet the living Word. As a result, Nathanael moves from scepticism to bold Christological confession. In John's Gospel, the decision to be a disciple is inseparable from the decision one makes about the identity of Jesus.

COLLECT

Almighty and everlasting God,
who gave to your apostle Bartholomew grace
truly to believe and to preach your word:
grant that your Church
may love that word which he believed
and may faithfully preach and receive the same;
through Jesus Christ your Son our Lord,
who is alive and reigns with you,
in the unity of the Holy Spirit,
one God, now and for ever.

Reflection by **John Perumbalath**

Friday 25 August

Psalms **88** (95)
Micah 5.2-end
Mark 6.14-29

Mark 6.14-29

'... greatly perplexed; and yet he liked to listen to him' (v.20)

John the Baptist's proclamation was both perplexing and interesting to Herod. John's intervention in the marital circumstances of Herod and Herodias reminds us that the gospel speaks to our corporate and political concerns. The concern was not just about a violation of Levitical law by Herodias being technically married to two brothers (who were her uncles too) but also about marriage being used as a means to fortify the royal court's alliances with others. Corruption in high places cannot be excluded from the scope of gospel proclamation. Herod was perplexed and possibly angry about John's personal attack on him, but he knew that John was 'a righteous and holy man'.

A key element in this episode is the relationship between God's messengers and the earthly powers. We should not be surprised when we are crushed by political or religious powers despite some signs of positive inclination. Both John and Jesus are sent to death by rulers who appreciated their goodness, but who were too weak and too influenced by popular opinion. As power structures are guided by ambition, fear, envy and compromise, the followers of Christ become victims.

This is the only account in Mark's Gospel that is not directly about Jesus. Yet it is not told here as an interlude in the mission of the Twelve but to foreshadow the fate of Jesus and to suggest that his mission will go on in spite of official opposition to it.

COLLECT

O God, you declare your almighty power
most chiefly in showing mercy and pity:
mercifully grant to us such a measure of your grace,
that we, running the way of your commandments,
may receive your gracious promises,
and be made partakers of your heavenly treasure;
through Jesus Christ your Son our Lord,
who is alive and reigns with you,
in the unity of the Holy Spirit,
one God, now and for ever.

Reflection by **John Perumbalath**

Psalms 96, **97**, 100
Micah 6
Mark 6.30-44

Saturday 26 August

Mark 6.30-44

'You give them something to eat' (v.37)

The disciples find in Jesus' words an insensitive and impossible demand. They are worried about the scarcity of food and want to exclude the crowd; Jesus creates plenty and includes all of them. Jesus asks them to 'go and see' what the people have. If we are to see what God can do in order to meet humanity's need, we must offer what we have, however little that is.

To share the little we have, we need compassion. Jesus' response to the crowd is not irritation but compassion because they were like 'sheep without a shepherd', an image of aimlessness and wandering. The first thing that Jesus did with them was to teach them. Teaching is part of his compassionate response to the directionless crowd.

But feeding them with the word was not enough; they are physically exhausted and hungry. Teaching cannot satisfy their physical hunger; they need material food. This is not a question of either this or that. Also, the strong echo of sacramental language is clear in verse 41 – 'blessed', 'broke' and 'gave'. The story becomes part of the sacrament; its words become living bread that satisfies our deepest hunger.

The disciples find themselves at odds with what Jesus wants them to do. Are they tired and fractious? In an overworked and stressed-out world, it is essential to listen to Jesus' invitation to go away and rest for a while. Solitude and rest are the very environment out of which fruitful ministry grows.

COLLECT

God of glory,
the end of our searching,
help us to lay aside
all that prevents us from seeking your kingdom,
and to give all that we have
to gain the pearl beyond all price,
through our Saviour Jesus Christ.

Reflection by **John Perumbalath**

Monday 28 August

Psalms **98**, 99, 101
Micah 7.1-7
Mark 6.45-end

Mark 6.45-end

'... they did not understand about the loaves, but their hearts were hardened' (v.52)

The saga of the failure of the Twelve in understanding Jesus continues. They didn't understand the significance of the feeding miracle and now Jesus offers them another epiphany. The divine character of Jesus' walk on water is clear. They know from the Hebrew Scriptures the descriptions of God appearing on the waters (Job 9.8; 38.16). Jesus' intention to 'pass them by' evokes an image of God's presence (Exodus 33.19,22). They should hear the formula of divine self-revelation, 'I Am,' in 'It is I' from Jesus' mouth.

But the disciples have hardened hearts. This is a description originally applied to hostile outsiders (Mark 3.5) – those who witnessed Jesus' miracles and journeyed with him are no better than the worst unbelievers! Often, we discover that our understanding of something we know well is not as secure as we thought. We face the challenge of constantly overcoming our hard heartedness and disbelief. We must take comfort from the fact that Jesus will still have the same disciples in his company, giving them further opportunities, as they continue to ask questions about his identity.

There is a message for the suffering Church in this story of danger and rescue: Jesus will not abandon his followers. God is there to help us through the difficulties of life. Mark portrays Jesus as the one who appears when his disciples are in trouble and also in the midst of ordinary people in their daily lives and practical needs.

COLLECT

Almighty and everlasting God,
you are always more ready to hear than we to pray
and to give more than either we desire or deserve:
pour down upon us the abundance of your mercy,
forgiving us those things of which our conscience is afraid
and giving us those good things which we are not worthy to ask
but through the merits and mediation
of Jesus Christ your Son our Lord,
who is alive and reigns with you,
in the unity of the Holy Spirit,
one God, now and for ever.

Reflection by **John Perumbalath**

Psalms **106*** (*or* 103)
Micah 7.8-end
Mark 7.1-13

Tuesday 29 August

Mark 7.1-13

'You abandon the commandment of God and hold to human tradition' (v.8)

The 'tradition of the elders' referred to interpretations, procedures and regulations that grew around the written law, the Torah. The Pharisees were committed to help people live the Torah, and for this purpose, they thought the tradition – the oral law – was equally important. But what is designed to aid faithfulness and obedience might become a heavy burden for people (cf. Matthew 23.4).

Jesus condemns elevating human tradition over true devotion to God. Pharisees were concerned about ceremonial purity and the sacredness of vows. The word used for 'defiled' means 'common' or 'communal'. The issue here is not one of hygiene, but a kind of ceremonial 'cleanness' that was difficult for ordinary people to achieve. Clearly, you had to be of a certain class in order to belong to the true religion!

Jesus then turns to the concern about vows. He picks up an example by comparing the commandment to honour one's parents with the tradition that allowed people to avoid this sacred responsibility. By taking an oath, *corban*, people could set aside their property for the use of the temple for religious purposes, making it unavailable for use by their parents. Jesus finds that this practice nullifies the command of God. The unintended consequence of this zealous tradition is economic hardship and injustice.

Jesus is not advocating abandonment of tradition but its radical reassessment in the light of Scripture and our new context.

COLLECT

God of constant mercy,
who sent your Son to save us:
remind us of your goodness,
increase your grace within us,
that our thankfulness may grow,
through Jesus Christ our Lord.

Reflection by **John Perumbalath**

Wednesday 30 August

Psalms 110, **111**, 112
Habakkuk 1.1-11
Mark 7.14-23

Mark 7.14-23

'... do you also fail to understand?' (v. 18)

In yesterday's reading, Jesus was speaking to the Pharisees and scribes. The audience of verses 14-15 is the crowd. The rest of today's reading is private instruction to the disciples.

Jesus rejects the ritual understanding of uncleanness in favour of a prophetic and ethical one. Instruments of human defilement emerge from within the heart, the seat of moral sensibility. All the vices Jesus refers to here violate the social contract. It is easier to follow some ritual practices than to transform our hearts. But that's the challenge posed by the gospel.

In the list that Jesus provides, attitudes and actions are intermingled. Jesus does not seem to think that one is more sinful than the other. Our attitudes and actions reflect the orientation of our heart. The heart of holiness is not a matter of distancing from 'unclean' foods, objects or persons. It has more to do with a choice to love God and neighbour.

Jesus challenges us to examine the religious practices we pursue and ask why we pursue them. We also need to assess how those practices affect ourselves and others. Moral rigidity and self-satisfaction are no proof of holiness. Washed hands are nothing compared to our attitudes and actions that do damage to others. Defilement is not only about what we do but also about how that impacts others. Jesus' emphasis is on what defiles our relationships.

COLLECT

Almighty and everlasting God,
you are always more ready to hear than we to pray
and to give more than either we desire or deserve:
pour down upon us the abundance of your mercy,
forgiving us those things of which our conscience is afraid
and giving us those good things which we are not worthy to ask
but through the merits and mediation
of Jesus Christ your Son our Lord,
who is alive and reigns with you,
in the unity of the Holy Spirit,
one God, now and for ever.

Reflection by **John Perumbalath**

Psalms 113, **115**
Habakkuk 1.12 – 2.5
Mark 7.24-30

Thursday 31 August

Mark 7.24-30

'For saying that, you may go...' (v. 29)

Jesus provides an example of how to lose an argument graciously.

Jesus is found with the wrong person in the wrong place! A Jewish teacher would not normally engage with a gentile woman in a dialogue like this. And, unlike other Jewish teachers, Jesus has made a trip to the gentile places. Earlier in this chapter, some Jewish leaders had argued with Jesus about defilement and purity. As if to show them where he stood on these issues, he goes straight to non-Jewish territories, enters a house there, and begins a dialogue with a woman.

Yet he makes a harsh statement. Although many interpreters try to explain away the problem by defining 'dog' positively, we need to accept that this is an insulting remark. The dialogue presents an honest picture of Jesus. Jesus is weary and under constant attack from the Jewish leaders. He has tried to get away from it all, but is pursued by people. The offending remark represents the then prevalent Jewish approach to gentiles. Nevertheless, the dialogue is transforming and Jesus grants her request. With this act, Jesus has moved across all kinds of boundaries: theological, geographical, ethnic and gender.

Despite being initially compared to a dog, the woman is affirmed and lifted up as an example. Rather than succumbing to her limitations, she brings them into light and calls them into question. In her persistent, altruistic, courageous and inventive approach, the woman serves as a shining example of faith.

COLLECT

God of constant mercy,
who sent your Son to save us:
remind us of your goodness,
increase your grace within us,
that our thankfulness may grow,
through Jesus Christ our Lord.

Reflection by **John Perumbalath**

Friday 1 September

Psalm **139**
Habakkuk 2.6-end
Mark 7.31-end

Mark 7.31-end

'They brought to him a deaf man who had an impediment in his speech' (v. 32)

Jesus continues his ministry in the gentile territories of Decapolis. It is not the faith of the deaf man with the speech impediment that brings about his healing but that of his faithful companions. Mark also makes a big deal about the response to the healing from those companions, not from the healed man. The man, without speech and hearing, is possibly unaware of Jesus and unable to ask him for help on his own. Those who can't come to Jesus on their own may need to be brought to Jesus. Indeed, many – if not most – people need some support to turn to Jesus.

Speech and hearing play a symbolic role in Mark's narrative. Jesus' disciples show increasing difficulty in understanding what Jesus is telling them. They are in need of a miracle of heart that will help them hear and understand. Our understanding is normally expressed to others through speaking. The companions of the healed man spoke or 'proclaimed', as in other stories of healing. Believers need to recognize the need to speak about their experience of Jesus.

Jesus tells them, as in many other instances, not to tell anyone of this saving experience. This pattern is a common one in Mark: Jesus orders silence, yet everybody talks. Jesus does not want to be known in his true identity until it will be clear that suffering rather than power lies at the core of that identity.

COLLECT

Almighty and everlasting God,
you are always more ready to hear than we to pray
and to give more than either we desire or deserve:
pour down upon us the abundance of your mercy,
forgiving us those things of which our conscience is afraid
and giving us those good things which we are not worthy to ask
but through the merits and mediation
of Jesus Christ your Son our Lord,
who is alive and reigns with you,
in the unity of the Holy Spirit,
one God, now and for ever.

Reflection by **John Perumbalath**

Psalms 120, **121**, 122
Habakkuk 3.2-19*a*
Mark 8.1-10

Saturday 2 September

Mark 8.1-10

'They ate and were filled' (v.8)

The first feeding story (Mark 6.35-44) was initiated by the disciples' concern for the crowd. In this story, Jesus takes the initiative. There is a specific function for each of these stories in Mark's narrative. This story takes place in a predominantly gentile context. The earlier story had numbers and images related to the history of Israel – reminding us of the 'five' books of the law, 'twelve' tribes, shepherd; those references are absent here.

Jesus came to feed gentiles as well as Jews. Gentiles are entitled to more than 'crumbs' (cf. 7.28). Mark's narrative was addressing the early Church where the inclusion of gentile Christians as equal partners with Jewish Christians was the central issue. When we read Mark, we must reflect on the central issues of inclusion and exclusion in our time.

This episode is also about the disciples' failure to understand. They ask, 'How can one feed these people ...?' Jesus had fed a multitude a short while ago and in a similar situation to this one; yet they don't seem to remember what happened before. How many more episodes will they need before they get some understanding of the power and grace of Christ?

The feeding also points forward to the Last Supper. It is unlikely that Mark's audience would have missed the eucharistic allusions in Jesus taking, giving thanks, breaking and giving. Just as Jesus fed both Jews and Gentiles in the lands around Galilee, so he still feeds his followers.

COLLECT

God of constant mercy,
who sent your Son to save us:
remind us of your goodness,
increase your grace within us,
that our thankfulness may grow,
through Jesus Christ our Lord.

Reflection by **John Perumbalath**

Monday 4 September

Psalms 123, 124, 125, **126**
Haggai 1.1-11
Mark 8.11-21

Mark 8.11-21

'... no sign will be given' (v.12)

Whether he is exasperated or wounded, Jesus' deep sigh reflects a weariness as he faces the latest in the Pharisees' tests and questions. Freshly returned from feeding 4,000 people with just seven loaves and a few fish, Jesus could be forgiven for thinking that the Pharisees had more than enough information, stories and testimony to determine his identity.

The religious leaders are not satisfied. They want a 'sign from heaven', evidence on their own terms. Jesus refuses. He will not be manipulated, cajoled or pressured into meeting the Pharisees' demands. Neither will he endlessly adjust the trajectory of his mission to respond to the preferences of others.

This is not to exclude the Pharisees from the kingdom of Heaven – the same invitation of love and welcome is extended to them as it is to all people, but it is to make clear the authority of Jesus. He is not building a democratic coalition or establishing his authority by gathering support from different parties. Jesus' authority arises from who he is: the way, the truth and the life.

Jesus' deep sigh might prompt reflection in us. Are there times when we are inclined to want the gospel presented on our own terms, despite the signs of the kingdom all about us? How might we resist the temptation to temper the demands of discipleship to suit others' preferences? Certain of his vocation and identity, Jesus does not engage in fruitless debate but simply presses on. May we do likewise.

COLLECT

Almighty God,
who called your Church to bear witness
that you were in Christ reconciling the world to yourself:
help us to proclaim the good news of your love,
that all who hear it may be drawn to you;
through him who was lifted up on the cross,
and reigns with you in the unity of the Holy Spirit,
one God, now and for ever.

Reflection by **Vanessa Conant**

Psalms **132**, 133
Haggai 1.12 – 2.9
Mark 8.22-26

Tuesday 5 September

Mark 8.22-26

'Can you see anything?' (v.23)

This story of the blind man at Bethsaida occurs only in Mark's Gospel and, uniquely among the miracle stories, shows the healing to be, initially, only partially effective. If we were to look at this account in isolation, we might wonder why Mark chose to include it; what are we to make of the fact that Jesus has to lay hands on the man's eyes for a second time in order for him to see clearly?

We might find some insight if we consider the way that Mark has chosen to structure these central passages of the Gospel. Two stories of blindness bracket Jesus' teaching on what it means to be a disciple. In the first, we see a man whose sight has improved but who needs further healing before it is fully restored. In the second, Bartimaeus is immediately healed.

These two stories offer us a helpful metaphor for the journey of discipleship. We may begin like the blind man, by seeing only in part, just as the disciples struggle to understand both the facts of Jesus' impending death and resurrection and the related costs of following him.

Three times in the following chapters, Jesus responds to the disciples' confusion or denial with further teaching, encouraging them to know his call and his commission. We accompany them in this study, invited to deepen our knowledge and our commitment until, like Bartimaeus, we find we are able to see.

COLLECT

Almighty God,
you search us and know us:
may we rely on you in strength
and rest on you in weakness,
now and in all our days;
through Jesus Christ our Lord.

Reflection by **Vanessa Conant**

Wednesday 6 September

Psalm **119.153-end**
Haggai 2.10-end
Mark 8.27 – 9.1

Mark 8.27 – 9.1

'But who do you say that I am?' (8.29)

The question Jesus poses to his disciples is not a theological quiz. This is not a rabbi, testing his students to make sure that they have understood the material. Jesus is asking both if they have grasped the truth of who he is *and* what difference that truth will make to them.

The same question faces every person who places their trust and hope in Jesus Christ. We cannot respond to the question of his identity without revealing something of our own. If we say that Jesus is the Son of God, if we believe that healing and hope are to be found in him alone, then we must reckon with what that means for the shape of our living.

Peter's confession of faith is followed swiftly by words of rebuke to Jesus. The Messiah should not – *cannot* surely – suffer in this way at the hands of the elders? Jesus' response is sharp: Peter cannot declare faith in Christ without accepting that the promised redemption is cruciform in shape. The glory for which Peter longs can only be fulfilled through suffering, service and sacrifice.

If we are willing to be known for what we believe, we must also make choices that correlate with this faith. We cannot choose only half the picture. Responding to Jesus' enquiry is much more than making a statement about who Christ is; it is committing ourselves to walking with Jesus, all the way to the cross.

COLLECT

Almighty God,
who called your Church to bear witness
that you were in Christ reconciling the world to yourself:
help us to proclaim the good news of your love,
that all who hear it may be drawn to you;
through him who was lifted up on the cross,
and reigns with you in the unity of the Holy Spirit,
one God, now and for ever.

Reflection by **Vanessa Conant**

Psalms **143**, 146
Zechariah 1.1-17
Mark 9.2-13

Thursday 7 September

Mark 9.2-13

'... listen to him!' (v.7)

Mark writes with characteristic attention to detail to draw us into the mystery and awe of this moment: '... his clothes became dazzling white, such as no one on earth could bleach them.' No wonder Peter wants to capture this moment, to build booths, to stay in this place of glorious beauty.

The response to this hasty, frightened offer is a voice from heaven, echoing Jesus' baptism but speaking now directly to the disciples: 'This is my Son, whom I love. Listen to him'. Faced with ineffable mystery, Jesus' followers are called not to build some museum of holy encounter, but to listen closely and to respond to the call of discipleship.

Soon, the disciples will descend the mountain and find themselves in the pain and mess of human life. Soon, Jesus will speak for the second time of his coming death. The transfiguration is not offered as escapism from all of this, but as equipping strength for all that will follow.

It can be tempting, amid the challenges of daily life, to cling to memories of times when we did experience God's presence or when faith felt simpler. We may want to retreat into and preserve our own encounters with the dazzling brightness, however they may have appeared to us. In these moments, God reminds us to keep listening; the way of Jesus is not to remain on the mountaintop. Sustained by his presence, we are to follow him towards the cross, where brokenness and radiant glory meet.

COLLECT

Almighty God,
you search us and know us:
may we rely on you in strength
and rest on you in weakness,
now and in all our days;
through Jesus Christ our Lord.

Reflection by **Vanessa Conant**

Friday 8 September

Psalms 142, **144**
Zechariah 1.18 – end of 2
Mark 9.14-29

Mark 9.14-29

'... help me overcome my unbelief!' (v.24, NIV)

The desperate father stands in sharp contrast to the quarrelling disciples and teachers of the law. Here is a man aware of the smallness and inadequacy of his faith. Unlike those at the centre of the row, he has no confidence in his own powers to help his son. He has brought his child to Jesus because he is at the end of his resources and out of options.

This is a great risk of faith. After years of disappointment and suffering, the father has to trust again, and this is costly. His call for help to overcome his unbelief comes as a loud cry, a raw shout from the depths of his need.

There is no shame in his position. In this passage, the father serves as an example of hopeful belief. The disciples seem to have forgotten that their previous attempts to drive out demons were effective not because of their own power, but because of the power of Christ. The father comes to Jesus aware of his utter dependence and fragility and so is able to witness the healing for which he has prayed so urgently.

Here is invitation and assurance: true faith is found, not in certainty or arrogance, but in humble openness to Jesus with whom all things are possible.

COLLECT

Almighty God,
who called your Church to bear witness
that you were in Christ reconciling the world to yourself:
help us to proclaim the good news of your love,
that all who hear it may be drawn to you;
through him who was lifted up on the cross,
and reigns with you in the unity of the Holy Spirit,
one God, now and for ever.

 Reflection by **Vanessa Conant**

Psalm **147**
Zechariah 3
Mark 9.30-37

Saturday 9 September

Mark 9.30-37

'But they did not understand ...' (v.32)

In Chapters 8 and 9 of Mark's Gospel, the disciples' confusion and uncertainty weave between moments of conviction and clarity. By now, we are familiar with these oscillations between radical faith and utter bewilderment, and this is a pattern that will be repeated throughout the Gospel: the fisherman who will leave his nets at a word of invitation will later deny the one to whom he has pledged his life.

For the second time, Jesus predicts his death and resurrection and, for the second time, the disciples are mystified and afraid to ask Jesus to explain. Instead, they descend into argument and jockeying for position. Their distress at Jesus' description of his imminent death, their refusal to accept a Messiah who would die in this way or their embarrassed attempt to hide their confusion all prevent them from receiving the truth of the incarnation.

We too experience undulations of faith – moments of profound encounter can give way to crises of belief, heartfelt convictions can flounder in the face of circumstances we don't understand. How might we avoid the squabbles and failings of the disciples by asking our harder questions, seeking deeper understanding and being unafraid to admit our uncertainty?

The passage ends with Jesus embracing a child. Who better to represent humanity's curiosity, immaturity and unknowing? When it comes to our confusion and our questions, we have nothing to fear.

COLLECT

Almighty God,
you search us and know us:
may we rely on you in strength
and rest on you in weakness,
now and in all our days;
through Jesus Christ our Lord.

Reflection by **Vanessa Conant**

Monday 11 September

Psalms **1**, 2, 3
Zechariah 4
Mark 9.38-end

Mark 9.38-end

'... and we tried to stop him' (v.38)

Something powerful, undeniable and unsettling is happening. People are being released from the deathly grip of demons not by Jesus, not even by his chosen followers, but now by unknown people choosing to pray in his name. Perhaps it is only natural that the disciples are struggling to know how to respond. Should this power to drive out evil be given to just anyone? How naturally we draw boundary lines when we are uncertain; there is a security and a safety in knowing who is 'in' and who is 'out'.

Jesus urges his disciples to widen their perspective; there is a gracious welcome of the kingdom to anyone who gives all that they have in the costly ministry of driving out satanic forces in his name.

Likewise, even the simple act of offering water to a disciple will bring gracious reception into the community of Jesus' followers. His attention is on those whose actions reflect his character of merciful love, and the boundary is constantly being widened to include and to welcome.

To follow Jesus is to be expansive in our understanding of belonging, to be constantly mindful of our instinct to put up barriers and dividing lines, and to be open instead to the surprising and beautiful way in which the Holy Spirit works in both friend and stranger.

COLLECT

Almighty God,
whose only Son has opened for us
a new and living way into your presence:
give us pure hearts and steadfast wills
to worship you in spirit and in truth;
through Jesus Christ your Son our Lord,
who is alive and reigns with you,
in the unity of the Holy Spirit,
one God, now and for ever.

Reflection by **Vanessa Conant**

Psalms **5**, 6 (8)
Zechariah 6.9-end
Mark 10.1-16

Tuesday 12 September

Mark 10.1-16

'... let no one separate' (v.9)

In this passage, we are given a profound insight into what Jesus means when he said, 'I have come not to abolish the law but to fulfil it' (Matthew 5.17). Divorce was not uncommon in Jewish culture, and most debate centred around detailed points of law. Jesus refuses to enter into the minutiae of the Pharisees' legal interpretation and, instead, cuts straight to the heart of the argument.

Jesus' challenge is that the Pharisees' approach to Mosaic law neglects the spirit of the law, most particularly the protection of the most vulnerable. Divorce placed a woman at great risk. Without the protection of a wider family structure and without an explanation for the ending of her marriage, she was exposed both physically and economically.

The legal arguments tended to assume a man's perspective and focused on how he could legally divorce for his own benefit and financial enrichment. There was no consideration for how this could endanger the woman. Jesus is clear: marriage is not about gain or utility but about identity. The law is more demanding than the Pharisees understand.

At the end of the passage, Jesus speaks again for the vulnerable when the disciples try to stop people bringing children to him, those without rights or social status. In these two moments of encounter, Jesus teaches that the fulfilment of the law is to be found not in precise navigation of the rules but in the care and protection of those most in need.

COLLECT

Merciful God,
your Son came to save us
and bore our sins on the cross:
may we trust in your mercy
and know your love,
rejoicing in the righteousness
that is ours through Jesus Christ our Lord.

Reflection by **Vanessa Conant**

Wednesday 13 September

Psalm **119.1-32**
Zechariah 7
Mark 10.17-31

Mark 10.17-31

'... he was shocked and went away grieving' (v.22)

There is both tenderness and respect in the encounter between the young man and Jesus. He kneels before Jesus and addresses him with terms of honour. Jesus, in turn, looks at him and loves him. Yet the conversation between the aspiring disciple and his Teacher does not result in a confession of faith or commitment to follow. Instead, he goes away grieving.

It is clear from Jesus' teaching throughout the passage that we cannot earn our way to salvation. The disciples are shocked to learn that the wealthy – whose advantages would have been considered the result of divine blessing or favour – will struggle to enter the kingdom of God. Who then, they ask, can be saved? Jesus reminds them that hope is to be found not in our own goodness, but in God's saving love and mercy alone.

This doesn't mean that, for each of us, nothing must change. The rich young man serves as an example of the paradox of discipleship. Jesus offers him the eternal life he seeks to inherit, but it comes at the cost of the possessions to which he is wedded. It seems, in this moment, too much to ask.

Following Jesus is to live in this tension: our salvation comes to us as grace, but our discipleship demands a response. Kneeling with the young man and seeking to learn, can we relinquish our attachment to those things that prevent us from giving our all – or will we, too, go away grieving?

COLLECT

Almighty God,
whose only Son has opened for us
a new and living way into your presence:
give us pure hearts and steadfast wills
to worship you in spirit and in truth;
through Jesus Christ your Son our Lord,
who is alive and reigns with you,
in the unity of the Holy Spirit,
one God, now and for ever.

Reflection by **Vanessa Conant**

Psalms 2, 8, 146
Genesis 3.1-15
John 12.27-36*a*

Thursday 14 September

Holy Cross Day

John 12.27-36*a*

'... children of light' (v.36)

Far away from the solemnity of Holy Week and Easter, Holy Cross Day stops us in our tracks and calls for our attention. We return to the mystery of how a barbaric instrument of death was redeemed into the tree of life for all humankind. In this passage in John, the crowd hears the voice of God as thunder or the voice of an angel. How might we be called to hear the voice of God as we come to worship and adore the Christ who redeemed the world through his death on the cross?

On this feast day, we both celebrate and re-affirm our commitment to walk in the way of Jesus. The text contains both urgency and clarity. This is the last time Jesus will speak to the crowd and so this is the last opportunity for the world to make a decision. How will it respond to Jesus? How will we? The sharp focus of this moment calls the crowd to see how Jesus' crucifixion triumphs over powers of darkness, how his rising again will draw all people to him.

On this Holy Cross Day, we are invited to respond afresh to Jesus' urging. How will we be children of light, putting our trust and faith in the cross that brings our redemption and being people who work for that redemption in our own lives and communities?

COLLECT

Almighty God,
who in the passion of your blessed Son
made an instrument of painful death
to be for us the means of life and peace:
grant us so to glory in the cross of Christ
that we may gladly suffer for his sake;
who is alive and reigns with you,
in the unity of the Holy Spirit,
one God, now and for ever.

Reflection by **Vanessa Conant**

Friday 15 September

Psalms 17, **19**
Zechariah 8.9-end
Mark 10.35-45

Mark 10.35-45

'Are you able to drink the cup?' (v.38)

Again, the disciples have not understood. Their eagerness is for glory, but they have overlooked the suffering that lies ahead. Once again, Jesus teaches that the way of discipleship is one of costly self-denial; do James and John really know what they are asking?

Power and prestige are always enticing. It is not only the sons of Zebedee who long for honour; the disciples are enraged by the pair's jostling for position. Unpicking our longing for status, affirmation and privilege is challenging work.

Here, Jesus teaches what he will later demonstrate in a final meal with his disciples. The cup he drinks from will be the cup of his blood, poured out for many. Those who want to share in his glory must also be willing to share in the rejection, humiliation and violence he will encounter.

Sacrifice and servitude are not purposeless. They not only challenge the world's understanding of greatness and offer an alternative way of being human; Jesus' cup is both the sign of his self-giving love and an act that brings about redemption. Through the death and resurrection we commemorate in the Eucharist, Jesus brings new blessing and new life, nourishment, community, covenant and healing. We are invited to share in this work too.

In love, Jesus drinks the cup, trusting in the Father to strengthen him for all that lies ahead. So it is for us; only with his help can we do likewise.

COLLECT

Almighty God,
whose only Son has opened for us
a new and living way into your presence:
give us pure hearts and steadfast wills
to worship you in spirit and in truth;
through Jesus Christ your Son our Lord,
who is alive and reigns with you,
in the unity of the Holy Spirit,
one God, now and for ever.

Reflection by **Vanessa Conant**

Psalms 20, 21, **23**
Zechariah 9.1-12
Mark 10.46-end

Saturday 16 September

Mark 10.46-end

'My teacher, let me see again' (v.51)

In contrast to James and John, Bartimaeus seeks no special privileges. His is a simple and straightforward request, '... let me see again'. The petition alone is revealing of Bartimaeus' faith, for which Jesus praises him. Here is an exemplary disciple.

Unlike so many of those who fail to recognize who Jesus is, Bartimaeus, the blind man, has no difficulty in naming Jesus as royal. He calls out to the Son of David, a title that reflects Bartimaeus' understanding of Jesus as an agent of divine power.

In the preceding passages, we have seen the faith and commitment of others falter – even those closest to Jesus. Not so for Bartimaeus. He is persistent and courageous, ignoring the attempts to stop him reaching Jesus and facing down the rebukes that told him to be quiet. There was little social standing for blind people forced to beg for their survival, but Bartimaeus is not deterred by the hierarchies of his culture or society; he will seek healing from the one who can bring wholeness.

In Bartimaeus, we see expectation and hope. He trusts and believes that Jesus can bring him sight and so transform his life. He asks simply and confidently for what he needs and, receiving it, he follows Jesus along the road. May we learn from Bartimaeus' example, from his boldness, tenacity, trust and faith and may the eyes of our hearts see more clearly to follow Jesus on the way to the cross.

COLLECT

Merciful God,
your Son came to save us
and bore our sins on the cross:
may we trust in your mercy
and know your love,
rejoicing in the righteousness
that is ours through Jesus Christ our Lord.

Reflection by **Vanessa Conant**

Monday 18 September

Psalms 27, **30**
Zechariah 10
Mark 11.1-11

Mark 11.1-11

'Blessed is the one who comes in the name of the Lord!' (v.9)

The four Gospels are sometimes described as passion narratives with long introductions. This makes them unique as a style of writing. A conventional biography divides a person's life into balanced parts. Mark focuses six chapters out of sixteen on the final eight days of Jesus' life. For this span of eight days, time slows down, as it were. We move in minute detail through every episode of this season. The evangelist invites us to ponder the two great questions of the Gospel. The first: Who is this Jesus? The second: What is the meaning of his death and his resurrection? The course of our whole lives will turn on the answers we make.

Mark answers the questions through the way the Gospel tells the story. Much of the detail is not decoded for the reader but invites us to explore further. What is the meaning of this entry to Jerusalem? Why a colt that has never been ridden? Why this royal road, spreading palms and coats along the way?

As we seek answers to the questions we are drawn back to the Old Testament prophecies of the king who will come, the Messiah. We are drawn to Zechariah's prophecy about the humble king riding on a donkey (Zechariah 9.9); above all we are drawn to the vast expanse of Psalm 118 through the cry 'Hosanna!': a song of victory, not lament, which frames our understanding of what is unfolding before us.

And Jesus? Jesus is largely silent here, directing events in detail, looking around at everything. Who can this be?

COLLECT

God, who in generous mercy sent the Holy Spirit
upon your Church in the burning fire of your love:
grant that your people may be fervent
in the fellowship of the gospel
that, always abiding in you,
they may be found steadfast in faith and active in service;
through Jesus Christ your Son our Lord,
who is alive and reigns with you,
in the unity of the Holy Spirit,
one God, now and for ever.

Reflection by **Steven Croft**

Psalms 32, **36**
Zechariah 11.4-end
Mark 11.12-26

Tuesday 19 September

Mark 11.12-26

'... a house of prayer for all the nations' (v.17)

There are two prophetic actions here: signs that reveal God's purpose in the tradition of Amos and Jeremiah (see Jeremiah 19.10 for an example). The cursing of the fig tree happens within the circle of the disciples. The cleansing of the temple is Jesus' most public act of confrontation with the Jewish authorities and gives a final pretext for the chief priests and scribes to seek to kill Jesus, 'for they were afraid of him'. More is being overturned than chairs and tables.

Mark invites his readers to ponder the wider meaning of these signs in the story of salvation. It's not hard to see the fig tree as an echo of Isaiah's parable of the vineyard. God comes looking for the fruit of justice but finds only weeping (Isaiah 5). The purification of the temple echoes many prophetic attempts to cleanse Israel's centre of worship and prayer, especially Josiah's reforms (2 Kings 22). Both have a particular significance in the narrative of the passion. The role of the nation and of the temple is about to be changed profoundly by the death and resurrection of the Son of God.

Vital as these wider perspectives are, we must not miss the actual lessons Jesus draws from both symbolic actions that centre on prayer. Prayer is partly a matter of place – are we giving the right priority to worship and to the love of God in our lives? Prayer is even more a matter of the heart; faith and forgiveness are essential in our everyday faith.

COLLECT

Lord God,
defend your Church from all false teaching
and give to your people knowledge of your truth,
that we may enjoy eternal life
in Jesus Christ our Lord.

Reflection by **Steven Croft**

Wednesday 20 September

Psalm **34**
Zechariah 12.1-10
Mark 11.27-end

Mark 11.27-end

'By what authority are you doing these things?' (v.28)

This is the first of four questions asked in the temple precincts by different groups with very different motives. Jesus responds in different but equally salty ways to each. Mark gives us a picture of a Christ who is full of energy and creativity, able to craft a counterquestion that divides his opponents but also able to answer with rich crystals of truth that live long in the mind. Mark's portrait has moved from the prophet to the wise teacher, skilled in every form of debate.

This first question on authority is vital and is both answered and not answered. The word 'authority' takes us back to the very beginning of Jesus' ministry in Galilee: the crowds are astounded by his authority in teaching, healing and forgiving sins (Mark 1.22, 27; 2.10). Will this kind of charismatic authority be sufficient in Jerusalem? As elsewhere in Mark, Jesus avoids a direct answer but throws a question back to his inquisitors about the authority of the baptism of John.

As often with Mark, the reader who lingers and wonders and looks back in the story will find the answers continuing to unfold. There is only one possible answer to the question that the reader of Mark can give. Jesus is, in fact, claiming the same authority as John the Baptist but also a still greater authority as the one to whom the Baptist points.

COLLECT

God, who in generous mercy sent the Holy Spirit
upon your Church in the burning fire of your love:
grant that your people may be fervent
in the fellowship of the gospel
that, always abiding in you,
they may be found steadfast in faith and active in service;
through Jesus Christ your Son our Lord,
who is alive and reigns with you,
in the unity of the Holy Spirit,
one God, now and for ever.

Reflection by **Steven Croft**

Psalms 49, 117
1 Kings 19.15-end
2 Timothy 3.14-end

Thursday 21 September

Matthew, Apostle and Evangelist

2 Timothy 3.14-end

'All scripture is inspired by God and is useful …' (v.16)

'Then when we retire, we can write the gospels' sing the apostles in *Jesus Christ Superstar*. St Matthew's day is an excellent day to reflect on that process of writing and inspiration that gifted the world with four Gospels, each telling the story of Jesus in a way that is distinctive, each connecting with different cultures and with different stages of life and faith.

Like each of the Gospels, Matthew has a distinctive personality and emphases, but we will each understand only some of them in a single lifetime. Matthew is shaped by the Gospel's source material (primarily Mark and probably collections of Jesus' teaching). Matthew is shaped by the Jewish Christian community for whom the Gospel was first written, but also, undoubtedly, by the mature reflection and personality of the author.

2 Timothy 3 is both unhelpful and helpful as a way into understanding Matthew's creative process. Unhelpful because, in its context, 'all scripture' undoubtedly refers to the Old Testament texts. Only later does the Church affirm the Gospels and New Testament texts as authoritative to the same degree. But it is helpful because the unique word translated as 'inspired' captures something vital about the Gospel text, seen through the eyes of faith. The word means literally 'God-breathed'. It captures a sense of the Spirit, the breath of God, enlivening each part of the text; brooding over the writer in the act of creation; brooding over the readers as we each find new life as we hear the text today.

COLLECT

O Almighty God,
whose blessed Son called Matthew the tax collector
to be an apostle and evangelist:
give us grace to forsake the selfish pursuit of gain
and the possessive love of riches
that we may follow in the way of your Son Jesus Christ,
who is alive and reigns with you,
in the unity of the Holy Spirit,
one God, now and for ever.

Reflection by **Steven Croft**

Friday 22 September

Psalm **31**
Zechariah 14.1-11
Mark 12.13-17

Mark 12.13-17

'Is it lawful to pay taxes to the emperor, or not?' (v.14)

The way Mark tells the story of this second question does three things. The first is to continue the dramatic build-up to the arrest of Jesus by revealing the hostility of further factions among the leaders in Jerusalem. The Pharisees and Herodians come 'to trap him' – a word normally used of the capture of animals in a hunt. There is an irresistible momentum here.

The second is to offer a clear foundational principle for the Christian community after the resurrection. How were the Christians to live well in relation to the Roman Empire, which occupied most of the known world? Were they to withdraw like the Essenes to live out their lives in small faithful enclaves? Were they, like the Zealots, to attempt to establish by violence a theocracy, a state where the law of God was applied? Jesus' answer points to a better way, yet one that has integrity: a primary allegiance to God but a recognition that the normal situation, the starting point for debate, is one of compatible loyalties. This critical engagement proves vital in every generation for the wellbeing of the Church and the world, and of Christian mission.

But the third purpose is the place where Mark leaves us. Once again we stand with the interrogators. Jesus has been faced with a seemingly impossible dilemma. With them, we are amazed and we wonder and we keep asking the question: who is this who holds such deep wisdom and can read the hearts of humankind?

COLLECT

God, who in generous mercy sent the Holy Spirit
 upon your Church in the burning fire of your love:
grant that your people may be fervent
in the fellowship of the gospel
that, always abiding in you,
they may be found steadfast in faith and active in service;
through Jesus Christ your Son our Lord,
who is alive and reigns with you,
in the unity of the Holy Spirit,
one God, now and for ever.

Reflection by **Steven Croft**

Psalms 41, **42**, 43
Zechariah 14.12-end
Mark 12.18-27

Saturday 23 September

Mark 12.18-27

'... you are quite wrong' (v.27)

The Sadducees remind us that there was no universal agreement among Jews or Gentiles about the resurrection from the dead or about what happens when a person dies. The default belief then, as now, was simply an ending to life and meaningful existence. At the time of Jesus, belief in resurrection was growing, and had been embraced by the Pharisees, but not by a majority by any means. The religious landscape on death was not so very different from the present day.

But in the face of this question, Jesus is clear and unequivocal. There is no attempt to parry or to avoid an answer. In reverse order, the Sadducees are simply wrong; the truth of the resurrection rests in the very nature and essence of God, the great 'I AM', who cannot but give and sustain life to those God loves; the resurrection life will be fundamentally different from this life, not a simple continuation. The implication of verse 25 is that those who share it will retain our identity, but our relationships and the need to reproduce will be transformed.

Mark's Gospel is famously brief in its account of the resurrection of Jesus, but that resurrection is signposted all the way through the narrative and especially here. As an anxious Church casts about for points of clarity and certainty, here is a solid rock on which to place our feet in the fast-flowing river of our culture. Death is not the end. There will be resurrection. God is the God of the living not the dead. Christ is risen. Alleluia!

COLLECT

Lord God,
defend your Church from all false teaching
and give to your people knowledge of your truth,
that we may enjoy eternal life
in Jesus Christ our Lord.

Reflection by **Steven Croft**

Monday 25 September

Psalm **44**
Ecclesiasticus 1.1-10
or Ezekiel 1.1-14
Mark 12.28-34

Mark 12.28-34

'You are not far from the kingdom of God' (v.34)

In this sequence of four questions, Mark has saved the best until last. The overall impression is that Jesus prevails in the debate summarized in the Gospel's judgement that 'after that no one dared to ask him any questions'. Jesus' wisdom and ability to craft an answer to the testings is not in doubt. Now that wisdom enters territory familiar to the rabbis: the interpretation of Torah. Which of the 613 commandments in the Books of Moses is the greatest? Is there an overriding principle to be found?

The principle in Jesus' answer is clear and it is the principle of love, lifted up here above obedience or holiness. The life of the disciple is primarily relational. We are invited into a love affair with God, which animates every part of our lives and which overflows into love of everyone and everything around us: a response to the love we have received.

The love described is deeper than romantic love and the solid mutual love of friendship. This is *agape*: steadfast, constant self-giving and preference for God and neighbour. The twist in the answer is, of course, responding not with a single principle but with two commandments. These do have an order to them ('The first ... The second'). But they are to be held in perpetual tension. Jesus sets the rhythm of life here for every disciple and for every church.

COLLECT

O Lord, we beseech you mercifully to hear the prayers
of your people who call upon you;
and grant that they may both perceive and know
what things they ought to do,
and also may have grace and power faithfully to fulfil them;
through Jesus Christ your Son our Lord,
who is alive and reigns with you,
in the unity of the Holy Spirit,
one God, now and for ever.

 Reflection by **Steven Croft**

Psalms **48**, 52
Ecclesiasticus 1.11-end
or Ezekiel 1.15 – 2.2
Mark 12.35-end

Tuesday 26 September

Mark 12.35-end

'... all she had to live on' (v.44)

One of the best Christian mimes I've ever seen was about a man responding to the collection plate in church. He gives. The plate comes back. He puts in his wallet and cards. The plate returns and each time the man adds more: car keys, house keys, jacket, trousers, shoes. The plate comes back. Finally the man understands what is required. Slowly and carefully the man himself climbs onto the plate.

God does not seek our possessions. God is not looking for a tip in the form of our loose change or even a tithe in the form of our regular giving. God invites us to give our whole selves in response to the love of God poured out and demonstrated through Jesus our Lord.

This is the love and understanding demonstrated by the widow. The widow puts in more than all the others who contribute out of their abundance. This is not only because of what the gift means as a proportion of her wealth. The original translates literally as 'she threw in everything she has, *her whole life*'.

Every time I return to this story, I am profoundly moved: by the widow herself and her generosity; by the many examples of sacrificial giving I have seen and known across the years, but most of all by the one who comments on the gift. Again, we remember where we are in the passion story: here is one who is about to give his whole life.

COLLECT

Lord of creation,
whose glory is around and within us:
open our eyes to your wonders,
that we may serve you with reverence
and know your peace at our lives' end,
through Jesus Christ our Lord.

Reflection by **Steven Croft**

Wednesday 27 September

Psalm **119.57-80**
Ecclesiasticus 2
or Ezekiel 2.3 – 3.11
Mark 13.1-13

Mark 13.1-13

'And the good news must first be proclaimed to all nations' (v.10)

A handful of disciples sit by themselves with Jesus on the Mount of Olives looking over the Kidron valley. The skyline is dominated by the temple, the symbol of stability and security.

As Jesus speaks with them, one set of securities crumbles away in the light of Jesus' words to be replaced by another. It will be no use now placing trust in the temple or in human rulers or even nations. All will be shaken in the generations to come. Even families will come under pressure and fall apart.

So what then is left? Where should disciples place their trust? One place remains: the good news that must be proclaimed first to all the nations. Every word in verse 10 is worthy of careful reflection and meditation. The good news of Jesus – the very content of Mark's Gospel we are reading together – is the story of Jesus' life, death and resurrection. This good news is of significance not to one nation but to every nation; not for a single generation but for every generation to come.

This good news must be proclaimed for the sake of the whole world: so great is the responsibility laid on these disciples with great resources entrusted to them. This is a life-changing message. And this good news must be proclaimed 'first': not only a statement of the order in which things will happen but a challenge to the priorities of our lives.

COLLECT

O Lord, we beseech you mercifully to hear the prayers
of your people who call upon you;
and grant that they may both perceive and know
what things they ought to do,
and also may have grace and power faithfully to fulfil them;
through Jesus Christ your Son our Lord,
who is alive and reigns with you,
in the unity of the Holy Spirit,
one God, now and for ever.

Reflection by **Steven Croft**

Psalms 56, **57** (63*)
Ecclesiasticus 3.17-29
or Ezekiel 3.12-end
Mark 13.14-23

Thursday 28 September

Mark 13.14-23

'... do not believe it' (v.21)

To add to the challenges facing the people of God, in the midst of trauma and suffering there will be false messiahs and false prophets. The central claims of the Christian faith will be contested. Even the elect are in danger of being led astray.

This is one of the most cryptic and difficult passages in Mark. The references to the end times (and all the times to come) seem to give way now to a focus on the traumatic years around the destruction of Jerusalem by Roman armies in AD 70. Jesus draws insights from the book of Daniel: a desolating sacrifice will be set up in the temple. Commentators are not able to tell us definitively what this means.

But the lessons we need to draw are clear. The events Mark unfolds for us are of cosmic and global significance for all time. The disciples need to be prepared to face periods of great hardship and suffering, alongside the rest of this suffering world. In addition, we need to be alert to twists and distortions and false claims in our faith. Discernment is needed, combined with a willingness not to believe some claims made in the name of faith; watchfulness on the part of the whole Church; and a readiness to return continually to the words of Jesus to test what is said.

Today is a good day to assess where we are placing our trust and confidence and where we need to be more questioning of those who make claims in the name of our faith.

COLLECT

Lord of creation,
whose glory is around and within us:
open our eyes to your wonders,
that we may serve you with reverence
and know your peace at our lives' end,
through Jesus Christ our Lord.

Reflection by **Steven Croft**

Friday 29 September
Michael and All Angels

Psalms 34, 150
Tobit 12.6-end *or* Daniel 12.1-4
Acts 12.1-11

Acts 12.1-11

'... he did not realize that what was happening with the angel's help was real' (v.9)

There are times in most lives when we experience a particular sense of grace and help from heaven. There are times in most lives when, in moments of trial and suffering, it seems as though that help does not arrive.

In Luke and Acts, angels only appear at key moments in the story. This is one such point in the narrative: a crisis in the life of the Church. Herod has killed James and others. He turns his attention next to Peter in an attempt to deprive the Church in Jerusalem of its leader. Peter is delivered from the depths of the prison, whilst guarded by four squads of soldiers. Chains fall off wrists; guards fail to notice an escape; gates open of their own accord.

On this occasion, the angel does not come to deliver a message but acts as an agent and sign of deliverance. The angel reminds us on this feast day that, as Christians, we believe in a God who intervenes in the affairs of humankind, daily. The fervent prayers of the Church are vital in determining those interventions. Encounters like Peter's remain exceptional and extraordinary – that is why we celebrate them.

Jesus teaches all of his disciples to pray daily: deliver us from the time of trial. Such trials come in all our lives. Sometimes deliverance comes in the form of grace or resilience to bear suffering. But today we remember and give thanks that sometimes that deliverance will come in real and unexpected ways in answer to the prayers of the Church.

COLLECT

Everlasting God,
you have ordained and constituted
the ministries of angels and mortals in a wonderful order:
grant that as your holy angels always serve you in heaven,
so, at your command,
they may help and defend us on earth;
through Jesus Christ your Son our Lord,
who is alive and reigns with you,
in the unity of the Holy Spirit,
one God, now and for ever.

Reflection by **Steven Croft**

Psalm **68**
Ecclesiasticus 4.29 – 6.1
or Ezekiel 9
Mark 13.32-end

Saturday 30 September

Mark 13.32-end

'It is like a man going on a journey ...' (v.34)

Finally, at the end of all the head-scratching complexity of the apocalypse, the dire warnings, the confusions about the times, the dangers, we have a simple instruction and a parable we can understand. A man is going on a journey.

Like all images, this one is imperfect. There are some points that correspond to the reality Jesus is describing. The Lord is indeed going on a journey, walking in the way of the cross and of resurrection. We will return to that hard road in the very next verses. The Lord has entrusted to each of us, his servants, our own work to be done. We are not to be idle as we wait for the Master's return. We do not know when that return might be. Therefore our response is simple: to keep awake, to watch, to be good stewards of what has been entrusted to us.

But there is at least one paradox of the life of the Church not reflected in the parable. The Master is going on a journey but he is also still with us, present in our daily lives, accessible in our prayers, active in the life of the Church through the power and the presence of the Holy Spirit and the signs and tokens of his love, bread and wine.

It is the loving presence of Christ that enables us to wait patiently and long for his return.

COLLECT

Almighty God,
you have made us for yourself,
and our hearts are restless till they find their rest in you:
pour your love into our hearts and draw us to yourself,
and so bring us at last to your heavenly city
where we shall see you face to face;
through Jesus Christ your Son our Lord,
who is alive and reigns with you,
in the unity of the Holy Spirit,
one God, now and for ever.

Reflection by **Steven Croft**

Monday 2 October

Psalm **71**
Ecclesiasticus 6.14-end
or Ezekiel 10.1-19
Mark 14.1-11

Mark 14.1-11

'... he began to look for an opportunity to betray him' (v.11)

Here begins Mark's lengthy and detailed account of the passion of Jesus. It's two days before the Passover; the crowds are gathering in Jerusalem; the Roman guards are strategically placed to stamp down quickly on any hint of rebellion; the chief priests and scribes are plotting Jesus' downfall. We can feel the tension rising.

In the midst of it all, Jesus is in Bethany, eating and drinking and enjoying the company of friends. But even here among his closest companions, there is muttering and complaining and criticizing and plotting. As Jesus defends the one person who puts him and his needs first, anointing him generously and without restraint, another goes out into the night to betray him.

This may sound familiar to anyone who has experienced the feeling of discovering someone they trusted whispering and plotting in dark corners. Perhaps there is some comfort in remembering that Jesus faced the same undermining, the same betrayals.

The hardest thing then is remembering that he never stopped loving, never stopped forgiving, and understood somehow that greed, jealousy and ambition are all a part of our flawed human nature. He called out those whose behaviour was unjust and cruel; he brought their muttering in dark corners out into the light. And then he kept on keeping on.

COLLECT

Almighty God,
you have made us for yourself,
and our hearts are restless till they find their rest in you:
pour your love into our hearts and draw us to yourself,
and so bring us at last to your heavenly city
where we shall see you face to face;
through Jesus Christ your Son our Lord,
who is alive and reigns with you,
in the unity of the Holy Spirit,
one God, now and for ever.

 Reflection by **Jan McFarlane**

Psalm **73**
Ecclesiasticus 7.27-end
or Ezekiel 11.14-end
Mark 14.12-25

Tuesday 3 October

Mark 14.12-25

'... a man carrying a jar of water will meet you' (v.13)

So much of this passage is very familiar to us, the danger being, of course, that we skip through it and stop listening. Why not read the passage again, slowly, leaving a pause between every sentence to see what speaks to you anew?

What struck me was the verses that could have come straight from a detective novel or spy thriller. Jesus instructs the disciples to go to Jerusalem and to meet 'a man carrying a jar of water' whom they are to follow, to the place set aside for Jesus to share the Passover. It's all a bit mysterious, undercover, secretive.

But the confidentiality is crucial. Jesus knows that his time is short; that the religious authorities are out to get him; that one of his closest friends will betray him. He can't risk anyone knowing where he will be that night of all nights.

If Jesus issued those instructions today, there would be those who would point the finger and accuse him of a 'lack of transparency'. And yet there is a time and a place for proper confidentiality. Not everything can be shared openly; sometimes confidentiality is needed to protect an innocent party, or because the facts are not yet fully known, or because there is a plan in place that can't yet be shared. Sometimes it isn't appropriate to be told everything.

Gracious God,
you call us to fullness of life:
deliver us from unbelief
and banish our anxieties
with the liberating love of Jesus Christ our Lord.

COLLECT

Reflection by **Jan McFarlane**

Wednesday 4 October

Psalm **77**
Ecclesiasticus 10.6-8, 12-24
or Ezekiel 12.1-16
Mark 14.26-42

Mark 14.26-42

'You will all become deserters' (v.27)

It's not only Judas who betrays Jesus. One by one, all his disciples will fall away, leaving only his mother and 'the one whom Jesus loved' standing at the foot of the cross. The disciples are offended when Jesus tells them this will be so. Of course they are. None of us like to think of ourselves as duplicitous cowards.

And yet for Peter, as with the others, the cross becomes a stumbling-block. It's an embarrassment. It isn't how messiahs die. They can't argue back when Jesus is mocked and dressed in a purple robe and crowned with thorns as 'King of the Jews'. They're deeply humiliated and terrified. They are more concerned for themselves than for him. And one by one, they slink away.

There is a little part in all of us that stands with Peter and cries, in an offended manner, that we will never deny Jesus. But in one way or another, at some point, we will. It might be by not standing up for our faith when openly challenged. It might be by taking the easy way out and going with the flow. It might take the form of failing to recognize God's image in those around us, and failing to love them as God does. It might be more insidious – a slow but sure drifting-away, not praying as often as we once did, missing our daily 'quiet time', our church attendance slowly becoming less regular.

One by one, we quietly slink away.

COLLECT

Almighty God,
you have made us for yourself,
and our hearts are restless till they find their rest in you:
pour your love into our hearts and draw us to yourself,
and so bring us at last to your heavenly city
where we shall see you face to face;
through Jesus Christ your Son our Lord,
who is alive and reigns with you,
in the unity of the Holy Spirit,
one God, now and for ever.

Reflection by **Jan McFarlane**

Psalm **78.1-39***
Ecclesiasticus 11.7-28
or Ezekiel 12.17-end
Mark 14.43-52

Thursday 5 October

Mark 14.43-52

'The one I will kiss is the man' (v.44)

The irony of Judas' act of betrayal is that is it is successful precisely because he knows Jesus so well. Judas has left the Passover meal early, but he knows what Jesus will do next. He knows that Jesus will go to the Garden of Gethsemane to pray, and that his closest friends will be with him but are likely to be asleep. Jesus will, in effect, be alone and vulnerable. This is the moment.

To identify Jesus for the guards with a kiss seems the ultimate betrayal. The Greek word used in Mark's Gospel when Judas instructs the guards is the word used for the kiss of respect given by a disciple to his master, but the Greek word used at the moment of betrayal means an emotional kiss, one given by a good friend to a good friend. Is it only at this moment of betrayal that the full horror of what he has done becomes clear to Judas?

In the musical *Jesus Christ Superstar*, this moment is captured perfectly in composer Andrew Lloyd Webber's score. Jesus sings quietly and poignantly, 'Judas, must you betray me with a kiss?', and the question hangs in the air, challenging us all to remember the times when we have betrayed others, not by facing them openly and honestly, but through deceit disguised as affection.

COLLECT

Gracious God,
you call us to fullness of life:
deliver us from unbelief
and banish our anxieties
with the liberating love of Jesus Christ our Lord.

Reflection by **Jan McFarlane**

Friday 6 October

Psalm **55**
Ecclesiasticus 14.20 – 15.10
or Ezekiel 13.1-16
Mark 14.53-65

Mark 14.53-65

'... the chief priests, the elders, and the scribes were assembled' (v.53)

Why are the chief priests, elders and scribes all assembled in the dead of night, and on a major religious feast too, thus breaking their own rules? Jesus is condemned before he has even opened his mouth. This will never be a fair trial. And so he keeps quiet, breaking his silence, in Mark's account, only to ensure that he is tried for the truth – that he is indeed the Messiah.

The fact that Jesus is betrayed, arrested and tried at night, under cover of darkness, adds to the sense of drama, but also points to the underhand and deceitful way in which Jesus is being condemned. False testimonies are exchanged, and Jesus is defenceless in the hands of those who are determined to do away with him.

For many, the night has always been symbolic of fear, mystery and evil. The darkness can be disorientating. Those of us who sometimes spend the small hours tossing and turning, ruminating on real or perceived hurts, trying to solve seemingly intractable problems, could try handing ourselves over to God, and waiting for the clear light of day to help us to put things into perspective. Decisions made in the dead of night are not always the most rational. Better then to pray the words of the ancient office of Compline, or Night Prayer: 'From evil dreams defend our sight, from fears and terrors of the night.'

COLLECT

Almighty God,
you have made us for yourself,
and our hearts are restless till they find their rest in you:
pour your love into our hearts and draw us to yourself,
and so bring us at last to your heavenly city
where we shall see you face to face;
through Jesus Christ your Son our Lord,
who is alive and reigns with you,
in the unity of the Holy Spirit,
one God, now and for ever.

Reflection by **Jan McFarlane**

Psalms **76**, 79
Ecclesiasticus 15.11-end
or Ezekiel 14.1-11
Mark 14.66-end

Saturday 7 October

Mark 14.66-end

'And he broke down and wept' (v.72)

Already since Jesus told Peter that he would deny him three times before the cockerel crowed twice, there have been two mini betrayals on Peter's part. First, he has fallen asleep in the Garden of Gethsemane when Jesus has asked him to stay awake with him, on this of all nights. Then, although he follows Jesus to the house of Caiaphas the High Priest, he remains in the courtyard at a safe distance. He's there – but he's not there.

And then when his cover is blown, the three denials of his master and his friend follow one after the other. Probably in the heat of the moment, Peter is frightened and concerned most of all to save his own skin. But then the cockerel crows for a second time and with that piercing wake-up call, the full horror of what he has done hits him. He breaks down and weeps.

But that's not the end of the story for Peter. We think ahead to Jesus' resurrection appearances and his words to Peter, recorded for us by John, 'Do you love me? Feed my sheep' (John 21.15ff). Three times Jesus gives Peter the opportunity to cancel out each of his three denials. And Peter responds from his heart and is forgiven.

Jesus never gives up on Peter. And what a huge relief to know that, no matter how far we have strayed, we too are – in the words of the hymn – 'ransomed, healed, restored, forgiven'.

Gracious God,
you call us to fullness of life:
deliver us from unbelief
and banish our anxieties
with the liberating love of Jesus Christ our Lord.

COLLECT

Reflection by **Jan McFarlane**

Monday 9 October

Psalms **80**, 82
Ecclesiasticus 16.17-end
or Ezekiel 14.12-end
Mark 15.1-15

Mark 15.1-15

'Do you want me to release for you the King of the Jews?' (v.9)

Pilate doesn't have much time for those under his rule. He sees through the trumped-up charges of the members of the Sanhedrin council, and, if Jesus had answered his questions, Pilate might well have let him go. But Jesus remains silent and Pilate is baffled. He can see that there will be trouble if he refuses to take the charges against Jesus seriously, but he's uneasy too about condemning him. So he takes the easy way out and asks the crowds what they want him to do.

Angry crowds rarely make sensible and well-thought-through decisions. Few of us will ever forget the scenes on our television screens when a baying mob stormed Washington's Capitol Hill government buildings in January 2021 in the closing days of Donald Trump's presidency. Not many of us would have entrusted a life and death decision to such a crowd. But Pilate did.

Those who lead have to be the ones who make the final decision. They should, of course, consult trusted advisors and even test the temperature of a wider group, but the final decision must always be theirs, and they must bear the consequences of their actions. Pilate abdicated his responsibility, but the consequences of that attempted abdication come back to haunt him and are rehearsed weekly in our creeds. Pilate goes down in history as the one under whom Jesus was crucified.

COLLECT

Almighty and everlasting God,
increase in us your gift of faith
that, forsaking what lies behind
and reaching out to that which is before,
we may run the way of your commandments
and win the crown of everlasting joy;
through Jesus Christ your Son our Lord,
who is alive and reigns with you,
in the unity of the Holy Spirit,
one God, now and for ever.

Reflection by **Jan McFarlane**

Psalms 87, **89.1-18**
Ecclesiasticus 17.1-24
or Ezekiel 18.1-20
Mark 15.16-32

Tuesday 10 October

Mark 15.16-32

'And they crucified him' (v.24)

Mark is writing his Gospel between AD 50–70. His audience are Christians in Rome. He doesn't need to spell out the details of crucifixion. They know them already.

And us? The story of Jesus' crucifixion is so familiar to us and the older I get, the less I want to comment. The story speaks for itself. It needs no elaboration. It should reduce us to silence. We watch in silent horror, helplessness and awe as the Son of God, pure love, the one in whom we find compassion and forgiveness and hope, hangs on a cross. And in silence we fall to our knees.

My faith journey began in earnest when, as a student, a modern-day disciple of Jesus explained that if I had been the only person in the whole world and in the whole of history who could have been put right with God as a result of Christ's death, he still would have gone through with it. Because that's how much he loves me.

How do we respond to such love? Today we stand at the foot of the cross and see the dying Jesus looking at us with such depths of undeserved and unconditional love and consider again how we will respond. Perhaps with the words of Isaac Watts' famous hymn: 'Love so amazing, so divine, demands my soul, my life, my all.'

COLLECT

God, our judge and saviour,
teach us to be open to your truth
and to trust in your love,
that we may live each day
with confidence in the salvation which is given
through Jesus Christ our Lord.

Reflection by **Jan McFarlane**

Wednesday 11 October

Psalm **119.105-128**
Ecclesiasticus 18.1-14
or Ezekiel 18.21-32
Mark 15.33-41

Mark 15.33-41

'There were also women ...' (v.40)

Jesus dies. His male disciples, despite their earlier bravado, have all fled for fear of their lives. Jesus is abandoned and, in Mark's Gospel, he is surrounded only by his enemies and by those who have come to mock and taunt him. Though surrounded by the crowds, Jesus dies a lonely death.

And then in verse 40, we're told that Jesus hadn't been abandoned completely. Mark tells us that there were women there, standing at a distance maybe, but refusing to run away. Women who are given the dignity of being named and known, women 'looking on' – the Greek verb in the text means 'watching with sustained attention'. These were no casual onlookers. These were disciples: Mary from Magdala near Galilee; Mary the mother of the younger James and of Joses; Salome, the mother of James (the apostle) and John. They have been with Jesus since his Galilee days, following him, providing for him. Disciples.

A number of commentaries I have read while writing these reflections stop at verse 39. They don't mention these faithful women who refused to desert their teacher and friend. Perhaps the commentators haven't noticed them. Perhaps they are choosing to ignore them. But they can't be airbrushed out.

Whom do we, consciously or subconsciously, attempt to airbrush out of the life of the Church?

COLLECT

Almighty and everlasting God,
increase in us your gift of faith
that, forsaking what lies behind
and reaching out to that which is before,
we may run the way of your commandments
and win the crown of everlasting joy;
through Jesus Christ your Son our Lord,
who is alive and reigns with you,
in the unity of the Holy Spirit,
one God, now and for ever.

Reflection by **Jan McFarlane**

Psalms 90, **92**
Ecclesiasticus 19.4-17
or Ezekiel 20.1-20
Mark 15.42-end

Thursday 12 October

Mark 15.42-end

'... a respected member of the council' (v.43)

According to Jewish law, Jesus' body must be buried by the twelfth hour of the day of preparation for the Sabbath, before darkness falls and the Sabbath begins. But the disciples have fled, and there is no one to claim Jesus' body.

Then out of the shadows steps Joseph of Arimathea. He is a prominent member of the Sanhedrin Council, though Luke tells us he refused to be part of the plot to have Jesus falsely charged and executed (Luke 23.50-51). Showing immense courage, Joseph goes to Pilate and asks for Jesus' body, which he then lays in a rock-hewn tomb, with only Mary Magdalene and Mary the mother of Joses as witnesses.

Joseph of Arimathea risks everything in recovering this dead body. Members of the Sanhedrin will see him as a traitor. Pilate could easily accuse Joseph of being a follower of Jesus and therefore guilty of treason. The crowds will look on in amazement and disdain as this respectable Jew risks touching an unclean body, and puts his reputation well and truly on the line.

I'm always amused when, in the interest of good governance, churches have to consider 'reputational risk'. We are those who follow one who was born in a mucky stable, lived as an itinerant preacher, and died a criminal's death. Isn't our reputation already at risk?

COLLECT

God, our judge and saviour,
teach us to be open to your truth
and to trust in your love,
that we may live each day
with confidence in the salvation which is given
through Jesus Christ our Lord.

Reflection by **Jan McFarlane**

Friday 13 October

Psalms **88** (95)
Ecclesiasticus 19.20-end
or Ezekiel 20.21-38
Mark 16.1-8

Mark 16.1-8

'... and they said nothing to anyone, for they were afraid' (v.8)

The three women who had witnessed Jesus' crucifixion have returned, bravely, to his tomb to anoint his body with spices. It's important that they are named, so we name them again: Mary Magdalene, Mary the mother of James, and Salome. They witnessed Jesus' crucifixion because they refused to desert him. And they remain faithful to the end.

But what awaited them was beyond all comprehension. The heavy stone moved, the body of Jesus gone, a man in a white robe saying strange and perplexing things to them. How can they be anything but terrified? It all becomes too much for them and finally they run – and with all the horror of the past few days finally crashing down around them, they run and run and run – and say nothing to anyone.

Perhaps today we can spend time with this passage – it is where Mark's Gospel originally ended – and put ourselves in the shoes of these three women seeing what they saw, hearing what they heard, imagining how they felt, running with them as far as possible from this incomprehensible scene.

We know the rest of the story – but they didn't. And how much better that the first of the Gospels to be written ended here, with fear and incomprehension. Because how can anyone understand – truly understand – resurrection? Perhaps we can pray today for someone we know who cannot make this leap of faith, but who, deep down, longs to do so.

COLLECT

Almighty and everlasting God,
increase in us your gift of faith
that, forsaking what lies behind
and reaching out to that which is before,
we may run the way of your commandments
and win the crown of everlasting joy;
through Jesus Christ your Son our Lord,
who is alive and reigns with you,
in the unity of the Holy Spirit,
one God, now and for ever.

Reflection by **Jan McFarlane**

Psalms 96, **97**, 100
Ecclesiasticus 21.1-17
or Ezekiel 24.15-end
Mark 16.9-end

Saturday 14 October

Mark 16.9-end

'... while the Lord worked with them' (v.20)

I'm often accused of being too tidy-minded, liking things to be neat and orderly, with everything in its place and a place for everything. But I find myself strangely amused at the attempts to 'tidy up' the ending to Mark's Gospel. Matthew, Luke and John tell of the resurrection in much greater detail. The sudden ending of Mark stops us in our tracks.

Scholars tell us that today's verses were added to Mark's Gospel in the second century. Perhaps they felt more explanation and evidence of Jesus' resurrection was needed. An alternative shorter ending was also added in the fourth century.

To my mind both endings are clunky and don't really flow. So what if today we return to verse 8, and then add our own ending. What will our own ending be if it's left to us today to continue the story?

Will we run with Mary, Mary and Salome – run away from the resurrected Jesus who might make demands of us we're not ready to undertake? Will we align ourselves with the male disciples and refuse to believe? Will we hear Jesus' voice challenging our lack of faith?

Or will we allow ourselves to be convinced of the truth of Jesus' resurrection and commit ourselves once again to be those who 'Go into all the world and proclaim the good news to the whole creation'?

COLLECT

God, our judge and saviour,
teach us to be open to your truth
and to trust in your love,
that we may live each day
with confidence in the salvation which is given
through Jesus Christ our Lord.

Reflection by **Jan McFarlane**

Monday 16 October

Psalms **98**, 99, 101
Ecclesiasticus 22.6-22
or Ezekiel 28.1-19
John 13.1-11

John 13.1-11

'Lord, not my feet only but also my hands and my head!' (v.9)

The threads are coming together at last. The long awaited 'hour' has come when chronological time, God's time, and the disciples' time-to-respond are all coming into focus over the next few hours. And it's all symbolized in a supremely memorable action – the washing of feet. This isn't just about the humility of Jesus; this is about the nature of God and what God has been doing in Jesus. The Word who 'was with God, and who was God' (John 1.1), has laid aside the clothing of glory, taken our human nature, and loved to the uttermost, which now means the extremity of the cross.

So much is packed into these eleven verses. We generally marvel at the example Jesus gave of humility and service. But there's an even deeper significance in the words of Peter, 'not my feet only...' As followers of Jesus, we can't participate in his life and in the victory of the cross and resurrection without being thoroughly washed by him and identified with him. Peter, in his characteristic all-or-nothing style, stands for us feeble followers coming to realize that this Christian life isn't about believing certain doctrines and knowing certain rituals; it isn't about giving God the nod on Sundays along with the tail-end of our time and money. It's about being soaked in the love of God. This faith isn't intellectual entertainment; it's personal surrender. It's accepting God's active presence in our lives and aligning ourselves daily with God's unconditional love for the world.

No wonder I find it difficult.

COLLECT

O God, forasmuch as without you
we are not able to please you;
mercifully grant that your Holy Spirit
may in all things direct and rule our hearts;
through Jesus Christ your Son our Lord,
who is alive and reigns with you,
in the unity of the Holy Spirit,
one God, now and for ever.

Reflection by **John Pritchard**

Psalms **106*** (*or* 103)
Ecclesiasticus 22.27 – 23.15
or Ezekiel 33.1-20
John 13.12-20

Tuesday 17 October

John 13.12-20

'I have set you an example' (v.15)

It was my first Sunday evening in a new parish. I was tired, it was raining, and I discovered it was my job to haul the rubbish bins from the back of the church hall onto the main road for collection the next day. 'Surely not!' I thought. 'Was all my training for this?' Then I realized: yes it was. If I wasn't prepared to do the unpleasant, messy parts of ministry, then I hadn't understood it. And even then there would still be a danger, because as I did the small, unglamorous jobs, I might find myself being proud of my humility! Screwtape would be thrilled.

Jesus has given us a pattern of unselfconscious service of each other. It ought to come naturally to those of us who belong to a church, because this is where rich and poor, privileged and under-privileged, young and old, gay and straight meet together and find bread and wine on the table, and a towel and a bowl of water on the floor. The symbols say it all. The trouble is that we haven't always learned their lesson very well.

A man once asked his rabbi why people couldn't see the face of God any more. The rabbi answered, 'It seems that not many people can stoop that low.' But Jesus could.

COLLECT

Faithful Lord,
whose steadfast love never ceases
and whose mercies never come to an end:
grant us the grace to trust you
and to receive the gifts of your love,
new every morning,
in Jesus Christ our Lord.

Reflection by **John Pritchard**

Wednesday 18 October
Luke the Evangelist

Psalms 145, 146
Isaiah 55
Luke 1.1-4

Isaiah 55

'... you shall go out in joy, and be led back in peace' (v.12)

The story is told of Walt Disney's faithful housekeeper being given an envelope every Christmas which she failed to understand or to open. When she died, her executors found a large pile of such envelopes and it turned out that they had contained Disney share certificates that would have made her a very rich woman indeed. But she never knew it; she never grasped the significance of what she had been given.

In Isaiah 55, Israel is in exile in Babylon and is being encouraged to leave captivity behind. The people are wasting money on things that will never satisfy. Instead, they should come out and claim the blessings of the covenant God had originally made with David. It would be paradise regained (a repeated theme in Isaiah) as the mountains burst into song and the trees of the field clap their hands. This poetic image reaches across the ages and invites Christians today to enjoy the blessings of their new relationship with the Lord of creation. Why complain about the quality of the after-church coffee when you're being invited to enjoy the champagne of the kingdom – wine and milk that comes free ('without money and without price'). Do we sufficiently grasp the significance of what we've been given?

How, today, can we more fully enjoy the freedom and beauty of life shared with God?

COLLECT

Almighty God,
you called Luke the physician,
whose praise is in the gospel,
to be an evangelist and physician of the soul:
by the grace of the Spirit
and through the wholesome medicine of the gospel,
give your Church the same love and power to heal;
through Jesus Christ your Son our Lord,
who is alive and reigns with you,
in the unity of the Holy Spirit,
one God, now and for ever.

Reflection by **John Pritchard**

Psalms 113, **115**
Ecclesiasticus 24.23-end
or Ezekiel 34.1-16
John 13.31-end

Thursday 19 October

John 13.31-end

'I will lay down my life for you' (v.37)

We're well-practised at breaking promises. We do it politically (think climate change); we do it in our relationships (think marriage vows); we do it to ourselves (think diet in my case). So we understand Peter. He over-promises. He wants Jesus to understand how much he means to Peter, and he hasn't yet mastered the art of polite restraint.

Many of us love that desire to be wholehearted, to 'put it all out there'. I heard a young person talking about a well-used gap year and saying that she simply wanted 'to give everything for everything rather than nothing for nothing'. Similarly, we might love to be able to say that we would lay down our life for our faith, but in reality, we fear we're not up to that kind of promise. Fortunately, God knows the secrets of our hearts and is gentle with our limitations. He is the God of Psalm 139 who knits us together in our mother's womb and discerns our thoughts from afar. Some of us do, some don't, some will, some won't, turn out to be able to keep our promises.

The golden truth to which we hold is that, even when we are unreliable in keeping our promises, God is utterly reliable in keeping his. We may even deny him three times, and yet he will meet us on the seashore after breakfast and ask us simply, 'Do you love me?' No reprimand, no judgement. Just a gentle reminder and a renewed invitation: 'Follow me.'

COLLECT

O God, forasmuch as without you
we are not able to please you;
mercifully grant that your Holy Spirit
may in all things direct and rule our hearts;
through Jesus Christ your Son our Lord,
who is alive and reigns with you,
in the unity of the Holy Spirit,
one God, now and for ever.

Reflection by **John Pritchard**

Friday 20 October

Psalm **139**
Ecclesiasticus 27.30 – 28.9
or Ezekiel 34.17-end
John 14.1-14

John 14.1-14

'No one comes to the Father except through me' (v.6)

It's often said that the claim of Christians that Jesus is the only way to God the Father is offensive and arrogant. There are a number of things to say to that. One is that a man who washes feet and who willingly gives his life for others can hardly be described as arrogant. Another is that John was probably not thinking of the far reaches of empire when he wrote this, nor was he thinking as a twenty-first-century world citizen. He spoke of what he knew, and that was that Jesus is the one clear way to God for anyone who will listen. A further response to these bold words is that we do well to leave to God the faith and fate of those who have not heard or been convinced by the gospel. God is quite able to handle the problem.

The most important thing to take away is that for the believer, as Catherine of Siena said, 'all the way to heaven is heaven' because Jesus is the way there. He embodies the truth about heaven and he demonstrates the life of heaven. Christians don't need to get involved in a shouting match about the way to God. Sufficient to live the heavenly way of Jesus as we know it and to give thanks that Jesus takes us straight to the Father's heart.

That's enough good news for the start of any day.

COLLECT

O God, forasmuch as without you
we are not able to please you;
mercifully grant that your Holy Spirit
may in all things direct and rule our hearts;
through Jesus Christ your Son our Lord,
who is alive and reigns with you,
in the unity of the Holy Spirit,
one God, now and for ever.

Reflection by **John Pritchard**

Psalms 120, **121**, 122
Ecclesiasticus 28.14-end
or Ezekiel 36.16-36
John 14.15-end

Saturday 21 October

John 14.15-end

'I am in my Father, and you in me, and I in you' (v.20)

Rublev's famous fifteenth-century icon of the Trinity depicts three angels sitting equidistant from each other around a table with a cup laid on it. They have a harmony and elegance that fits well with the concept of the eternal Trinity. But the gift of the icon to so many believers is that there's a space at the table for us. We seem to be invited to share the very life of the Trinity, to participate in the life of God.

What's the purpose of our faith? It isn't to have somewhere nice to go on a Sunday morning. It isn't to be reminded how to be good or to learn more about Christian doctrine. It isn't to get a free pass to heaven. The purpose of our faith is to be drawn into the life of God so that the life-blood of God – the Spirit – flows through our veins. This is what Jesus is speaking of as he promises that through the events of the coming days the disciples will find that he will be 'in' his Father, and they will be 'in' him and he will be 'in' them. This is nothing less than sharing the life of God, now.

This is not a faith of small things. This is a faith of ultimate things. You can't get much more ultimate than sharing the very life of God. *That's what we're for.*

COLLECT

Faithful Lord,
whose steadfast love never ceases
and whose mercies never come to an end:
grant us the grace to trust you
and to receive the gifts of your love,
new every morning,
in Jesus Christ our Lord.

Reflection by **John Pritchard**

Monday 23 October

Psalms 123, 124, 125, **126**
Ecclesiasticus 31.1-11
or Ezekiel 37.1-14
John 15.1-11

John 15.1-11

'... apart from me you can do nothing' (v.5)

One of my many areas of incompetence is anything to do with plants, flowers or shrubs. I can be left alone with a lawnmower and hedge-clippers, but that's about it. If my wife weren't too polite, she might say, 'Apart from me you can do nothing.' If I'm to be any help in the garden, what I need is an attitude of complete dependence on her, but equally what she needs is my glad willingness. Then we can be truly fruitful.

As Jesus' 'hour' comes closer, his teaching becomes more urgent, and here he's laying it on the line. What the followers of Jesus are going to need in the future is a trust so profound it will be a kind of mutual in-dwelling. Without it, they (and we) will be able to do nothing, or at least nothing beautifully and with the watermark of Christ. That 'abiding' isn't easy for those of us brought up on a spiritual diet that involves gorging ourselves on the carbohydrates of words and the fatty food of dogmas. Most of us need a quieter faith, a deeper trust, a richer silence to screen out the cacophony of our noisy lives and the constant chatter in our heads. Then, as we abide gently in Christ and he in us, we might be fruitful.

In his book *Energy and Equity*, the social critic Ivan Illich said, 'Tell me how fast you go and I'll tell you who you are'. Jesus asks us to slow down to 'abiding' speed.

COLLECT

God, the giver of life,
whose Holy Spirit wells up within your Church:
by the Spirit's gifts equip us to live the gospel of Christ
and make us eager to do your will,
that we may share with the whole creation
the joys of eternal life;
through Jesus Christ your Son our Lord,
who is alive and reigns with you,
in the unity of the Holy Spirit,
one God, now and for ever.

Reflection by **John Pritchard**

Psalms **132**, 133
Ecclesiasticus 34.9-end
or Ezekiel 37.15-end
John 15.12-17

Tuesday 24 October

John 15.12-17

'I have called you friends' (v.15)

Here's a hypothetical test to find out who is your best friend: imagine putting your dog and your closest friend in the boot of the car for an hour. When you open the boot again, who's really happy to see you? By contrast, Jesus declares that even those who betray him or deny knowing him are his friends. They don't have to qualify for that affection; it's just given.

It's possible to see God's Big Story as one of friendship. Friends are made in Creation, but fall out in the Fall. These friends keep trying to maintain their friendship in the story of Israel, until our best, best friend comes in the person of Jesus whose death and resurrection cement the relationship. That intimate friendship continues in the life of the Church, and the new creation assures us that the friendship is forever. Friendship can act as a defining category for God's relationship with the world he loves.

The deepest friendships are based on sharing everything; Jesus made known to the disciples all that he heard from his Father. In true friendship the parties are on the same level, without a 'higher' and 'lower'. This is all breathtaking stuff in terms of a relationship with Christ, but Jesus assures his friends, both then and now, that we will share both the passion and the pain of love. There's no dodging the clear, commanding, no-nonsense core of friendship: 'Love one another.' And that means today.

God, our light and our salvation:
illuminate our lives,
that we may see your goodness in the land of the living,
and looking on your beauty
may be changed into the likeness of Jesus Christ our Lord.

COLLECT

Reflection by **John Pritchard**

Wednesday 25 October

Psalm **119.153-end**
Ecclesiasticus 35
or Ezekiel 39.21-end
John 15.18-end

John 15.18-end

'If the world hates you, be aware that it hated me before it hated you' (v.18)

Do you know of anyone who hates you? Even to be asked that question is painful. I'm not aware of anyone hating me (but that doesn't mean there isn't a whole secret society out there...). Hatred is a brutal word. Jesus used it in the style of classic Hebrew thought – it's hyperbole, exaggeration to get the point across. Nevertheless, he wasn't being paranoid. He was alerting the disciples to the reality they would soon be facing because 'the world' (i.e. all that's set against God, refusing his reign) would be on the attack.

This is the daily reality of 260 million Christians around the world. Christians in the West are more ignored or faintly ridiculed than persecuted, but 'hatred' in a variety of different senses isn't far off the mark. Jesus, of course, doesn't hate the world in return. 'God so *loved* the world that he gave his only son.' In one of his sermons, 'Loving Your Enemies', Martin Luther King said, 'Hate cannot drive out hate; only love can do that.' Trying to stop God loving is like trying to stop the ocean being wet.

The question we face is whether we can live with that same grace and resist the temptation to despise, demean or denigrate those who attack us. Do we have enough faith to believe that *ultimately* love always wins?

COLLECT

God, the giver of life,
whose Holy Spirit wells up within your Church:
by the Spirit's gifts equip us to live the gospel of Christ
and make us eager to do your will,
that we may share with the whole creation
the joys of eternal life;
through Jesus Christ your Son our Lord,
who is alive and reigns with you,
in the unity of the Holy Spirit,
one God, now and for ever.

 Reflection by **John Pritchard**

Psalms **143**, 146
Ecclesiasticus 37.7-24
or Ezekiel 43.1-12
John 16.1-15

Thursday 26 October

John 16.1-15

'When the Spirit of truth comes, he will guide you into all the truth' (v.13)

Truth is the one virtue with which Jesus identified himself (John 14.6). He knew how crucially important it is to be fiercely loyal to the truth, and yet that's precisely the virtue most at risk in our 'make-it-up-as-you-go-along' political and social culture. If truth is simply what I want it to be, then we're lost. This problem isn't new. Winston Churchill said: 'Men (sic) occasionally stumble over the truth, but most of them pick themselves up and hurry off as if nothing ever happened.'

Jesus knew the corkscrew nature of the human heart, always bending the truth to our own interests, so he emphasized that the coming Spirit would be a spirit of truth, a plumbline to rely on, speaking only what was to be heard in the heavenly realm. We are therefore on safe ground when we say, with philosopher Simone Weil, that Christ would want us to prefer truth to Christ, because before being Christ, he is truth. I have always thought that if we aim first for the truth, we'll soon come across Jesus.

I once saw a poster that said: 'That which can be destroyed by the truth, should be.' Perhaps our personal poster could be: 'Hold fast to Jesus, and live the truth.'

COLLECT

God, our light and our salvation:
illuminate our lives,
that we may see your goodness in the land of the living,
and looking on your beauty
may be changed into the likeness of Jesus Christ our Lord.

Reflection by **John Pritchard**

Friday 27 October

Psalms 142, **144**
Ecclesiasticus 38.1-14
or Ezekiel 44.4-16
John 16.16-22

John 16.16-22

'... your pain will turn into joy' (v.20)

Here's another key word in John's Gospel – joy. Jesus is delivering some heavy-duty messages in these chapters, and the dreadful events of the next hours will be deeply painful. So he wants the disciples to realize that the context, the big picture of what's happening, is ultimately and overwhelmingly joyful because it's the dawn of a new world. Don't despair when I leave, he's saying, joy is on its way.

Joy is deeper than the 'happenings' on which 'happiness' depends. It depends not on events but on knowing and trusting God. Joy is a deep-down smile in the presence of God, and it's one of the touchstones of the Christian life. I remember a retreat when I was a young priest where the elderly, experienced retreat conductor said to us: 'Never let the sorrows of this world – or of your ministry – hide from you the joy of Christ risen.' I've taken that with me ever since. Joy is like a homing beacon; it keeps us on track. If we lose it, we know we've wandered off the path somewhere along the way. We come from the joy of the Creator and return to the joy of the risen, ascended Lord – with many excursions into sorrow along the way.

There's one other thing to remember. If we have the joy of the Lord in our hearts, it's good to notify our face.

COLLECT

God, the giver of life,
whose Holy Spirit wells up within your Church:
by the Spirit's gifts equip us to live the gospel of Christ
and make us eager to do your will,
that we may share with the whole creation
the joys of eternal life;
through Jesus Christ your Son our Lord,
who is alive and reigns with you,
in the unity of the Holy Spirit,
one God, now and for ever.

Reflection by **John Pritchard**

Psalms 116, 117
Wisdom 5.1-16
or Isaiah 45.18-end
Luke 6.12-16

Saturday 28 October

Simon and Jude, Apostles

Luke 6.12-16

'... he called his disciples and chose twelve of them' (v.13)

Maybe it never happened to you, but many a hapless child has been the last one to be picked in a playground game of football. It feels like being rejected. I wonder what it felt like to those disciples who had been with Jesus for a while but who didn't get picked for his team? Did Jesus help them cope with their disappointment? Did they go home but turn up again whenever they could get time off work? Did they follow Jesus' fortunes from afar and try to put into practice what they could remember?

Jesus spent a whole night praying about his choice. It was vital to get it right because he was calling out a new Israel, twelve people instead of twelve tribes, with the future of the Kingdom Project in their hands. Luke shows us how, at key moments, Jesus soaked his decisions in prayer. (How prayerfully, really, do we approach our big decisions?)

In our churches, many will have the hard experience of not being chosen. They won't complain. They won't make a song and dance about it. They'll carry on serving the Lord, loving their neighbour, doing the small unnoticed things, sometimes even praying through the night. 'They also serve...' And they deserve to be noticed, affirmed and loved for their faithfulness.

Look around in church next Sunday.

COLLECT

Almighty God,
who built your Church upon the foundation
of the apostles and prophets,
with Jesus Christ himself as the chief cornerstone:
so join us together in unity of spirit by their doctrine,
that we may be made a holy temple acceptable to you;
through Jesus Christ your Son our Lord,
who is alive and reigns with you,
in the unity of the Holy Spirit,
one God, now and for ever.

Reflection by **John Pritchard**

Monday 30 October

Psalms 1, 2, 3
Ecclesiasticus 39.1-11
or Ecclesiastes 1
John 17.1-5

Ecclesiastes 1

'... all is vanity and a chasing after wind' (v.14)

This strange book from the Wisdom tradition is now commonly thought to have been written in or around the third century BCE by someone (not Solomon) known as the Teacher or the Gatherer, who, to be honest, doesn't sound like great company on Saturday night in the Dog and Duck. He comes across as weary, cynical and overcome with the meaninglessness of existence. But when we've got over our surprise at finding such a wayward document in the Bible, we might be ready to accept that for some people much of the time, and for most people some of the time, this is how life can seem. There's a disarming honesty about the Teacher. He's real.

It has to be said that perpetually smiley, shiny Christians who have never come close to an existential crisis or a moment of cosmic doubt and hopelessness, can be a bit of a pain. So let's give Ecclesiastes a chance. There are flashes of humour here and passages of moving beauty, and an underlying recognition that God is supreme.

That said, the big question we all face is meaning. It's fascinating that the most popular course at Harvard has been, for a while at least, 'The science of happiness'. The professor teaching the course says that these bright young people realize that it isn't intelligence, wealth or achievement that brings happiness – it's meaning.

COLLECT

Blessed Lord,
who caused all holy Scriptures to be written for our learning:
help us so to hear them,
to read, mark, learn and inwardly digest them
that, through patience, and the comfort of your holy word,
we may embrace and for ever hold fast
the hope of everlasting life,
which you have given us in our Saviour Jesus Christ,
who is alive and reigns with you,
in the unity of the Holy Spirit,
one God, now and for ever.

Reflection by **John Pritchard**

Psalms **5**, 6 (8)
Ecclesiasticus 39.13-end
or Ecclesiastes 2
John 17.6-19

Tuesday 31 October

Ecclesiastes 2

'Come now, I will make a test of pleasure' (v.1)

The Teacher decides that the pursuit of pleasure might be the answer to his quest for meaning. He's not alone in that. Every generation tries the golden goblet of self-indulgence, and every generation finds that it fails to satisfy the deepest needs of the heart. Nevertheless, the Teacher concludes that there's nothing better on offer than to eat and drink and find enjoyment in work – and yet that too is vanity and chasing after wind.

The solemn truth remains that the soul rusts with neglect. There's a profound longing for Something More to give life meaning, and it isn't found in the familiar trinity of money, sex and power. Even the atheist philosopher Bertrand Russell kept in his desk these words, written in a letter and found after his death: 'The centre of me is always and eternally a terrible pain, a searching for something transfigured and infinite. The beatific vision – God. I do not find it. I do not think it is to be found – *but the love of it is my life*.'

At least Bertrand Russell, like the Teacher, agonized over these ultimate questions. As our lives now get incomparably faster, noisier and more complex, there has to be some doubt that people will have time for such agonizing or allow enough stillness to hear the whisper of the Spirit moving over the face of the earth. But we have to hope we will, or we'll only ever be a shadow of our true selves.

COLLECT

Merciful God,
teach us to be faithful in change and uncertainty,
that trusting in your word
and obeying your will
we may enter the unfailing joy of Jesus Christ our Lord.

Reflection by **John Pritchard**

Wednesday 1 November
All Saints' Day

Psalms 15, 84, 149
Isaiah 35.1-9
Luke 9.18-27

Isaiah 35.1-9

'The wilderness and the dry land shall be glad' (v.1)

We can't know what language the saints use in heaven, but I imagine it's a language of love and beauty. Much of the language of our culture has become the literary equivalent of junk food that fills and fattens us without any of the joy and inspiration of the culinary arts. A modern day St John might well write, 'Once upon a time a very important baby was born,' rather than, 'The Word became flesh and lived among us'.

In Isaiah 35, the prophet uses a glorious palette of colours to excite the spirit and move us to celebrate our coming liberation. The first referent for this lovely passage is the return of the exiles from Babylon, but the further referent is to the restoration of all creation to harmony and peace. Only poetic language can do justice to such a glorious theme. Poet and novelist Robert Graves called poetry 'stored magic' and here you can see how that works, with evocative images piled up one on top of another. In his great essay, 'The Redress of Poetry', Seamus Heaney went even further, saying that poetry 'offers a clarification, a fleeting glimpse of a potential order of things *beyond confusion*'.

Isaiah 35 is just such a glimpse of an order of things beyond confusion, where the saints enjoy the language we can only reach for – the perfect love language of God.

COLLECT

Almighty God,
you have knit together your elect
in one communion and fellowship
in the mystical body of your Son Christ our Lord:
grant us grace so to follow your blessed saints
in all virtuous and godly living
that we may come to those inexpressible joys
that you have prepared for those who truly love you;
through Jesus Christ your Son our Lord,
who is alive and reigns with you,
in the unity of the Holy Spirit,
one God, now and for ever.

Reflection by **John Pritchard**

Psalms 14, **15**, 16
Ecclesiasticus 43.1-12
or Ecclesiastes 3.16 – end of 4
John 18.1-11

Thursday 2 November

Ecclesiastes 3.16 – end of 4

'... if they fall, one will lift up the other' (4.10)

The Teacher's torrid internal dialogue turns to the issue of injustice and oppression, but there are no more hopeful outcomes here than in his previous investigations. Humans suffer the same fate as animals, and envy damages us all. The one positive thought offered to us is the value of companionship in adversity, with the familiar image that 'a threefold cord is not quickly broken'.

Even in the era of the autonomous individual, friendship is seen as a universal good. Research in 2019 showed that the favourite television programme for older children and teenagers was still the American show *Friends*, although the series started in the 1990s. It may have changed by now, but the lasting importance of that theme of friendship is clear. The irony is that young people usually watch programmes about friendship alone. A recent American study says that since the 1990s, the number of adults who can name six close friends has dropped from 55% to 27%.

The Teacher rightly asks 'how can one keep warm alone?' Friendships emerge from openness, vulnerability, radical acceptance, listening and laughter. (I would certainly dispute the Teacher's assertion, 'I said of laughter, "It is mad"', Ecclesiastes 2.2.) Friendship is egalitarian, supportive and genuinely compassionate. Ultimately, friendship is sacrificial – which brings us back to Jesus who, incredibly, as we saw last week, calls us 'friends'. He it is who, if we fall, will lift us up.

COLLECT

Blessed Lord,
who caused all holy Scriptures to be written for our learning:
help us so to hear them,
to read, mark, learn and inwardly digest them
that, through patience, and the comfort of your holy word,
we may embrace and for ever hold fast
the hope of everlasting life,
which you have given us in our Saviour Jesus Christ,
who is alive and reigns with you,
in the unity of the Holy Spirit,
one God, now and for ever.

Reflection by **John Pritchard**

Friday 3 November

Psalms 17, **19**
Ecclesiasticus 43.13-end
or Ecclesiastes 5
John 18.12-27

Ecclesiastes 5

'God is in heaven, and you upon earth; therefore let your words be few' (v.2)

It's a salutary fact that we don't remember many sermons beyond the day we hear them. However, I still remember one address at a clergy day decades ago where the bishop preached on the wisdom of verse 2. He was saying it's a basic truth that God is God and we are not, so it behoves us not to weary God's people with endless words but rather to choose our words with care and humility and offer them with love.

Our society is drunk on words, drunk and disorderly. We spray them around indiscriminately, covering every precious silence with what T.S. Eliot called 'the slimy mud of words ... the sleet and hail of verbal imprecisions' (*Choruses from 'The Rock'*). Moreover, so many of the words we use in church have been chewed so often there are no nutrients left in them and they've lost their taste. In the presence of God – whose home is in heaven while ours is on earth – we would do well to be more discerning in what we say, and spend more time listening and being attentive to God and to others. We might then recognize the truth of what the great Polish-American poet Czesław Miłosz said when he accepted the Nobel Prize for Literature some years ago: 'One word of truth sounds like a pistol shot.'

That's the word we're listening for in worship, in preaching, in listening to friends. And that's the word that God sometimes asks us to utter – maybe even today.

COLLECT

Blessed Lord,
who caused all holy Scriptures to be written for our learning:
help us so to hear them,
to read, mark, learn and inwardly digest them
that, through patience, and the comfort of your holy word,
we may embrace and for ever hold fast
  the hope of everlasting life,
which you have given us in our Saviour Jesus Christ,
who is alive and reigns with you,
in the unity of the Holy Spirit,
one God, now and for ever.

Reflection by **John Pritchard**

Psalms 20, 21, **23**
Ecclesiasticus 44.1-15
or Ecclesiastes 6
John 18.28-end

Saturday 4 November

Ecclesiastes 6

'... if he does not enjoy life's good things, ... a stillborn child is better off than he' (v.3)

The Teacher is still not a happy man, but at least he's decided that it's better to make the most of the good things around him while he's here. '... who knows what is good for mortals while they live the few days of their vain life?' That's still the underlying theme but it goes with a grim determination to enjoy what he can.

There is, however, a more positive and faithful way of adopting this strategy. The rabbis said that God's first question to us after this life will be, 'So, did you enjoy my creation?' It's our call. Faith shouldn't inhibit our capacity for life but rather enhance it. The poet Emily Dickinson was more in tune with the Poet from Galilee when she wrote, 'Life is so marvellous I hardly have time for anything else!'

Of course, life is also tragic, but the possibility of abundant life (John 10.10) keeps on emerging through the cracks. A character in Marilynne Robinson's *Gilead* says: 'There are a thousand thousand reasons to live this life, every one of them sufficient.' If we dig through the substrata of life, we come to a bedrock that Christians identify as the love of God. The truth about life is love; and the truth about love is God.

Everything else follows.

Merciful God,
teach us to be faithful in change and uncertainty,
that trusting in your word
and obeying your will
we may enter the unfailing joy of Jesus Christ our Lord.

COLLECT

Reflection by **John Pritchard**

Monday 6 November

Psalms **2**, 146 *or* 27, **30**
Isaiah 1.1-20
Matthew 1.18-end

Matthew 1.18-end

'"... they shall name him Emmanuel", which means, "God is with us."' (v.23)

Matthew sets the birth of Jesus at the end of a long genealogy stretching from Abraham to Joseph, marking significant phases in the history of God's people. So when today's reading begins with conception of Jesus by the Holy Spirit, it is in the context of hundreds of years of human errors, inconsistencies, irregularities and divine punishments in Israel's past. The point is to show that God's interventions in human history are rarely straightforward. They often come as a result of human fallibility. Even best of us – Joseph was a righteous man – are prone, as Joseph was, to misinterpret the ways of God.

This can be unnerving, but it is also a great consolation. 'God writes straight with crooked lines' is perhaps an over-familiar phrase, but it is intended to affirm the biblical insight that God achieves his perfect plan through deeply imperfect people. The angel sent to Joseph is sent to invite him to do something risky and unconventional. But this is not to satisfy some egoistical need of Joseph's to be different, but to obey a God who sees further than we can see and has designs more fulfilling than we can imagine. As we face today's particular challenges, God is with us.

COLLECT

Almighty and eternal God,
you have kindled the flame of love in the hearts of the saints:
grant to us the same faith and power of love,
that, as we rejoice in their triumphs,
we may be sustained by their example and fellowship;
through Jesus Christ your Son our Lord,
who is alive and reigns with you,
in the unity of the Holy Spirit,
one God, now and for ever.

 Reflection by **Angela Tilby**

Psalms **5**, 147.1-12 *or* 32, **36**
Isaiah 1.21-end
Matthew 2.1-15

Tuesday 7 November

Matthew 2.1-15

'Where is the child ... ?' (v.2)

Matthew is clear that Jesus is the Messiah for all people. His reign will eventually stretch beyond the Jewish world into which he was born. The visit of the gentile wise men at the beginning of the Gospel has a parallel at the end, when the risen Jesus commands his followers to make disciples of all nations (Matthew 28.16-20). So Matthew's Gospel both begins and ends with the universality of Christ. But Matthew's Gospel also shows that Christian life can only be lived in the here and now, in particular places and in response to particular circumstances. The universal Christ is not an abstract Christ. He is encountered in the immediate, the local and the specific.

This is why the search of the wise men does not end at Herod's palace. The wise men do not expect to be directed to Bethlehem, but they are guided ironically, through Herod's interpreting of Scripture, at 'the place' and in 'the house'. It is not part of Joseph's plan to have to flee into Egypt. But he does so, and he finds refuge there.

It is our Christian responsibility to become increasingly sensitive to God's guidance by paying attention to the specific detail of our daily experience. God guides us not only through our dreams and desires, but also through setbacks and opposition. We should not be surprised to be surprised.

COLLECT

God of glory,
touch our lips with the fire of your Spirit,
that we with all creation
may rejoice to sing your praise;
through Jesus Christ our Lord.

Reflection by **Angela Tilby**

Wednesday 8 November

Psalms **9**, 147.13-end *or* **34**
Isaiah 2.1-11
Matthew 2.16-end

Matthew 2.16-end

'... he made his home in a town called Nazareth' (v.23)

The story of the Holy Innocents is one of the most unbearable parts of Scripture. It fulfils one of the bleakest prophecies of the Old Testament (Jeremiah 31.15). The loss of children is a loss of the future, and the slaughter of the innocents sets the birth of Christ in a tragic light. No wonder they are seen as martyrs, witnesses to the significance of Christ's coming, foreshadowing his future sacrifice.

It is significant that, in his ministry, Jesus welcomed children for themselves (Matthew 19.13-15), seeing them as specially blessed by God, capable of receiving revelation that adults are often blind to (Matthew 11.25). Today's reading might provide an opportunity to reflect on our own experience of childhood with its mix of blessings and hurts. It is always good to be thankful for the sheer gift of existence, the care we received as children and the sense of childhood wonder at the world. But we can also mourn the bereavements of childhood: any times when our vulnerability caused us pain or sorrow.

None of us choose the circumstances into which we are born. Joseph would have preferred to return to Bethlehem. But Nazareth was where Jesus was brought up. So we seek God in the facts, in what really happened, rather than in the fantasies of what might have been.

COLLECT

Almighty and eternal God,
you have kindled the flame of love in the hearts of the saints:
grant to us the same faith and power of love,
that, as we rejoice in their triumphs,
we may be sustained by their example and fellowship;
through Jesus Christ your Son our Lord,
who is alive and reigns with you,
in the unity of the Holy Spirit,
one God, now and for ever.

Reflection by **Angela Tilby**

Psalms 11, **15**, 148 *or* **37***
Isaiah 2.12-end
Matthew 3

Thursday 9 November

Matthew 3

'This is my Son, the Beloved ...' (v.17)

There are very few passages in Scripture where the triune God is revealed directly. This account of the baptism of Jesus is one of those rare passages, and artists have made much of it, depicting the Father affirming Jesus from above as John baptizes him, and the Holy Spirit descending on him in the form of a dove.

Today's reading invites us to think about our own baptism, whether or not we remember it. Baptism affirms each individual life as precious to God and potentially fruitful. We are named. We are blessed. The wilderness in which Jesus was baptized reminds us that our baptismal promises require us to be separated from 'the world'. The water of baptism both cleanses us and immerses us in the life of the Trinity. The baptized life is one of continuous discernment, of separation from what is false and an ever-greater appreciation of the reality of God. It takes time to understand how distorted our lives are by fear, greed and egoism. Baptism makes us disciples, students, learning to live in self-giving love and the joy of true belonging.

John's warning to the Pharisees and Sadducees reminds us that baptism is not a ritual add-on – it needs our daily recognition that we are created for the kingdom. The water of baptism, as a preacher once put it, never quite dries off.

COLLECT

God of glory,
touch our lips with the fire of your Spirit,
that we with all creation
may rejoice to sing your praise;
through Jesus Christ our Lord.

Reflection by **Angela Tilby**

Friday 10 November

Psalms **16**, 149 *or* **31**
Isaiah 3.1-15
Matthew 4.1-11

Matthew 4.1-11

'If you are the Son of God ...' (v.3)

Jesus' confrontation with Satan is meant by Matthew and the other Gospel writers to prepare Christians for the reality of spiritual struggle. Jesus cannot simply rest on the affirmation given in his baptism. He needs his vocation to be tested. The affirmation he has received at his baptism needs to be worked out and proved in real life.

As for Jesus, so for us. A placid, conflict-free life is not a Christian one. The peace of the kingdom has to be fought for again and again by the choices we make when faced with unavoidable decisions. Practical Christianity is like exercise. We grow stronger, more flexible and more resilient by working our spiritual muscles, and everyday life is a perfect arena for meeting temptation.

Satan presents his three temptations in the guise of reasonable strategies for Jesus to receive recognition of his Messiahship. There is a warning here about the temptation to find pragmatic reasons for actions that we suspect may not quite be compatible with our professed faith. Yet the more sensitive we become to the life of the Spirit within us, the more we will be aware of the way faithlessness can present itself in the guise of prudence. It is often tempting to take short cuts which ultimately do harm, or to advance our favoured agenda at others' expense. And we should always remember that the devil knows how to quote Scripture. 'If you are a Christian ... '

COLLECT

Almighty and eternal God,
you have kindled the flame of love in the hearts of the saints:
grant to us the same faith and power of love,
that, as we rejoice in their triumphs,
we may be sustained by their example and fellowship;
through Jesus Christ your Son our Lord,
who is alive and reigns with you,
in the unity of the Holy Spirit,
one God, now and for ever.

Reflection by **Angela Tilby**

Psalms **18.31-end**, 150
or 41, **42**, 43
Isaiah 4.2 – 5.7
Matthew 4.12-22

Saturday 11 November

Matthew 4.12-22

'... he said to them, "Follow me ..."' (v.19)

It is striking that Jesus does not start his mission with a master plan. Instead he progresses step by step, waiting for the right moment before taking action. Matthew the Evangelist is hypersensitive to Scripture, and shows us, sometimes in minute detail, how Jesus fulfils the words of the prophets. But he also shows Jesus exercising caution, sensitive to the politics of the moment. This is why he withdraws from Nazareth to quieter Capernaum after the arrest of John. He begins his preaching ministry by imitating John's message of repentance, and he begins to call his followers almost randomly from among the fisherfolk of the Sea of Galilee. It is very much one step at a time.

In the Christian life, we can sometimes feel very driven by the need to see results, to be sure that we are making a difference. Much contemporary talk of 'mission' seems to be driven by anxiety and the need to see measurable outcomes from our efforts. But the kingdom often comes in small steps, and may involve periods of uncertainty, waiting and even withdrawal. Often, in retrospect, we find that the fallow and apparently unproductive times in our Christian lives were actually periods of deep change and growth. Discipleship is as much about patience and waiting as it is about doing and action.

COLLECT

God of glory,
touch our lips with the fire of your Spirit,
that we with all creation
may rejoice to sing your praise;
through Jesus Christ our Lord.

Reflection by **Angela Tilby**

Monday 13 November

Psalms 19, **20** *or* **44**
Isaiah 5.8-24
Matthew 4.23 – 5.12

Matthew 4.23 – 5.12

'Then he began to speak, and taught them ...' (5.2)

The Sermon on the Mount is often regarded as the high point of Christian ethics, the new law of the kingdom, which both sums up and surpasses the law given to Moses on Mount Sinai. But we should notice the order in which Matthew sets out Jesus' actions and words. Matthew sets the sermon *after* the call of the disciples and after Jesus' tour of Galilee with them. Before he preaches to the masses, he heals and cures, teaching in small communities and local synagogues, changing the lives of those he encounters and bringing release to those burdened by sickness.

In this way, Jesus makes the kingdom real before he speaks about it to the gathered crowds. The crowd who listen are the crowd who are already blessed, who have already experienced the liberation of God's rule. There is no oppressive moralism in the teaching of Jesus, no talking down to people, no implication that God's care is conditional on their good behaviour.

As Christian disciples, we need to earn the right to speak about God, and we only gain that right by demonstrating our care and genuine concern. Pray today that you may see those you encounter through the eyes of Jesus, that you may be a blessing, and not a burden, to those you meet.

COLLECT

Almighty Father,
whose will is to restore all things
in your beloved Son, the King of all:
govern the hearts and minds of those in authority,
and bring the families of the nations,
divided and torn apart by the ravages of sin,
to be subject to his just and gentle rule;
who is alive and reigns with you,
in the unity of the Holy Spirit,
one God, now and for ever.

Reflection by **Angela Tilby**

Psalms **21**, 24 *or* **48**, 52
Isaiah 5.25-end
Matthew 5.13-20

Tuesday 14 November

Matthew 5.13-20

'... let your light shine' (v.16)

Matthew's Gospel holds together two truths. The first is that the teaching of Jesus is subversive and revolutionary. This is what is implied by the teaching of the Sermon on the Mount. The people who are blessed by God are not those we might expect to be blessed, but rather the poor, the grieving and the persecuted.

But then there is the countertruth. This teaching is not so revolutionary after all, because it reflects the way God's world actually is: 'not one stroke of a letter will pass from the law until all is accomplished'. The revolutionary law of the Sermon on the Mount turns out to be more exacting, more searching than that taught by the scribes and Pharisees.

It is important in our everyday discipleship to remember that Jesus' teaching, revolutionary though it is, is also continuous with Jewish tradition, and has its counterparts with other faith traditions. That is why when people adopt Christianity for themselves they sometimes speak of how 'something clicked'. Deep down we know that we belong to one another and depend on one another. But we can only appreciate that when we know at the same time that our uniqueness is recognized. We need both the salt of truth and the light of kindness in order to bear witness to Our Lord, and also the insight to recognize those qualities in others. The demands of Jesus sometimes come to us as blessings in disguise.

COLLECT

God, our refuge and strength,
bring near the day when wars shall cease
and poverty and pain shall end,
that earth may know the peace of heaven
through Jesus Christ our Lord.

Reflection by **Angela Tilby**

Wednesday 15 November

Psalms **23**, 25 *or* **119.57-80**
Isaiah 6
Matthew 5.21-37

Matthew 5.21-37

'Let your word be "Yes, Yes" or "No, No"' (v.37)

'Purity of heart', said the Danish theologian Søren Kierkegaard, 'is to will one thing.' At the heart of Jesus' Jewish faith was the *Shema*, 'Hear, O Israel, the Lord is our God, the Lord is one'. The call of God to us is a call to integration, to become one, even as God is one.

Our potential for inner unity is broken by conflict, whether with another person or by the war of conflicting desires within ourselves. Jesus speaks to our condition in the most radical terms, tearing out the wrong-seeing eye and cutting off the offending hand. These instructions are not, of course, to be taken literally, but they are meant to bring it home to us that we can never find our true humanity unless we are prepared to search our hearts and endure the painful revelation of our own contradictions.

The way of integrity means the renunciation of some of our cherished desires. But Jesus knows the way we are. It is better not to make pretend promises, that we cannot keep, than to break them. It may be uncomfortable, but Jesus' teaching suggests we need to be able to aspire to true integrity while accepting our constant need for mercy and forgiveness. For many, the Jesus prayer, 'Lord Jesus Christ, Son of God, have mercy on me, a sinner' is a daily step towards purity of heart.

COLLECT

Almighty Father,
whose will is to restore all things
in your beloved Son, the King of all:
govern the hearts and minds of those in authority,
and bring the families of the nations,
divided and torn apart by the ravages of sin,
to be subject to his just and gentle rule;
who is alive and reigns with you,
in the unity of the Holy Spirit,
one God, now and for ever.

Reflection by **Angela Tilby**

Psalms **26**, 27 *or* 56, **57** (63*)
Isaiah 7.1-17
Matthew 5.38-end

Thursday 16 November

Matthew 5.38-end

'Love your enemies and pray for those who persecute you' (v.44)

Jesus' challenging call to love our enemies is hard to hear for those who are oppressed by the wickedness or indifference of others. But the background to this radical non-conformity is the blessing we have already received. Those who follow Jesus need to dwell in the reality that they are, indeed, blessed by God. It remains the case that we are precious children of God, with the dignity that goes with that status, whatever circumstances we find ourselves in. While we cannot always feel charitable towards those who make life difficult for us, we can strive to be just and fair, looking at our circumstances as though through God's eyes. God does not favour the righteous or the unrighteous but provides for both equally.

Sometimes, we need to extend the command to love our enemies to ourselves, especially if circumstance and experience have led us to a point where we have become our own worst enemy. Compassion for self and self-care are not self-indulgence. It is justice to who we are in God's eyes, and may be the point at which we begin to understand Jesus' strange and countercultural demand, to pray for those who persecute us.

Who do we think of as our enemies today, and what might happen if we took the Lord's command seriously and prayed for them?

COLLECT

God, our refuge and strength,
bring near the day when wars shall cease
and poverty and pain shall end,
that earth may know the peace of heaven
through Jesus Christ our Lord.

Reflection by **Angela Tilby**

Friday 17 November

Psalms 28, **32** *or* **51**, 54
Isaiah 8.1-15
Matthew 6.1-18

Matthew 6.1-18

'... pray to your Father, who is in secret' (v.6)

We speak today of 'virtue-signalling' as a way of gaining social approval without making any real demand on ourselves. Jesus' warnings about hypocrisy indicate an age-old danger for those seeking the approval of others through ostentatiously pious practices. It is indeed very agreeable to be admired, and few of us can resist what can sometimes be a temptation. Yet Jesus understands how the desire to be loved, liked and approved of, however natural, can lead us away from true integrity. That is why he insists on a 'secret' relationship with God, and on the self-discipline to keep our good deeds out of the public eye. If our light is truly to shine before others, we should not be drawing attention to it.

Jesus then gives a form of prayer that has been precious to Christians from the beginning. The Lord's Prayer is not original. It is the kind of prayer any observant Jew would have made to God. Jesus gives the prayer to assure those who follow him that they belong to him. As Paul would say, the Spirit of Jesus cries 'Abba, Father,' and the Lord's Prayer is the pledge that we share in Christ's sonship. We do not need to strive to be prayerful people, but we do need to ensure that there is time and space in our lives to be alone with God.

COLLECT

Almighty Father,
whose will is to restore all things
in your beloved Son, the King of all:
govern the hearts and minds of those in authority,
and bring the families of the nations,
divided and torn apart by the ravages of sin,
to be subject to his just and gentle rule;
who is alive and reigns with you,
in the unity of the Holy Spirit,
one God, now and for ever.

Reflection by **Angela Tilby**

Psalm **33** *or* **68**
Isaiah 8.16 – 9.7
Matthew 6.19-end

Saturday 18 November

Matthew 6.19-end

'Today's trouble is enough for today' (8.34)

Much of Jesus' teaching is about living as sons and daughters of the kingdom of God, and that means learning to live without anxiety. Phrases such as 'look at the birds of the air', 'consider the lilies of the field', 'Solomon in all his glory was not clothed like one of these' are memorable because they focus on how nature reveals the creator in sometimes unexpected ways. Jesus would not be such an attractive figure were he only a moral teacher. What makes him compelling is his immediate sense of God's providence. He communicates wonder and freedom, demonstrating that goodness is not a dour quality, but an expression of beauty and truth.

Children of the kingdom are rich even when they are poor, as the seventeenth-century Anglican poet Thomas Traherne said: 'Your enjoyment of the world is never right until every morning you awake in heaven.' More prosaically, we know how good it is for our mental health to immerse ourselves in the natural world. Jesus knows our needs. But he also knows how we are torn apart by our fears and compulsions, especially if we are poor, anxious or vulnerable, as many of his followers have always been.

What can you do today to stop yourself worrying too much about tomorrow and about all the unknowns of the future?

God, our refuge and strength,
bring near the day when wars shall cease
and poverty and pain shall end,
that earth may know the peace of heaven
through Jesus Christ our Lord.

COLLECT

Reflection by **Angela Tilby**

Monday 20 November

Psalms 46, **47** *or* **71**
Isaiah 9.8 – 10.4
Matthew 7.1-12

Matthew 7.1-12

'Ask, and it will be given to you ...' (v.7)

This last fortnight before Advent Sunday and the beginning of the new ecclesial year falls in what many of us know as the 'Kingdom Season'. Next Sunday is the celebration of Christ the King, and we reflect that all of history ends with him risen, ascended, glorified and enthroned, ruling over all. But the kingdom is not just beyond space and time: its coming is woven through Matthew's Gospel.

Indeed, immediately before the Sermon on the Mount, Matthew tells us 'Jesus went throughout Galilee ... proclaiming the good news of the kingdom' (Matthew 4.23). So we should realize that the kingdom is close, and we are experiencing what it is to live under Christ's just and peaceful rule wherever we find the behaviour and attitudes that Jesus teaches in these chapters – today, for example, neither dishing out condemnation nor finding ourselves condemned by others, and treating others as we would be treated.

But it's not yet like that everywhere, all the time. That's why we pray 'thy kingdom come'. That's why Jesus tells us 'Ask ...', while teaching us through the Sermon of the last week or so what we should be asking for: the kingdom-shaped and kingdom-shaping gifts that Christmas brings, delivered through the incarnation of the eternal Word made flesh for our salvation. Perhaps it's not too early to start thinking about what sort of Christmas gift you most want, or most need, this year.

COLLECT

Heavenly Father,
whose blessed Son was revealed
to destroy the works of the devil
and to make us the children of God and heirs of eternal life:
grant that we, having this hope,
may purify ourselves even as he is pure;
that when he shall appear in power and great glory
we may be made like him in his eternal and glorious kingdom;
where he is alive and reigns with you,
in the unity of the Holy Spirit,
one God, now and for ever.

Reflection by **Sarah Rowland Jones**

Psalms 48, **52** *or* **73**
Isaiah 10.5-19
Matthew 7.13-end

Tuesday 21 November

Matthew 7.13-end

'Enter through the narrow gate ...' (v.13)

Journeying into the heartlands of Christ's kingdom isn't always an easy or straightforward route to follow; it may take us into territory we'd rather avoid. It requires commitment and consistency, which may well mean self-denial. This is what the narrow gate demands.

Living as a citizen of this kingdom means far more than just brandishing what seems to be an appropriate passport when it's convenient for us – 'Lord, Lord ...' It takes more than this to pass the citizenship test, and even this is not just a matter of knowing the rules or passing an exam. We have to be able to demonstrate that we live in accordance with the kingdom's customs and culture, and that we follow the sustained patterns of living that produce good fruit.

That may feel daunting. Can we keep it up, by our own efforts? Can we truly 'walk the walk'? Well, we can when we have Jesus as our travel guide. He doesn't hand out maps and tell us to get on with it. He walks with us, leading us forward, and has the necessary provisions, even equipment, for us to keep on journeying – as we noted yesterday, we just have to ask.

Perhaps the image of building on rock resonates more for you. It's equally hard and demanding – but if you're short of equipment or tools, or just need nourishment to keep up the work, the solution is the same. Just ask.

COLLECT

Heavenly Lord,
you long for the world's salvation:
stir us from apathy,
restrain us from excess
and revive in us new hope
that all creation will one day be healed
in Jesus Christ our Lord.

Reflection by **Sarah Rowland Jones**

Wednesday 22 November

Psalms **56**, 57 *or* **77**
Isaiah 10.20-32
Matthew 8.1-13

Matthew 8.1-13

'I do choose. Be made clean!' (v.3)

The Sermon on the Mount has ended. Matthew's summation of Jesus' teaching on the kingdom gives way to a different form of instruction. We learn by watching Jesus, witnessing how the kingdom plays out in his own life and in the way he treats others.

First, we have the healing of the man with leprosy. The kingdom comes to him not merely through physical cure. For him, the kingdom also means healing his relationship with his faith community, no longer ostracized and distanced by the ritual uncleanness of his infectious condition.

Then we have the centurion's remarkable faith. It seems to me that in his utter acknowledgement of Jesus as Lord, Christ's kingdom has come to him so fully that all he asks is for its grace to touch his servant in distress. His desire is wholly aligned with Jesus' clear choice to restore all who are his own distressed servants.

Reading these accounts during the kingdom season highlights how the kingdom comes to us in two ways. Like the man with leprosy, we receive its healing. Like the centurion, we should be drawn into its life. It's worth noting that, though we often speak of being called to 'build the kingdom' (a phrase we do not find in the gospels), the picture in Scripture is of the kingdom coming as gift. Our task is to seek it as treasure, to lay hold of it, to strive to enter it – to do what we need to, just to receive this precious gift.

COLLECT

Heavenly Father,
whose blessed Son was revealed
to destroy the works of the devil
and to make us the children of God and heirs of eternal life:
grant that we, having this hope,
may purify ourselves even as he is pure;
that when he shall appear in power and great glory
we may be made like him in his eternal and glorious kingdom;
where he is alive and reigns with you,
in the unity of the Holy Spirit,
one God, now and for ever.

Reflection by **Sarah Rowland Jones**

Psalms 61, **62** *or* **78.1-39***
Isaiah 10.33 – 11.9
Matthew 8.14-22

Thursday 23 November

Matthew 8.14-22

'He took our infirmities and bore our diseases' (v.17)

Today, we read that Jesus cured all who were sick who were brought to him – yet today, illness of one sort or another abounds. So many are brought to the Lord in the prayers of the faithful. Yet not all prayers are answered in the way we might want. There are no easy answers.

What does this mean for our sense of the coming of the kingdom? Surely the kingdom isn't absent where sickness and suffering are found? Coming alongside those in need of healing seems to be so closely woven with Jesus' preaching of the kingdom.

Perhaps we might ponder how such situations can be opportunities for Jesus to come close, his kingdom coming in the particular ways we most need it, and are most open to receiving it. When my husband, Justus, was dying of cancer, it was certainly a struggle, but we found a sense of God's all-encompassing *shalom* peace assuring us that we were safe in the palm of his hand no matter what. We also found fresh spiritual and theological depths – the latter being the specific extra comfort most needed perhaps by fairly academic clergy!

Justus found insights into the incarnation and Christ's mortality that he could uniquely and powerfully share. I found a capacity to care that I doubted I had. Others' prayers seemed to lift us. With hindsight, I see that the kingdom was profoundly present for us and for those who supported us.

COLLECT

Heavenly Lord,
you long for the world's salvation:
stir us from apathy,
restrain us from excess
and revive in us new hope
that all creation will one day be healed
in Jesus Christ our Lord.

Reflection by **Sarah Rowland Jones**

Friday 24 November

Psalms **63**, 65 *or* **55**
Isaiah 11.10 – end of 12
Matthew 8.23-end

Matthew 8.23-end

'What sort of man is this ...?' (v.27)

My passport has a page of Notes. Some relate to my rights, including to live and work in the UK without immigration restrictions. There are also passport holders' responsibilities, to ensure it is kept safe, and that any loss, theft or destruction, is immediately reported. Furthermore, the passport remains the property of the Crown.

My citizenship of the kingdom also brings expectations from my side, and lays obligations upon me; and all this is expressed under the rule of its King. He sets the terms. Sometimes they are not easy for us to understand, and sometimes they are not easy for us to live with.

When Jesus was asleep, the disciples wanted him awake. But when he was awake, he could be more than disconcerting, leaving the disciples amazed, awed, even a little afraid of his capacities – yet they stuck with him. But the healing of the two demoniacs was seen by the local townspeople as so disruptive that they asked him to leave. It was one thing to heal those they considered possessed, but upsetting their economic wellbeing (even if invested in unclean pigs) was a step too far. His was a kingdom in which they knew for certain that they did not want citizenship.

Some people have dual nationality, holding passports from two different countries. This is not an option for citizens of the kingdom, and we need to recognize this, even when we find it uncomfortable.

COLLECT

Heavenly Father,
whose blessed Son was revealed
to destroy the works of the devil
and to make us the children of God and heirs of eternal life:
grant that we, having this hope,
may purify ourselves even as he is pure;
that when he shall appear in power and great glory
we may be made like him in his eternal and glorious kingdom;
where he is alive and reigns with you,
in the unity of the Holy Spirit,
one God, now and for ever.

 Reflection by **Sarah Rowland Jones**

Psalm **78.1-39** *or* **76**, 79
Isaiah 13.1-13
Matthew 9.1-17

Saturday 25 November

Matthew 9.1-17

'Go and learn ... mercy, not sacrifice' (v.13)

Another day, another boat, another town, and more challenging insights into living under the reign of Christ. Yes, we have the assurance that the forgiveness of sins flows from his hand, as well as his depictions of feasting, and newness of life.

There is challenge too. Like Matthew, we are called to follow, while being given no indication of where the journey will take us, or what it will entail. We can only know that in travelling through the kingdom's terrain, its ruler will be our guide. Feasting and newness of life are on the cards, though we may not be able to anticipate in advance how these will present themselves.

It comes with brain teasers along the way: what does it mean for the kingdom to be about God's desire for mercy, not sacrifice, and for the call to follow to be for sinners? Mercy-shaped living works two ways. First, we need to acknowledge our state as sinners and recognize our need for mercy. We need a big, all-encompassing mercy. And often we need extra mercy, extra compassion, extra grace, in specific issues of woundedness, brokenness, difficulty, wrongdoing, or ... well, just consider where you might need mercy today.

Second, we should also be ready to show mercy. Perhaps today, pray to keep alert to recognize situations where Christ-like, kingdom-shaped, mercy-sharing may be being called out of you. For me, it means life-long learning, through going, and doing.

COLLECT

Heavenly Lord,
you long for the world's salvation:
stir us from apathy,
restrain us from excess
and revive in us new hope
that all creation will one day be healed
in Jesus Christ our Lord.

Reflection by **Sarah Rowland Jones**

Monday 27 November

Psalms 92, **96** *or* **80**, 82
Isaiah 14.3-20
Matthew 9.18-34

Matthew 9.18-34

'"Do you believe?" ... "Yes, Lord."' (v.28)

There's a lot happening in the kingdom of God. 'While ... suddenly ... as [he] went on ... after ...' How does this busy schedule read to you? Does it seem like Jesus' life is hectic and exhausting, full of interruptions and derailments? Or do you see a man in control of events, steadily working through each next issue as it arises before him – no sweat!

Sometimes, we can find that reading the Bible is a matter of letting the Bible read us. If this passage stirs up in us a sense of one thing after another, perhaps it is because that's how our own life feels. If we read Scripture with an open heart, it can resonate with our own emotions, at times helping us recognize what we hadn't known was within us. It's worth pausing, and checking in where the words resonate with us today.

When we recognize our starting point, we can then sit with the passage meditatively for a little longer. As we re-read – consciously recognizing and acknowledging the parallels with our own lives – we can invite Jesus' presence, sense his kingdom coming into what it is that we are facing today and the way our circumstances make us feel. Perhaps we need to grow in reassurance that he is in control. Perhaps we know that already. Either way, may he give us grace to reach the point of echoing 'Yes, Lord!'

COLLECT

Eternal Father,
whose Son Jesus Christ ascended to the throne of heaven
that he might rule over all things as Lord and King:
keep the Church in the unity of the Spirit
and in the bond of peace,
and bring the whole created order to worship at his feet;
who is alive and reigns with you,
in the unity of the Holy Spirit,
one God, now and for ever.

Reflection by **Sarah Rowland Jones**

Psalms **97**, 98, 100 *or* 87, **89.1-18**
Isaiah 17
Matthew 9.35 – 10.15

Tuesday 28 November

Matthew 9.35 – 10.15

'The kingdom of heaven has come near' (10.7)

Years ago, a wise Christian said to me, 'A need is not a call'. Here, Jesus himself acknowledges that kingdom living can sometimes be very demanding. In response, we should pray – but not that the Lord of the harvest will give us the capacity to work 28-hour days, 9 days a week, as some of us sometimes feel we ought! No, we should pray he will send more labourers.

None of us can do everything, and none of us is called to do everything. We should often say 'no' to some things, in order to say a better 'yes' to those that require our attention. It's also worth remembering that where this yes and no lie may well shift over time.

But judging what deserves a yes or no requires careful discernment. In the book of Acts, we find that the disciples will travel far and wide, with funds, clothes, staffs, food and other resources. But they can do that safely, because they've already been taught to rely not on these, but – through doing without them – on Jesus himself and his provisioning. They've learnt to sit light to the rest. The kingdom of heaven has come near to them, as well as their hearers.

Sometimes, my attempts to do too much are bound up with relying on false resources – my imagined competence or a desire to prove I can cope with anything. I need to be reminded it's not all down to me, but to Jesus.

COLLECT

God the Father,
help us to hear the call of Christ the King
and to follow in his service,
whose kingdom has no end;
for he reigns with you and the Holy Spirit,
one God, one glory.

Reflection by **Sarah Rowland Jones**

Wednesday 29 November

Psalms 110, 111, **112**
or **119.105-128**
Isaiah 19
Matthew 10.16-33

Matthew 10.16-33

'... be wise as serpents and innocent as doves' (v.16)

Jesus tells the citizens of his kingdom not to be afraid of those who malign, even persecute us. With every hair on our head counted, the promise of being upheld by the Father's Spirit, and the assurance of our true value in God's eyes, such fears are wrongly placed.

Our concerns should lie elsewhere. What undermines our life within the kingdom of God? What threatens our capacity to live with integrity as it citizens? Where are we tempted to live like uncommitted foreigners, rather than permanent residents? What stops us being true disciples, who become like our teacher?

My sense of what disturbs me today is different from what I'd have identified ten, twenty, or more, years ago. Perhaps it's different for you. Sometimes I find unwarranted fears get tangled up with other challenges. But whatever I find I'm wrestling with, I find my capacity to lay hold fully of Christ's promises that he will see me through are very much helped by pulling it all into the light, and telling it, if not from the rooftops, then at least to Christian companions or perhaps my spiritual director. Putting it out there helps me firmly own Christ's promises, as well as being testimony to others. In the light, I, and others, can see more clearly how Christ roots me in his kingdom.

COLLECT

Eternal Father,
whose Son Jesus Christ ascended to the throne of heaven
that he might rule over all things as Lord and King:
keep the Church in the unity of the Spirit
and in the bond of peace,
and bring the whole created order to worship at his feet;
who is alive and reigns with you,
in the unity of the Holy Spirit,
one God, now and for ever.

Reflection by **Sarah Rowland Jones**

Psalms 47, 147.1-12
Ezekiel 47.1-12
or Ecclesiasticus 14.20-end
John 12.20-32

Thursday 30 November
Andrew the Apostle

John 12.20-32

'Sir, we wish to see Jesus' (v.21)

The Feast of St Andrew – Galilean fisherman, Apostle of Christ, martyred on a saltire cross, patron saint of Scotland and many other places and causes – falls as one Church year ends and another begins.

Andrew is a helpful saint for Christian beginnings, and for those encouraging Christian beginnings in others. All Andrew does is help Philip bring to Jesus the Greeks who want to see him. The two disciples only need to be recognizable as living signposts to Jesus, visibly citizens of Christ's kingdom. They don't have to persuade or explain, nor worry about having the right answers. They just need to invite others to join them in Christ's presence, and meet him for themselves. My own Christian journey found its turning point when I kept company with friends as they kept company with Jesus, and I encountered him for myself.

He is also helpful for Christian conclusions. Jesus' words to Andrew, Philip, and the Greeks, encourage perseverance and affirm our destiny. Through letting go of the things of this world, we will have empty hands ready to receive the awaiting gift of eternal life in overflowing abundance beyond our imagining. We will be caught up into the Father's glorification of the Son as he draws all people to himself. Andrew brings us to Christ, who invites us to be with him, for eternity.

Who has been as Andrew to you? To whom can you be an Andrew?

COLLECT

Almighty God,
who gave such grace to your apostle Saint Andrew
that he readily obeyed the call of your Son Jesus Christ
and brought his brother with him:
call us by your holy word,
and give us grace to follow you without delay
and to tell the good news of your kingdom;
through Jesus Christ your Son our Lord,
who is alive and reigns with you,
in the unity of the Holy Spirit,
one God, now and for ever.

Reflection by **Sarah Rowland Jones**

Friday 1 December

Psalm **139** *or* **88** (95)
Isaiah 22.1-14
Matthew 11.2-19

Matthew 11.2-19

'Go and tell John what you hear and see' (v.4)

Even John the Baptist had doubts about whether Jesus was the long-awaited Messiah. Sometimes, what we see of Jesus' redeeming presence and love at work doesn't fit our expectations of what it means to be the Christ.

Yet the remarkable actions of Jesus are not themselves the heart of the issue. Instead, they variously fulfil Old Testament's expectations around what the Messiah's coming will bring – John's Gospel calls them 'signs' pointing to who Jesus really is. The list Jesus gives here echoes the passage from Isaiah 61.1-2, read by Jesus in the synagogue in Nazareth (Luke 4.16-21). It's a sort of manifesto of all that will characterize his unfolding ministry.

John longed to see the Messiah, but was fearful of misunderstanding what he'd heard. The disciples also struggled to grasp that the Messiah would be servant of all and submit to death, rather than be a powerful ruler in a royal palace. Others seemed to understand only too well, but were sufficiently perverse to insist on rejecting the Lordship of Christ, however he came.

Christ's kingdom often comes in subtle and subversive guise, and I often find my assumptions about Jesus are too small, or off beam. Then the choice is this: will I perversely sit with an expectation that suits my priorities, or will I be ready to have heart, mind, and soul subverted with a fuller understanding of Christ the King and his kingdom.

COLLECT

Eternal Father,
whose Son Jesus Christ ascended to the throne of heaven
that he might rule over all things as Lord and King:
keep the Church in the unity of the Spirit
and in the bond of peace,
and bring the whole created order to worship at his feet;
who is alive and reigns with you,
in the unity of the Holy Spirit,
one God, now and for ever.

Reflection by **Sarah Rowland Jones**

Psalm **145** *or* 96, **97**, 100
Isaiah 24
Matthew 11.20-end

Saturday 2 December

Matthew 11.20-end

'... and I will give you rest' (v.28)

Today the old Church year ends. Tomorrow is Advent Sunday, and a new year begins. The Lectionary compilers have given us a passage that very satisfactorily ties up loose ends, and gives reassurance that isn't so very far from saying 'and they all lived happily ever after'.

But first, as in any rollicking story, it seems the baddies must be vanquished. 'Woe to you ... woe to you ...' There will be judgement. 'All things' have been handed to the Son, who overcomes. All that exalts itself in competition with Christ's own kingly rule will be brought down. All that has held out against his sovereignty will be brought in line. The standards of the world, including so-called wisdom and intelligence, will be found wanting.

Yet this is a vanquishing whose final word is redemptive love. Gentleness will prove more powerful than strength and coercion. Humility will triumph over status and pride. All of us are embraced with the promise that in our weariness and the burdensomeness of life, we can come home to the ultimate rest and peace. This is the sure and certain promise of the kingdom that is not yet. And on the way, the kingdom with us now, can be – truly is – an easy yoke, and a light burden.

What else can the last word be? Your kingdom come, your will be done. Amen.

COLLECT

God the Father,
help us to hear the call of Christ the King
and to follow in his service,
whose kingdom has no end;
for he reigns with you and the Holy Spirit,
one God, one glory.

Reflection by **Sarah Rowland Jones**

Seasonal Prayers of Thanksgiving

Advent

Blessed are you, Sovereign God of all,
to you be praise and glory for ever.
In your tender compassion
the dawn from on high is breaking upon us
to dispel the lingering shadows of night.
As we look for your coming among us this day,
open our eyes to behold your presence
and strengthen our hands to do your will,
that the world may rejoice and give you praise.
Blessed be God, Father, Son and Holy Spirit.
Blessed be God for ever.

Christmas Season

Blessed are you, Sovereign God,
creator of heaven and earth,
to you be praise and glory for ever.
As your living Word, eternal in heaven,
assumed the frailty of our mortal flesh,
may the light of your love be born in us
to fill our hearts with joy as we sing:
Blessed be God, Father, Son and Holy Spirit.
Blessed be God for ever.

Epiphany

Blessed are you, Sovereign God,
king of the nations,
to you be praise and glory for ever.
From the rising of the sun to its setting
your name is proclaimed in all the world.
As the Sun of Righteousness dawns in our hearts
anoint our lips with the seal of your Spirit
that we may witness to your gospel
and sing your praise in all the earth.
Blessed be God, Father, Son and Holy Spirit.
Blessed be God for ever.

Lent

Blessed are you, Lord God of our salvation,
to you be glory and praise for ever.
In the darkness of our sin you have shone in our hearts
to give the light of the knowledge of the glory of God
in the face of Jesus Christ.
Open our eyes to acknowledge your presence,
that freed from the misery of sin and shame
we may grow into your likeness from glory to glory.
Blessed be God, Father, Son and Holy Spirit.
Blessed be God for ever.

Passiontide

Blessed are you, Lord God of our salvation,
to you be praise and glory for ever.
As a man of sorrows and acquainted with grief
your only Son was lifted up
that he might draw the whole world to himself.
May we walk this day in the way of the cross
and always be ready to share its weight,
declaring your love for all the world.
Blessed be God, Father, Son and Holy Spirit.
Blessed be God for ever.

Easter Season

Blessed are you, Sovereign Lord,
the God and Father of our Lord Jesus Christ,
to you be glory and praise for ever.
From the deep waters of death
you brought your people to new birth
by raising your Son to life in triumph.
Through him dark death has been destroyed
and radiant life is everywhere restored.
As you call us out of darkness into his marvellous light
may our lives reflect his glory
and our lips repeat the endless song.
Blessed be God, Father, Son and Holy Spirit.
Blessed be God for ever.

Ascension Day

Blessed are you, Lord of heaven and earth,
to you be glory and praise for ever.
From the darkness of death you have raised your Christ
to the right hand of your majesty on high.
The pioneer of our faith, his passion accomplished,
has opened for us the way to heaven
and sends on us the promised Spirit.
May we be ready to follow the Way
and so be brought to the glory of his presence
where songs of triumph for ever sound:
Blessed be God, Father, Son and Holy Spirit.
Blessed be God for ever.

From the day after Ascension Day
until the Day of Pentecost

Blessed are you, creator God,
to you be praise and glory for ever.
As your Spirit moved over the face of the waters
bringing light and life to your creation,
pour out your Spirit on us today
that we may walk as children of light
and by your grace reveal your presence.
Blessed be God, Father, Son and Holy Spirit.
Blessed be God for ever.

From All Saints until the day before
the First Sunday of Advent

Blessed are you, Sovereign God,
ruler and judge of all,
to you be praise and glory for ever.
In the darkness of this age that is passing away
may the light of your presence which the saints enjoy
surround our steps as we journey on.
May we reflect your glory this day
and so be made ready to see your face
in the heavenly city where night shall be no more.
Blessed be God, Father, Son and Holy Spirit.
Blessed be God for ever.

The Lord's Prayer and The Grace

Our Father in heaven,
hallowed be your name,
your kingdom come,
your will be done,
on earth as in heaven.
Give us today our daily bread.
Forgive us our sins
as we forgive those who sin against us.
Lead us not into temptation
but deliver us from evil.
For the kingdom, the power,
and the glory are yours
now and for ever.
Amen.

(or)

Our Father, who art in heaven,
hallowed be thy name;
thy kingdom come;
thy will be done;
on earth as it is in heaven.
Give us this day our daily bread.
And forgive us our trespasses,
as we forgive those who trespass against us.
And lead us not into temptation;
but deliver us from evil.
For thine is the kingdom,
the power and the glory,
for ever and ever.
Amen.

The grace of our Lord Jesus Christ,
and the love of God,
and the fellowship of the Holy Spirit,
be with us all evermore.
Amen.

An Order for Night Prayer (Compline)

Preparation

The Lord almighty grant us a quiet night and a perfect end.
Amen.

Our help is in the name of the Lord
who made heaven and earth.

A period of silence for reflection on the past day may follow.

The following or other suitable words of penitence may be used

Most merciful God,
we confess to you,
before the whole company of heaven and one another,
that we have sinned in thought, word and deed
and in what we have failed to do.
Forgive us our sins,
heal us by your Spirit
and raise us to new life in Christ. Amen.

O God, make speed to save us.
O Lord, make haste to help us.

Glory to the Father and to the Son
and to the Holy Spirit;
as it was in the beginning is now
and shall be for ever. Amen.
Alleluia.

The following or another suitable hymn may be sung

Before the ending of the day,
Creator of the world, we pray
That you, with steadfast love, would keep
Your watch around us while we sleep.

From evil dreams defend our sight,
From fears and terrors of the night;
Tread underfoot our deadly foe
That we no sinful thought may know.

O Father, that we ask be done
Through Jesus Christ, your only Son;
And Holy Spirit, by whose breath
Our souls are raised to life from death.

The Word of God

Psalmody

One or more of Psalms 4, 91 or 134 may be used.

Psalm 134

1 Come, bless the Lord, all you servants of the Lord, ◆
you that by night stand in the house of the Lord.

2 Lift up your hands towards the sanctuary ◆
and bless the Lord.

3 The Lord who made heaven and earth ◆
give you blessing out of Zion.

Glory to the Father and to the Son
and to the Holy Spirit;
as it was in the beginning is now
and shall be for ever. Amen.

Scripture Reading

One of the following short lessons or another suitable passage is read

You, O Lord, are in the midst of us and we are called by your name; leave us not, O Lord our God.

Jeremiah 14.9

(or)

Be sober, be vigilant, because your adversary the devil is prowling round like a roaring lion, seeking for someone to devour. Resist him, strong in the faith.

1 Peter 5.8,9

(or)

The servants of the Lamb shall see the face of God, whose name will be on their foreheads. There will be no more night: they will not need the light of a lamp or the light of the sun, for God will be their light, and they will reign for ever and ever.

Revelation 22.4,5

The following responsory may be said

Into your hands, O Lord, I commend my spirit.
Into your hands, O Lord, I commend my spirit.
For you have redeemed me, Lord God of truth.
I commend my spirit.
Glory to the Father and to the Son
and to the Holy Spirit.
Into your hands, O Lord, I commend my spirit.

Or, in Easter

Into your hands, O Lord, I commend my spirit.
  Alleluia, alleluia.
Into your hands, O Lord, I commend my spirit.
  Alleluia, alleluia.
For you have redeemed me, Lord God of truth.
Alleluia, alleluia.
Glory to the Father and to the Son
and to the Holy Spirit.
Into your hands, O Lord, I commend my spirit.
  Alleluia, alleluia.

Keep me as the apple of your eye.
Hide me under the shadow of your wings.

Gospel Canticle

Nunc Dimittis (The Song of Simeon)

Save us, O Lord, while waking,
and guard us while sleeping,
that awake we may watch with Christ
and asleep may rest in peace.

1 Now, Lord, you let your servant go in peace:
your word has been fulfilled.

2 My own eyes have seen the salvation
which you have prepared in the sight of every people;

3 A light to reveal you to the nations
and the glory of your people Israel.

Luke 2.29-32

Glory to the Father and to the Son
and to the Holy Spirit;
as it was in the beginning is now
and shall be for ever. Amen.

Save us, O Lord, while waking,
and guard us while sleeping,
that awake we may watch with Christ
and asleep may rest in peace.

Prayers

Intercessions and thanksgivings may be offered here.

The Collect

Visit this place, O Lord, we pray,
and drive far from it the snares of the enemy;
may your holy angels dwell with us and guard us in peace,
and may your blessing be always upon us;
through Jesus Christ our Lord.
Amen.

The Lord's Prayer (see p. 331) may be said.

The Conclusion

In peace we will lie down and sleep;
for you alone, Lord, make us dwell in safety.

Abide with us, Lord Jesus,
for the night is at hand and the day is now past.

As the night watch looks for the morning,
so do we look for you, O Christ.

[Come with the dawning of the day
and make yourself known in the breaking of the bread.]

The Lord bless us and watch over us;
the Lord make his face shine upon us and be gracious to us;
the Lord look kindly on us and give us peace.
Amen.

Table of readings

Joshua 1.1-9 **136**

1 Samuel 2.1-10 **168**

2 Samuel 15.17-21 **196**

2 Chronicles 17—18, 20, 22—24, 26, 28—30, 32—36 **166–7, 169–74, 176–183**

Ezra 1, 3—5, 7—9 **184–8, 190–2**

Nehemiah 1—2, 5—9, 12—13 **194–5, 197–204**

Esther 1—8 **205–12**

Proverbs 4.10-18 **142**

Ecclesiastes 1—6 **298–9, 301–3**

Song of Solomon 1—3, 5—8 **124–9**

Isaiah 7.10-15 **233**
Isaiah 35.1-9 **300**
Isaiah 42—56 **10–11, 13–31**
Isaiah 49.1-6 **193**
Isaiah 55 **288**
Isaiah 57.15-end **37**
Isaiah 58 **33**
Isaiah 59—62 **38–43**
Isaiah 62.6-10 **137**
Isaiah 63 **32, 45**

Jeremiah 1—25 **82–3, 85–105, 107–10, 112–17**
Jeremiah 26.12-15 **34**

Ezekiel 47.1-12 **12**

Malachi 3.1-6 **189**

Matthew 1—11 **304–24, 326–7**
Matthew 3.13-end **162**
Matthew 9.35—10.20 **163**
Matthew 12.22-32 **164**
Matthew 13.54-end **106**
Matthew 18.1-10 **36**

Mark 1—16 **226–32, 234–40, 242–58, 260–4, 266–71, 273–85**

Luke 6.12–16 **297**
Luke 8.1-3 **213**
Luke 9.46-56 **215**
Luke 22—23 **118–121**

John 1.29-34 **44**
John 1.43-end **241**
John 2.18-22 **123**
John 12.20-32 **325**
John 12.27-36*a* **259**
John 13—18 **286–7, 289–96**
John 17—20 **70–81**
John 20—21 **130–35**

Acts 2.37-end **154**
Acts 12.1-11 **272**

Romans 5.12-end **111**
Romans 12.1-5 **67**

1 Corinthians 1—14, 16 **46–59, 61–6, 68–9**
1 Corinthians 2—3 **159–60**
1 Corinthians 10.1-17 **175**
1 Corinthians 12.1-13 **161**
2 Corinthians 11—13 **214, 216–17**

Galatians 5.13-end **158**

Ephesians 2—6 **138–41, 143–7**
Ephesians 6.10-20 **165**

Philippians 3.1-14 **60**

1 Timothy 6.6-19 **84**
2 Timothy 3.14-end **265**

Hebrews 7. [11-25] 26-end **157**
Hebrews 10.1-10 **122**

James 1—5 **218–25**

1 Peter 1—5 **148–53, 155–6**

1 John 2.1-11 **35**